EQUINE
Massage

A PRACTICAL GUIDE

Second Edition

JEAN-PIERRE HOURDEBAIGT, LMT

BICENTENNIAL
1807
⊕WILEY
2007
BICENTENNIAL

Wiley Publishing, Inc.

CONTENTS

FIGURES

PREFACE

Congratulations! You have made a wonderful investment in your future by purchasing this revised edition of *Equine Massage: A Practical Guide*. This book is a complete course on equine massage, hydrotherapy, stretching, and much more. In time, the knowledge you gain from this book will allow you to increase your understanding of your horse's locomotor system, as well as improve your palpation skills and your finesse of muscular tension evaluation and massage skills.

Until the advent of the holistic health movement, massage as a form of therapy had been neglected in human health care in traditional Western medicine, and almost totally ignored in animal health care. The massage touch has a very strong healing influence on horses of all ages and conditions. It is widely used to prevent and relieve stress as well as to assist in recovery from injuries. Massage techniques safely affect the whole body by regulating the circulatory, muscular, and nervous systems and their interdependent functioning. Massage will relax your animal when excitable, and give him strength and flexibility when tired. It helps to dispel toxins and increase oxygenation for a better metabolism, leading to enhanced performance and shorter recuperation time. Over time, it also will help soften sharp character traits.

Life is a constant process of learning that brings deeper understanding and appreciation of one's skill. The inspiration for this book originated with my first experience with equine massage more than 25 years ago. Since then, I have had the privilege to share valuable information with many other equine professionals as well as the students who attended my hands-on practical sessions.

The athlete horse has received so much attention in the last few years that new modalities have become part of equine maintenance, and myofascial massage has become mainstream in the last 10 years. Also, saddle fitting has become a very important topic of discussion, as has the study of muscular compensation. With this revised edition, I am very pleased to bring you the latest valuable information on all these topics to improve your massage performance.

This book is not intended to be used as a substitute for the medical advice of a licensed veterinarian. Rather, it is designed to give practical assistance to the horse owner or equine professional to better cope with everyday situations in the lives of our equine friends.

Regular massage applications create a great bonding experience between you and your horse. One of the most valuable and pleasurable experiences in my life has been to see this book bring great satisfaction to both horses and owners.

I hope you, too, will benefit from it.

Jean-Pierre Hourdebaigt, LMT
President Massage Awareness Inc.

ACKNOWLEDGMENTS

To all horses, thank you for sharing with me your majesty, stories, needs, and secrets, and for inspiring me to write this book.

To horse people, my gratitude for your years of participation in my seminars; for sharing your knowledge; and for giving me your feedback, support, and encouragement. Like your horses, you have been a source of inspiration to me. I also wish to thank the following people:

Brigitte Hourdebaigt, whose love and encouragement make my life a beautiful reality.

Cindy Teevens, for her support over the years, for her knowledge of and talent for desktop publishing and photography.

Shari Seymour and Colleen Boyle, whose artistic talents and illustrations brought this book to life.

Shaun Finucane, D.V.M., from Sydenham Veterinary Services, for verifying the medical content of the book.

Cathy Brown, for giving me support and encouragement throughout.

Helene Coulombe, for her valuable professional input.

Burt, Nancy, and Jennifer Grundy, for allowing us to photograph their beautiful animals.

INTRODUCTION

Performance horses, like human athletes, work very hard to achieve top results. Strong emphasis has been put on training, nutrition, and preventive and palliative care to help horses reach their maximum potential: to run faster, to jump higher, and to accurately execute technically difficult maneuvers. Unfortunately, such performances result in more injuries, pain, and prematurely worn-out animals. For a while, strong drugs were the solution to these problems—the "miraculous fix"—but over time, the industry realized the not-so-desirable, occasionally negative, side effects of these drugs.

The horse world has strongly benefited from the progress of modern medicine. The development and application of sports therapy for humans has progressed tremendously in the last several decades. The benefits of alternative treatments such as massage therapy, physiotherapy, chiropractic, acupuncture, and herbology no longer need to be proven. Such therapies have become widely accepted and recognized by the traditional medical community.

Sports massage therapy techniques have kept pace with the changing methods of training, playing a very important role in prevention therapy and in recovery from injury. These massage techniques have led to a much richer relationship with the animal, resulting in better care for their needs. Through this evolution, the horse has kept his noble and loyal character, his heart, and his ever readiness for flight.

A more holistic approach using alternative medicine is now preferred by many trainers and riders. "Holistic" means that in order to create an environment for the maintenance or restoration of health, we must consider the horse in his totality—the sum of his physical and psychological traits—rather than treat each symptom separately. We must take into consideration all the various factors affecting both the internal and external environment of the horse. How we view this complex totality can affect the animal for good or ill. Any dysfunction of the musculoskeletal system requires that an overall assessment be made as to the causative factors. We know that the body will strive to heal, repair, and maintain itself—if the right conditions are present. In order to help with the healing capacity of the body, the horse's emotional stability, lifestyle, nutritional balance, exercise, and hygiene programs, as well as structural soundness, are our responsibility. Massage therapy helps us to trigger the body into getting itself back to optimal health.

If you don't correct the factors responsible for the problems you are treating (whether postural, occupational, habitual, emotional, or musculoskeletal in origin), the treatment of symptoms provides only short-term value, and chances are good that the symptoms may return!

Massage therapy is the manipulation of the soft tissues of the body in order to achieve specific goals of drainage, relaxation, or stimulation, and of resolving muscle-related problems such as trigger points and stress points. It contributes to the overall economy of the body and to its ability to function efficiently. It greatly improves circulation, thereby promoting a good supply of nutrients to the muscle groups. Massage therapy also reduces stress on the nervous system, helping the psychophysiologic self-regulation factors between body and mind. Massage therapy's healing function has been known to speed up recovery from injury.

Furthermore, massage increases our emotional bonding with the animal—and especially the young horse—which learns to relax and accepts being handled better. Not all animals enjoy being touched. "Touch shyness" is an indication of problems or a phobia. Careful and frequent applications of gentle massages will lessen the phobia.

Massage is a terrific diagnostic tool. You will be able to feel and detect any abnormalities and problems much sooner than by sight. Massage will help you avoid possible complications that could be very costly to treat.

Massage therapy is easily learned, easily applied, and costs very little. It is one of the oldest forms of therapy; it has been used by people from ancient times to the present. Forms of equine massage therapy were practiced by the ancient Chinese and Romans and more recently by the Hopi Indians of the western United States.

BEGINNING YOUR JOURNEY

In this book, you will find everything you need and want to know about massage movements, pressures, rhythms, techniques, and sequences. Different routines are specially designed for different situations. You will learn about the various areas of stress in a working animal and how these areas of stress can be present in horses of various disciplines. You will learn how to apply myofascial massage, how to treat equine temporomandibular dysfunction syndrome and equine compensation syndrome, and you will also learn how improper saddle fitting can be corrected through massage and what you can do to ensure a proper fit.

After you have satisfied your curiosity and familiarized yourself with the content by scanning the book, proceed with the study of the material. Before you begin chapter 1, review the basic anatomical terms presented in figure IN.1. These basic terms will help you remain oriented throughout your study of this book. I recommend that you then proceed to read the book from cover to cover. Finally, go through it again, this time taking notes, and duplicating the drawings. This will help you fully absorb the material presented.

Maximizing Your Study

Having a life doesn't leave much free time for hobbies or studies. For your academic studying, 1-hour sessions work best. It is easier and faster to study little sections at a time than large ones at once. For your hands on palpation sessions, 1-hour sessions work best, too. The compliance of the horse you will practice on will also play a factor.

Good habits are the key to success. To get a good start, spend at least 1 hour a day minimum, up to 5–6 hours of study per week in the beginning. Be creative and stay focused. The few moments spent each day on studying are a small price to pay for the knowledge, happiness, and success that will be yours when finished with this home study course.

In order to get the most out of your study of massage, it's important that you make sure you've absorbed all of the material you've read. If, at any point in the text, you become confused, go back and review the previous sections. Doing so should clear up any confusion. You can't afford to progress in your education with parts of your knowledge remaining unclear. It would make your overall study much harder, and would ultimately affect your performance.

At first, absorbing all the information in this guide may seem to be a rather large task to undertake. But remember, the equine massage knowledge you are developing will stay with you for a lifetime. Take it one step at a time, and before you know it, you will have absorbed a lot and feel pretty confident. Persist and you will succeed. Read and study every day!

Making It a Fun Experience

Quiz yourself regularly over each chapter and each chart. Doing so will really help you grasp the essence of this material. To help my students, I offer various musculoskeletal charts, a stress point location poster, and work books containing hundreds of questions. These tools can be found on my website at www. massageawareness.com.

A part of making the learning process a fun experience is to give yourself rewards as you complete each section of the course.

Enjoy the learning process. Relax, take lots of deep breaths, and smile. Do not forget to appreciate the learning experience you are going through, as well as the deep bond you are developing with your horse during the hands-on periods.

On Going Learning

Be patient in your learning process as everything takes time to mature. As you combine this material with your instincts as a horse person, you will soon be confident in your evaluation and palpation of the equine muscular anatomy, and in the application of massage techniques and routines. Your horse will love you for it.

The key to the successful use of massage therapy is the ability to sense accurately what your hands are feeling, to have a knowledge of the structures worked on, and to understand the movement or technique being employed and what its effect will be. Much practice is required. Learn to "see" with your hands and listen to your horse's body "telling its own tale." This is the most efficient way to contribute to proper maintenance and therapy. Let's stop horsing around and get to it.

Enjoy your newfound awareness.

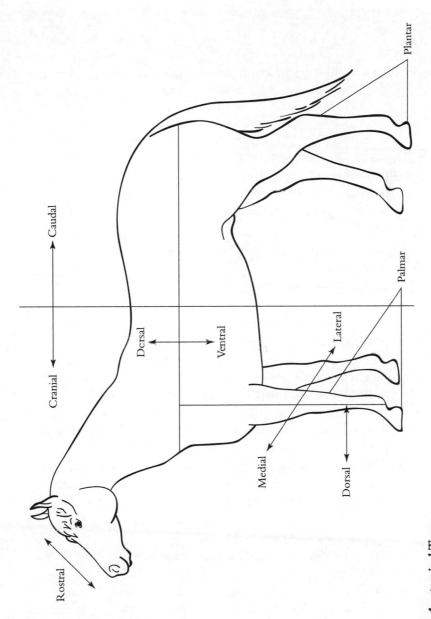

IN.1 Horse Anatomical Terms

1

ANATOMY AND PHYSIOLOGY OF THE HORSE

For massage therapy to be effective, its practitioner must have a good knowledge of a horse's makeup. In this chapter, we will examine the systems of the horse and the way in which these systems work together to promote the horse's health. To begin, we have:

* The nervous system (brain, spinal cord, sensory and motor nerves), which controls all the other systems.

* The respiratory system (trachea and lungs), which transmits oxygen to the bloodstream and removes carbon dioxide.

* The cardiovascular system (heart, blood, arteries, and veins), which conveys nutrients, oxygen and other essential components throughout the body.

* The lymphatic system (lymph channels and lymph glands), which provides a cleansing, filtering, and defense mechanism to deal with anything that could have a toxic effect on the body (lactic acid, bacteria, and viruses).

* The endocrine system, which is composed of glands that permit a range of functions in the body systems.

* The digestive system (mouth, stomach, intestines, and bowel), which extracts nutrients from food and eliminates waste.

* The urinary system (bladder and kidneys), which removes excess water and unwanted substances by filtering the blood through the kidneys.

* The reproductive system, which ensures the continuance of the species.

* The skeletal system, which is the bony frame that supports the body. Within the skeletal system there are joints which permit part of the bony frame to articulate (move).

* The muscular system, which provides the power and means to move the bony frame.

These systems are described briefly so that you can understand how each functions and relates to the other systems. More detailed information is beyond the scope of this book.

THE NERVOUS SYSTEM

The nervous system integrates and controls every body function; it processes all information and governs all commands to the body. In the nervous system we find:

❖ The central nervous system (CNS) consists of the brain and spinal cord, which perform very specific functions. The CNS is often compared to a complex computer.

❖ The peripheral nervous system (PNS) consists of numerous pairs of nerves that exit the spinal column at the vertebral level (spinal bones). There are sensory nerves (or afferent nerves) which carry information from the body to the CNS, and there are motor nerves (or efferent nerves) which carry information from the CNS to the body parts.

❖ The specialized sensory organs.

Complex in their makeup, nerve tissues are composed of many filaments that are very susceptible to pressure. In a case of severe trauma, when significant or strong pressure is applied to a nerve, nerve impulses can stop traveling along it. As a consequence, two things can happen: a loss of sensation or feedback from the nerve area to the CNS; and degeneration with eventual shrinking of the tissue in the immediate area of the affected nerve, as a result of lost motor nerve impulses from the CNS to the body part.

A *sweeney* is a typical example of a loss of motor nerve conduction. It is caused by a direct trauma to the point of the horse's shoulder. In this case, the suprascapular nerve that activates the muscles of the scapula is damaged.

The functioning of the nervous system is ensured by the autonomic nervous system (ANS), which maintains a stable internal environment. The ANS governs the vital organs and their complex functions that are normally carried out involuntarily, such as breathing, circulation, digestion, elimination, and the immune response. This system has two major divisions: the sympathetic and the parasympathetic. Both originate in the brain.

The *sympathetic division* causes the body to respond to danger, adversity, stress, anger, and pleasure by increasing the heart rate, blood pressure, air exchange volume, and blood flowing to muscles— all of which are needed for the horse to spring into action. The sympathetic division is responsible for the horse's "fight or flight" reaction. General stimulation of the sympathetic division results in

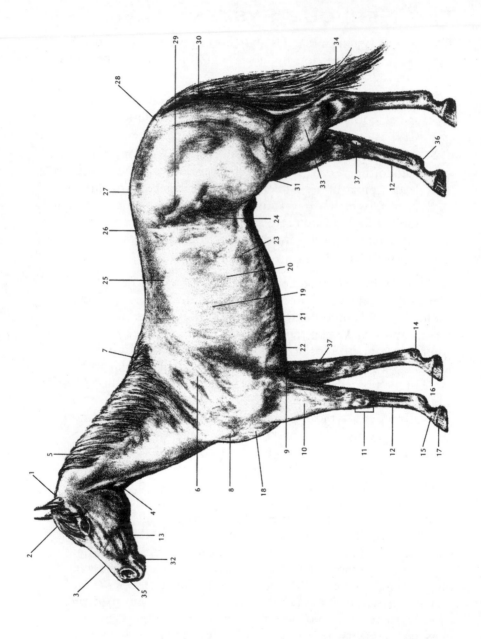

1.1 Points of the Horse

(1) poll
(2) forelock
(3) bridge of the nose
(4) throatlatch
(5) crest
(6) shoulder
(7) withers
(8) point of shoulder
(9) elbow
(10) forearm
(11) knee
(12) cannon
(13) jaw

(14) ergot
(15) pastern
(16) coronet
(17) hoof wall
(18) chest
(19) ribs
(20) costal arch
(21) xiphoid process of sternum
(22) girth
(23) belly
(24) flank
(25) back
(26) loins

(27) croup
(28) dock
(29) point of hip
(30) point of buttock
(31) stifle
(32) chin
(33) gaskin
(34) hock
(35) muzzle
(36) fetlock
(37) chestnut

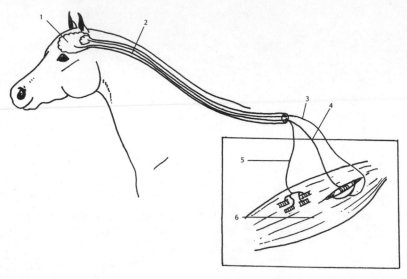

1.2 Nervous System

(1) brain
(2) spinal cord
(3) afferent nerve, Golgi apparatus
   sensory nerve

(4) afferent nerve, muscle spindle
   sensory nerve
(5) efferent motor nerve
(6) muscle

mobilization of resources to prepare the body to act or to deal with emergencies. (The warm–up routine in chapter 6 is designed to stimulate the nervous system.) The *parasympathetic division* monitors body functions during times of rest, sleep, digestion, and elimination, when the body is not ready to go into action. General stimulation of the parasympathetic division promotes relaxation and vegetative functions of the body such as breathing, circulation, digestion, immune response, and reproduction. (The relaxation routine in chapter 6 is designed to relax the nervous system.)

THE RESPIRATORY SYSTEM

The respiratory system includes the nose, mouth, pharynx, windpipe (or trachea), bronchial tubes, and lungs.

* ❖ The larynx is the organ of the voice.
* ❖ The lungs are somewhat elastic (expandable) and filled with numerous sacs (pulmonary alveoli) like a sponge. In the lungs, the blood takes on oxygen and gives off carbon dioxide (or waste).
* ❖ The diaphragm is a large, flat, muscular organ that separates the thoracic and abdominal cavities. Its action aids inhalation, expiration, and defecation.

Proper breathing is essential for good body metabolism. An exchange of oxygen and carbon dioxide is necessary for the body to remain vital and healthy. The horse's respiratory system also plays an important role in regulating his body heat and in maintaining the acid-base pH balance.

Oxygen is integral to the anabolic and catabolic processes that occur naturally in all structures. The oxygen/carbon dioxide exchange rate depends on how clean the lung tissues are, the depth of respiration, the animal's temperature (which causes expansion or dilation of blood vessels in tissues), and the rate of respiration. The rate of breathing for a horse at rest is around 12 to 16 breaths per minute; during heavy exercise, the rate is between 120 and 180. A cool-down period after strenuous exercise is essential to allow more time for the lungs to exchange gases, release toxins, and take in fresh oxygen.

Depth of respiration is very important. A girth that is too tight restricts the expansion of the rib cage. An improperly fitted saddle and a rider's tense legs also restrict the expansion of the rib cage, consequently limiting lung capacity.

Muscular problems such as *chronic stress points* (small spasms) and *trigger points* (areas of lactic acid build-up) will restrict the muscle action required to expand and contract the rib cage. (The recuperation massage routine in chapter 6 is designed to assist this problem.) Massage will help release any undue tension and relieve stress and trigger points around the rib cage, thus allowing for deeper breathing. (The stress point check-up massage routine in chapter 10 is designed to help you recognize potential stress point locations in and around the rib cage area.)

Massage indirectly assists in the oxygenation of tissues by increasing circulation throughout the body. Massage also relaxes the nervous system, thus allowing for deeper and steadier breathing, and better oxygen/CO_2 gas exchange.

THE CIRCULATORY SYSTEM

The circulatory system consists of the cardiovascular system and the lymphatic system. Circulation has a number of functions:

- ❖ Distributing oxygen and nutrients to every cell of a horse's body.
- ❖ Carrying antibodies to fight infections that invade the body.
- ❖ Removing metabolic waste and carbon dioxide.
- ❖ Distributing heat throughout the body, thereby regulating the horse's temperature.

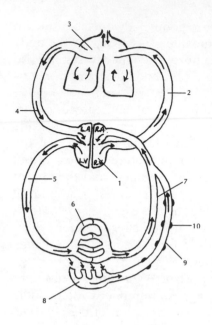

1.3 Circulatory System

(1) heart
(2) pulmonary artery
(3) lungs
(4) pulmonary vein
(5) artery
(6) blood capillaries
(7) vein
(8) lymph capillaries
(9) lymphatic vessel
(10) lymph node

THE CARDIOVASCULAR SYSTEM

The bulk of circulatory work is done by the cardiovascular system, which is made up of the heart, arteries, veins, capillaries, and the blood that flows through them. This is a closed-circuit system.

Arterial blood carries oxygen, nutrients, immune defense agents, glandular secretions, and blood-clotting agents throughout the body. Arterial blood circulation is generated by the pumping action of the heart and the contraction of the arterial wall muscles.

The normal heart rate at rest is 28 to 40 beats per minute, and up to between 210 and 280 beats per minute during exercise. The heart forces blood into the arteries, to the *arterioles* (smaller arteries) and then to the *capillaries* (minute blood vessels in the tissues), where the oxygen/carbon dioxide and nutrients/waste exchanges occur.

The blood returns via the *venules* (small veins) to the veins, to the heart, to the lungs, then back again to the heart for another cycle into the arteries. The venous blood transports metabolic waste and carbon dioxide from the cells of the tissues to the heart and lungs (where the oxygen/carbon dioxide exchange takes place). The venous return of blood is assisted by the movement of the large locomotor muscle groups of the body. Veins are equipped with little cuplike valves to prevent the backward flow of blood. Each muscle contraction squeezes the venous blood in one direction, toward the heart.

Normal functioning of all body tissue depends on the proper circulation of blood. However, after an injury it is even more important that an adequate supply of blood—bearing nutrients, oxygen, and healing material—reaches the site of injury. The blood will also remove waste, debris, or any toxins formed as a result of the injury.

The circulatory system controls the horse's body temperature. When the body is cold, the capillaries in those parts of the body farthest away from the heart constrict. Blood circulation is therefore reduced in the extremities, keeping most of the blood at the body's core in order to warm vital organs (brain, heart, and lungs.) Conversely, if the body is hot, the capillaries dilate, allowing more blood through the capillaries that are near the surface of the skin. Therefore, heat from the core of the body is released through the skin.

The pressure of massage movements has an effect on the circulation of blood throughout the body. Chapter 6 contains massage routines that can be used to deal with problems related to, or caused by, poor circulation.

THE LYMPHATIC SYSTEM

The lymphatic system plays an important role in the body's defense mechanism in that it contains *lymphocytes* (white blood cells that aid in fighting viral and bacterial infections). It is the body's first line of defense. When the body is injured, an increase of lymphatic fluid occurs at the site of trauma and produces swelling.

The lymphatic system consists of a network of small vessels containing lymphatic fluid and structures called *lymph nodes* (which are like miniature cleansing factories). There are twice as many lymph vessels as there are blood vessels. This system also filters and removes debris and waste material.

The lymphatic system sends fluid in only one direction—from the periphery of the body toward the heart. The circulation of the lymphatic fluid is slow, almost sluggish. Like veins, lymph vessels are equipped with cup-shaped valves to prevent backflow of the fluid. Muscle activity, breathing movements, and peristaltic activity of the bowels all contribute to the flow of lymphatic fluid.

Lack of exercise can contribute to *lymphatic congestion*, which results in swelling in the limbs. Overloading the lymphatic system as a result of too much exercise can cause a buildup of toxins, which leads to an inflammation of the lymph vessels and lymph nodes.

Following an injury, reduced muscular activity contributes to the slowing of lymphatic circulation. Massage with light drainage (effleurage movements) will assist lymphatic circulation. (Chapter 6 offers a recuperation routine that can help speed up recovery. Basically, the purpose of the recuperation routine is to prevent lactic

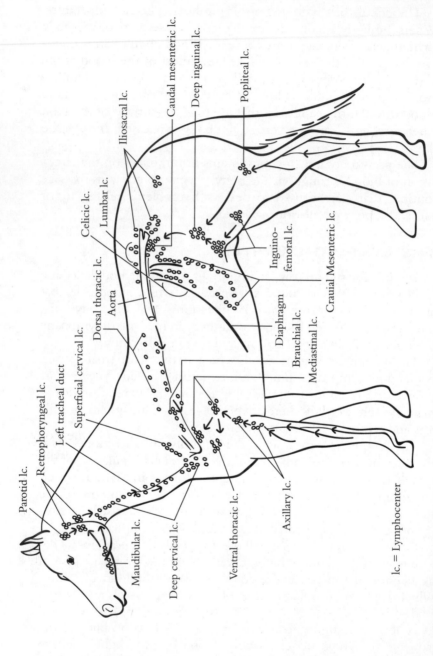

Caudal mesenteric lc.

Deep inguinal lc.

Popliteal lc.

Iliosacral lc.

Celicic lc.

Lumbar lc.

Dorsal thoracic lc.

Aorta

Superficial cervical lc.

Left tracheal duct

Retrophoryngeal lc.

Parotid lc.

Maudibular lc.

Deep cervical lc.

Ventral thoracic lc.

Axillary lc.

Inguino-femoral lc.

Crauial Mesenteric lc.

Diaphragm

Brauchial lc.

Mediastinal lc.

lc. = Lymphocenter

1.4 The Lymphatic System: *Lymphocenters made of lymphnodes.*

acid buildup after heavy training, racing, or competition. This routine will help prevent muscle stiffness, cramps, or tying up.) Massage does not directly affect the following four systems, but it does assist with the circulation of fluids (blood and lymph), allowing more nutrients and oxygen to reach the associated tissues. Massage also relaxes the central nervous system, contributing to an improved overall functioning of these four systems.

THE ENDOCRINE SYSTEM

Made up of glands and associated organs, the endocrine system produces and releases hormones directly into the bloodstream. These hormones regulate growth, development, and a variety of other functions, including reproduction and metabolism.

THE DIGESTIVE SYSTEM

The digestive system alters the chemical and physical composition of food so it can be absorbed and utilized by the horse's body. The gastrointestinal tract is a musculo-membranous tube that extends from the mouth to the anus (approximately 100 feet long). The digestive organs of the horse are the mouth, pharynx, esophagus, stomach, small intestine, cecum, large intestine, and anus. A healthy digestive tract is vital for the efficient assimilation of food. A balanced diet is very important for good performance and general well-being.

THE URINARY SYSTEM

The urinary system maintains the balance of fluids in the body and eliminates waste products from the body. The urinary system consists of a pair of kidneys, the ureters, the bladder, and the urethra. The kidneys provide a blood-filtering system to remove many waste products, and to control water balance, pH, and the level of many electrolytes. The kidney filtrate is urine, which is conveyed to the bladder by the 2 ureters. From there it is evacuated via the urethra. Proper urinary functioning avoids kidney failure and all its consequences: swelling, toxicity, and weight loss.

THE REPRODUCTIVE SYSTEM

The reproductive system ensures the continuation of the species. The male reproductive system consists of the testicles, the accessory glands and ducts, and the external genital organ. The female reproductive system consists of the ovaries, oviducts, uterus,

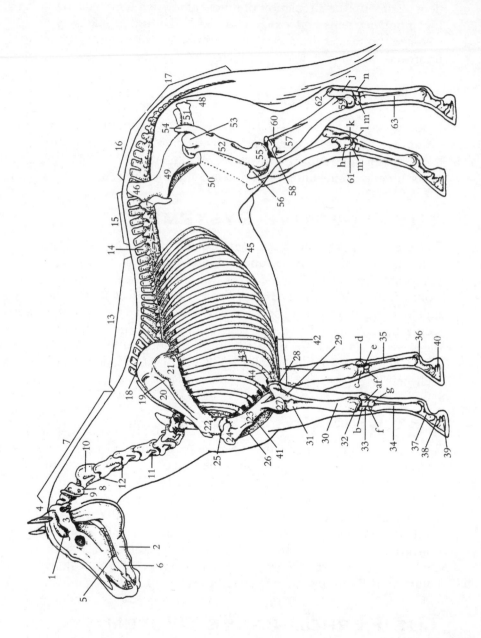

1.5 Skeleton of the Horse

(1) cranium
(2) mandible
(3) zygomatic arch
(4) poll
(5) teeth
(6) bar
(7) cervical vertebrae [7]
(8) atlas, first cervical vertebra
(9) wings of atlas
(10) axis (second cervical vertebra)
(11) expanded transverse process of fifth cervical vertebra
(12) intervertebral foramina, for passage of spinal nerves and blood vessels
(13) thoracic vertebrae [18]
(14) last thoracic vertebra
(15) lumbar vertebrae [6]
(16) sacrum [5 fused vertebrae]
(17) coccygeal vertebrae [usually 18]
(18) scapula
(19) scapular spine (bone ridge)
(20) supraspinous fossa of scapula
(21) infraspinous fossa of scapula
(22) neck of scapula
(23) humerus
(24) head of humerus
(25) point of shoulder

(26) deltoid tuberosity of humerus
(27) lateral condyle of humerus
(28) olecranon process of the ulna (point of elbow)
(29) ulna
(30) radius
(31) head of radius
(32) lateral styloid process of radius
(33) carpus [a] ulnar carpal bone (pyramidal or cuneiform), [b] intermediate carpal bone (lunate or semilunar), [c] radial carpal bone (scaphoid), [d] accessory carpal bone (pisiform), [e] second carpal carpal bone (trapezoid), [f] third carpal bone (os magnum), [g] fourth carpal bone (unciform)
(34) cannon (large metacarpal bone)
(35) splint bone (small metacarpal bone)
(36) proximal sesamoid bones (paired)
(37) long pastern bone (first phalanx)
(38) short pastern bone (second phalanx)
(39) pedal or coffin bone (third phalanx)
(40) distal sesamoid bone (navicular bone)
(41) sternum (breastbone)
(42) xiphoid cartilage of sternum
(43) rib
(44) costal cartilage

(45) costal arch
(46) tuber sacral (point of croup)
(47) tuber coxae (point of hip or haunch)
(48) tuber ischii (point of buttock or seat bone)
(49) ilium
(50) pubis
(51) ischium
(52) femur
(53) head of femur
(54) greater trochanter of femur (cranial and caudal part)
(55) lateral condyle of femur
(56) patella
(57) tibia
(58) lateral condyle of tibia
(59) lateral malleolus of tibia
(60) fibula
(61) tarsus (hock), [h] talus (astragalus or tibial bone), [j] calcaneus (os calcis or fibular tarsal bone), [k] central tarsal bone (scaphoid), [l] fused first and second tarsal bones (small cuneiform), [m] third tarsal bone (great cuneiform), [n] fourth tarsal bone (cuboid)
(62) tuber calcanei (point of hock or tuber calcis)
(63) cannon (large metatarsal)

vagina, and external genitalia. Proper fluid circulation and relaxation of the nervous system will ensure peak performance for reproduction purposes.

THE SKELETAL SYSTEM

The skeletal system serves as a framework for the horse's body, giving the muscles something to work against, and defining the animal's overall size and shape. The skeleton also protects the horse's vital internal tissues and organs. For example, the skull protects the brain; the rib cage protects the lungs and heart; the vertebral column protects the spinal cord. The skeleton is made up of over 200 bones.

BONES

Bones vary in size and shape according to their function. With the exception of the enamel-covered teeth, bones are the body's hardest substances and can withstand great compression, torque, and tension. A tough membrane called the *periosteum* covers and protects the bones and provides for the attachment of the joint capsules, ligaments, and tendons. Injury to the periosteum may result in undesirable bone growths such as splints, spavin, and ringbone. Bones are held together by *ligaments*; muscles are attached to the bones by *tendons*.

The articulating surface of the bone is covered with a thick, smooth cartilage that diminishes concussion and friction.

Long bones are found in the limbs; short bones in the joints; flat bones in the rib cage, skull, and shoulder; and irregularly shaped bones in the spinal column and limbs.

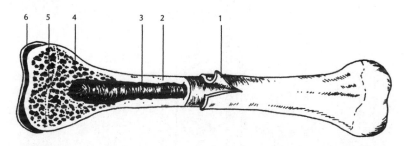

1.6 A Bone

(1) periosteum   (4) spongy bone with marrow cavities
(2) compact bone   (5) epiphyseal plate
(3) medullary cavity   (6) articulate hyaline cartilage

The *long bones* of the limbs (humerus, radius, femur, tibia, cannon bones) function mainly as levers and aid in the support of weight.

Short bones, found in complex joints such as the knee (carpus), hock (tarsus), and ankle (fetlock), absorb concussion.

Flat bones protect and enclose the cavities containing vital organs: skull (brain) and ribs (heart and lungs). Flat bones also provide large areas for the attachment of muscles.

Components of the skeleton of the horse are as follows:

- ❖ The skull consists of 34 irregularly shaped bones.
- ❖ The spine consists of 7 cervical vertebrae, 17 to 19 thoracic vertebrae (usually 18), 5 to 6 lumbar vertebrae (sometimes fused together), and 5 fused sacral vertebrae (the sacrum). The tail consists of 18 coccygeal vertebrae, although this number can vary considerably.
- ❖ The rib cage consists of 18 pairs (usually) of ribs springing from the thoracic vertebrae, curving forward and meeting at the breastbone (sternum).
- ❖ The forelegs carry 60 percent of the horse's body weight. Comprising the forelegs are the shoulder blade (scapula), humerus, radius, knee (8 carpal bones), cannon, splints, long and short pasterns, and the pedal (or coffin) bone.
- ❖ Comprising the hind legs are the pelvis (ilium, ischium, pubis), femur, tibia and fibula, the tarsus or hock (7 bones), cannons and splints, pasterns (long and short), and the pedal (or coffin) bone.

THE JOINTS

Joints are the meeting places between two bones. Movement of the horse is dependent upon the contraction of muscles and the corresponding articulation of the joints.

Some joints in the horse's body are not movable, but most are and permit a great range of motion.

The ends of the bones are lined with hyaline cartilage, which provides a smooth surface between the bones and acts as a shock absorber when compressed—for example, during takeoff and landing while jumping, and for torque during quick turns.

The *joint capsule,* also known as the capsular ligament, is sealed by the synovial membrane, which produces a viscous, lubricating secretion, the synovial fluid.

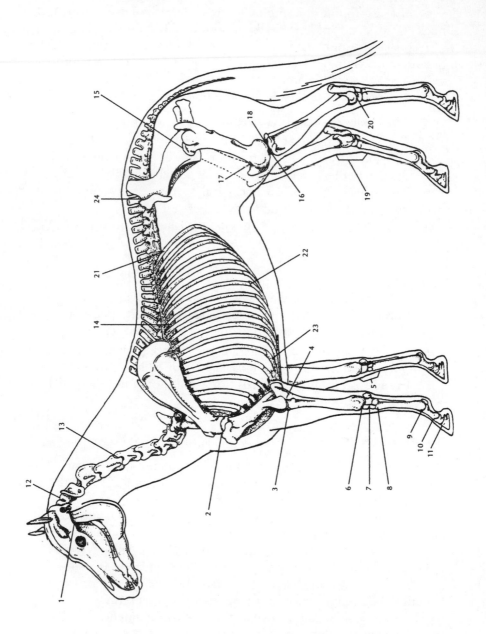

1.7 Joints of the Horse

(1) jaw joint (temporomandibular joint [TMJ])
(2) shoulder joint
(3) humeroradial component of elbow joint
(4) humeroulnar component of elbow joint
(5) knee joint (carpus or wrist)
(6) radiocarpal joint
(7) intercarpal joint
(8) carpometacarpal joint

(9) fetlock joint
(10) pastern joint
(11) coffin joint
(12) atlanto-occipital joint
(13) cervical intervertebral disc joint
(14) thoracic intervertebral disc joint
(15) hip joint
(16) stifle joint

(17) femoropatellar component of stifle joint
(18) femorotibial component of stifle joint
(19) hock joint (tarsus)
(20) talocrural joint
(21) costovertebral joint
(22) costochondral joint
(23) costosternal joint
(24) sacroiliac joint

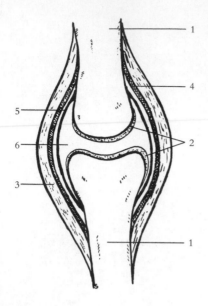

1.8 A Joint

(1) bone
(2) hyaline cartilage
(3) ligament
(4) fibrous capsule
(5) synovial lining
(6) joint cavity (with synovial fluid)

THE LIGAMENTS

A ligament is a band of connective tissue that links one bone to another (*tendons* connect muscles to bones). Ligaments are made up of collagen fiber, a fibrous protein found in the connective tissue. Ligaments have a limited blood supply. Consequently, if a ligament is injured, say by a sprain, it tends to heal slowly and sometimes incorrectly.

Most ligaments are located around joints to give extra support (capsular ligaments and collateral ligaments) or to prevent an excessive or abnormal range of motion and to resist the pressure of lateral torque (a twisting motion). (See figure 1.10, page 24.) The horse experiences lateral torque when turning sharply.

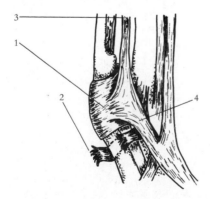

1.9 Ligaments of the Fetlock Joint

(1) palmar annular ligament, which provides strong support
(2) example of a torn ligament, the digital annular ligament
(3) suspensory ligament (superior sesamoidean part)
(4) suspensory ligament extension to common digital extensor tendon

Ligaments have little contracting power and therefore must work in conjunction with muscle action. Within very narrow limits, ligaments are somewhat elastic but are inflexible enough to offer support in normal joint play. If overstretched or repeatedly stretched, a ligament might lose up to 25 percent of its strength. Such a ligament may need surgical stitching to recover its full tensile strength. Severe ligament sprain will lead to joint instability.

Several ligamentous structures help support and protect the vertebral column, pelvis, neck, and limbs from suddenly imposed strain.

THE MUSCULAR SYSTEM

There are three classes of muscles: smooth, cardiac, and skeletal. The *smooth* and *cardiac muscles* are involuntary, or autonomic; they play a part in the digestive, respiratory, circulatory, and urogenital systems.

For the most part, *skeletal muscles* are voluntary; they function in the horse's movements. In massage, we are concerned with the more than 700 skeletal muscles that are responsible for the movement of the horse.

There are two types of skeletal muscle fibers: slow twitch fibers (ST) and fast twitch fibers (FT).

Slow twitch fibers are aerobic fibers; they need oxygen in order to do their job. Thus ST fibers require a good supply of blood to bring oxygen to them and to remove waste products created during exercise. ST fibers have strong endurance qualities.

Fast twitch fibers are anaerobic fibers; they do not need oxygen to work and therefore are able to deliver the quick muscular effort required for a sudden burst of speed. However, FT fibers are only able to perform for short periods of time.

The ratio of ST to FT fibers is genetically inherited. Careful selective breeding can emphasize these features in a horse. For example, the muscles of the Quarter Horse are mostly FT fibers, and the breed is noted for its dazzling sprint. On the other hand, a heavy horse, such as a draft horse, has more ST fibers and is noted for its strength and endurance abilities. Whether we are talking about FT or ST fibers, a muscle is made up of a fleshy part and two tendon attachments. The fleshy part, or *muscle belly*, is the part that contracts in response to nervous command. During contraction, the muscle fibers basically fold on themselves, shortening the fibers and resulting in muscle movement. The muscle belly is made up of many muscle fibers arranged in bundles, with each bundle wrapped in connective tissue (*fascia*). The fascia covers, supports, and separates the muscle bundles and the whole muscle

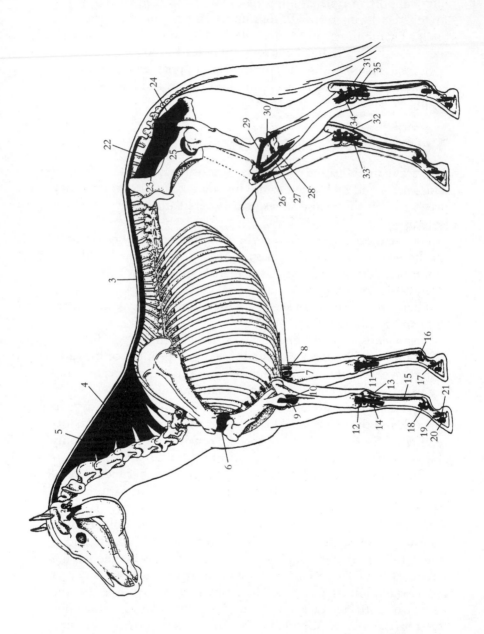

1.10 Ligaments of the Horse

(1) lateral ligament of jaw joint
(2) caudal (posterior) ligament of jaw joint
(3) supraspinous ligament
(4) funicular part of nuchal ligament
(5) lamellar part of nuchal ligament
(6) capsular ligament of shoulder joint
(7) medial collateral ligament of elbow joint
(8) medial transverse radioulnar ligament
(9) lateral collateral ligament of elbow joint
(10) lateral transverse radioulnar ligament
(11) medial collateral ligament of carpal joint
(12) lateral collateral ligament of carpal joint
(13) distal ligament of accessory carpal bone

(14) dorsal ligaments of carpal joints
(15) suspensory ligament (superior
  sesamoidean ligament derived from
  interosseous muscle)
(16) distal or inferior sesamoidean ligaments
(17) medial collateral ligament of fetlock joint
(18) lateral collateral sesamoidean ligament
  (fetlock joint)
(19) lateral collateral ligament of pastern joint
(20) lateral collateral ligament of coffin joint
(21) suspensory ligament of navicular bone
(22) dorsal sacroiliac ligament
(23) lateral sacroiliac ligament

(24) sacrosciatic ligament
(25) capsular ligament
(26) medial patellar ligament
(27) middle patellar ligament
(28) lateral patellar ligament
(29) lateral femoropatellar ligament
(30) lateral collateral ligament of stifle joint
(31) ligament connecting talus and calcaneus
(32) branches of medial collateral ligament
(33) medial collateral ligament of tarsal joint
(34) lateral collateral ligament of tarsal joint
(35) calcaneometa tarsal ligament (plantar
  ligament)

itself. This arrangement allows for greater support, strength, and flexibility in the movement between each of the muscle groups.

TENDONS

The tendon is the portion of the muscle that attaches to the bone. It is made up of *connective tissue*—a dense, white, fibrous tissue much like that of a ligament. The *origin tendon* is the tendon that attaches the muscle to the least movable bone; the *insertion tendon* attaches the muscle to the movable bone, so that on contraction the insertion is brought closer to the origin. Tendons attach to the periosteum of the bone; the fibers of the tendon blend with the periosteum fibers because of their similar collagen make-up. Tendons can be fairly short, or quite long as is seen with the flexor and extensor muscles of the lower legs. Usually, tendons are rounded but they can be flattened like the tendons that attach along the spine.

Because of their high-tensile strength, tendons can endure an enormous amount of tension, usually more than the muscle itself can produce; consequently, tendons do not rupture easily. They are not as elastic as muscle fibers, but they are more elastic than ligament fibers.

Tendons can "stress up" after heavy exercise, meaning that they can stay contracted. Gentle massage and stretching exercises will loosen residual tension. (See the neuromuscular technique in chapter 5.) Inflamed tendons are at great risk of being strained or overstretched. The horse has no muscles below the knee or hock; consequently, many leg muscles have long tendons that run down the legs over the joints. These tendons are protected by sheaths, or tendon bursae. Chronic irritation of the sheath can result in excess fluid production and soft swellings. Cold hydrotherapy (chapter 4) and massage will help increase circulation and keep inflammation down. If the inflammation persists, check with your veterinarian.

MUSCLES

Muscles come in all shapes and sizes. Some are small, some are large; some are thin, some are bulky. Look at the muscle charts to note the variety of shapes in the horse's muscle structure.

Muscles act together to give the horse his grace and power. Muscles work in three different ways: isometric contraction, concentric contraction, and eccentric contraction.

Isometric contraction occurs when a muscle contracts without causing any movement. During standing, for example, isometric contraction ensures stability.

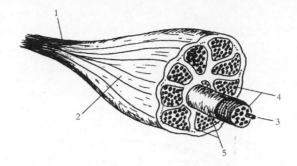

1.11 Cross-Section of a Skeletal Muscle

(1) tendon
(2) muscle belly
(3) muscle fiber (containing thick and thin filaments)
(4) bundles (made up of fibers)
(5) fascia

Concentric contraction occurs when a muscle shortens as it contracts, causing articular movements. Concentric contraction is
mostly seen in regular movements such as *protraction* (forward
movement) or *retraction* (backward movement) of the limbs, and in
any movement of the neck or back.

Eccentric contraction occurs when a muscle gradually releases as it
elongates. Eccentric contraction assists regular movements to
avoid jerky, unstable actions; it also plays a role in shock absorption during the landing phase of jumping.

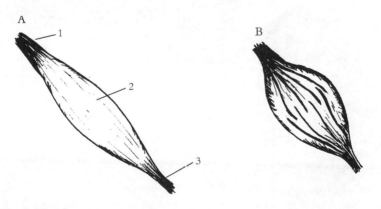

1.12 A Muscle

(A) Relaxed   (B) Contracted
   [1] origin tendon
   [2] muscle belly
   [3] insertion tendon

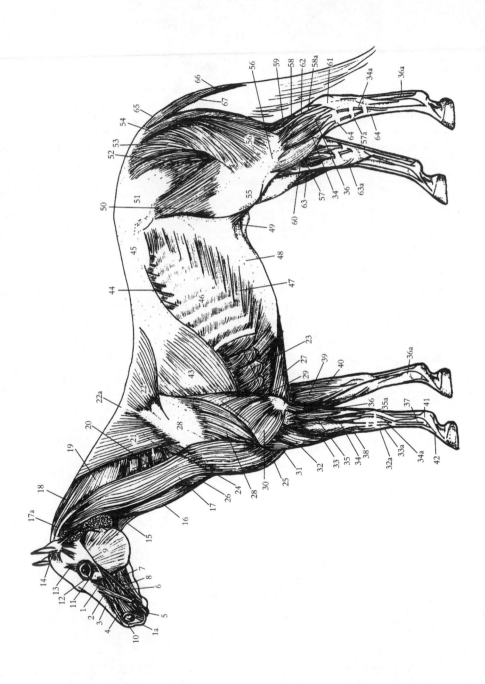

1.13 Superficial Muscles of the Horse

(1, 1a) levator muscle of upper lip and its tendon
(2) levator muscle of upper lip and nostril wing
(3) dorsal part of lateral nasal muscle
(4) lateral nostril dilator muscle
(5) orbicular muscle of the mouth
(6) buccinator muscle
(7) depressor muscle of lower lip
(8) zygomatic muscle
(9) masseter muscle
(10) transverse nasal muscle
(11) depressor muscle of lower eyelid
(12) orbicular muscle of the eye
(13) corrugator supercilii muscle
(14) auricular muscles
(15) sternothyrohyoid and omohyoid muscles
(16) sternomandibular part of sternocephalic muscle and tendon
(17, 17a) brachiocephalic muscle and tendon
(18) cervical part of rhomboid muscle
(19) splenius muscle
(20) cervical part of ventral serrate muscle
(21) cervical part of trapezius muscle
(22) thoracic part of trapezius muscle
(22a) tendinous intersection between the two parts of trapezius muscle

(23) thoracic part of ventral serrate muscle
(24) cranial deep pectoral muscle (anterior part of deep pectoral)
(25) cranial superficial pectoral muscle (anterior part of superficial pectoral)
(26) remains of skin muscle of neck
(27) caudal deep pectoral muscle (posterior part of deep pectoral)
(28) deltoideus muscle
(29) long head of triceps
(30) lateral head of triceps
(31) brachialis muscle
(32, 32a) radial carpal extensor muscle and tendon
(33, 33a) common digital extensor muscle and tendon
(34, 34a) lateral digital extensor muscle and tendon
(35, 35a) lateral carpal flexor muscle and its two tendons, long and short
(36, 36a) deep digital flexor muscle and tendon
(37) superficial digital flexor tendon
(38) oblique carpal extensor muscle
(39) medial carpal flexor muscle
(40) middle carpal flexor muscle

(41) suspensory ligament (superior sesamoidean section)
(42) extensor branch of suspensory ligament, attaching to common digital extensor tendon
(43) latissimus dorsi muscle
(44) caudal part of dorsal serrate muscle
(45) lumbodorsal fascia (thoracolumbar fascia)
(46) external intercostal muscle
(47) external abdominal oblique muscle
(48) aponeurosis (broad and flattened tendon of attachment)
(49) remains of skin muscle in fold of flank
(50) tensor muscle of lateral fascia of thigh (musculus tensor fasciae latae, or TFL)
(51) gluteal fascia
(52) superficial gluteal muscle
(53) biceps femoris muscle (part of hamstring group)
(54) semitendinosus muscle (part of hamstring group)
(55) lateral femoral fascia
(56) lateral crural fascia
(57, 57a) long digital extensor muscle
(58) Achilles tendon of triceps surae muscle
(58a) lateral head of gastrocnemius muscle

(continued)

1.13 *Superficial Muscles of the Horse* (continued)

(59) soleus muscle
(60) popliteal muscle
(61) common calcaneal tendon (the aggregate of tendons attached to tuber calcanei, i.e., Achilles tendon, superficial digital flexor tendon, and accessory or tarsal tendon from the hamstring muscles)

(62) accessory or tarsal tendon (from musculus biceps femoris and musculus semitendinosus of the hamstring group of muscles)
(63) cranial tibial muscle (anterior part of flexor metatarsi)

(63a) medial tendon of insertion of the cranial tibial muscle (cunean tendon or cuneiform insertion)
(64, 64a) annular ligaments
(65) short tail levator muscles
(66) long tail levator muscles
(67) tail depressor muscles

Skeletal muscles are highly elastic and have strong contractile power. They respond to motor nerve impulses; as a result, the contraction mechanism is a generated process. The release process is not a generated process, but rather is a natural relaxation of the muscle as a result of the cessation of the motor nerve impulses that originally "asked" the muscle to contract.

When a muscle develops a *contracture,* the muscle fibers stay contracted, eventually resulting in a spasm—at which point the natural relaxation process will not happen. Pain and motion problems will develop as a result.

Muscles are equipped with two types of sensory nerve endings: the Golgi apparatus and the muscle spindle. The *Golgi apparatus* nerve endings send feedback impulses to the brain as to the whereabouts of the muscles; this process is referred to as *proprioception.* The Golgi nerve endings are mostly located where the muscles and the tendons come together.

The nerve endings of the muscle spindle prevent overstretching of the muscle fibers. As its name implies, this nerve fiber coils around the length of the muscle bundle. Reaching a given length, the muscle spindle fires nerve impulses that trigger a fast reflex motor nerve reaction to induce immediate contraction of the muscle fibers. Thus the overstretching and potential tearing of fibers is prevented. This is a safety reflex mechanism.

When a muscle overstretches, a spasm often results. This is a *tetanic* (violent) contraction of a muscle in response to overstretching or trauma, whereby the muscle is unable to release its rigidity. A *microspasm,* on the other hand, is a small spasm occurring in just a few fibers of the muscle bundle. Microspasms have a cumulative effect over a period of time, resulting in a full spasm.

Sometimes a muscle is stretched past its limit and muscle fibers will tear. This causes an immediate muscle spasm and triggers an inflammation response, with swelling at the site of injury. As part of the healing process, new connective tissue is laid down in an irregular, scattered pattern within the muscle fiber arrangements. Unfortunately this scar tissue reduces the muscle's tensile strength, flexibility, and elasticity. Massage therapy can reduce the amount of scar tissue by applying deep kneadings and frictions after proper warm-up of the tissues. Also, stretching is a great technique for prevention and reduction of the formation of scar tissue.

A heavily exercised muscle will often develop light inflammation within its fibers. This is a normal process that promotes formation of new muscle fibers. But it is important to keep any inflammation under control to avoid the formation of scar tissue. To keep inflammation down, use cold hydrotherapy, ultrasound,

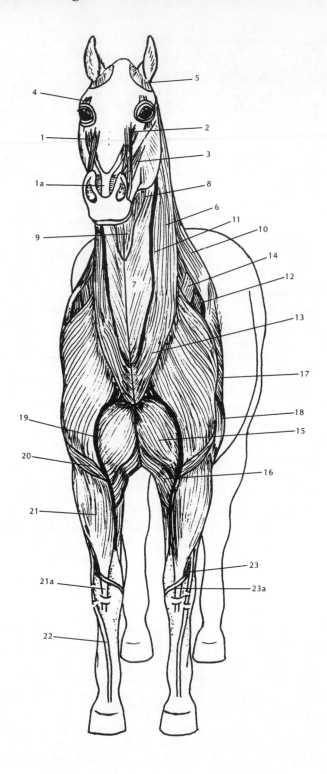

1.14 Muscles of the Horse, Front View

(1, 1a) levator muscle of upper lip and tendon
(2) levator muscle of upper lip and nostril wing
(3) lateral nostril dilator muscle
(4) corrugator supercilii muscle
(5) interscutular muscle
(6) brachiocephalic muscle
(7) sternomandibular part of sternocephalic muscle
(8) omohyoid muscle
(9) sternothyroid muscle
(10) cervical part of trapezius muscle
(11) jugular vein
(12) supraspinous muscle
(13) remains of skin muscle in the neck
(14) cranial deep pectoral muscle
(15) cranial superficial pectoral muscle
(16) caudal superficial pectoral muscle
(17) long head of triceps muscle
(18) lateral head of triceps muscle
(19) cephalic vein
(20) brachial muscle
(21, 21a) radial carpal extensor muscle and tendon
(22) common digital extensor tendon
(23, 23a) oblique carpal extensor muscle and tendon

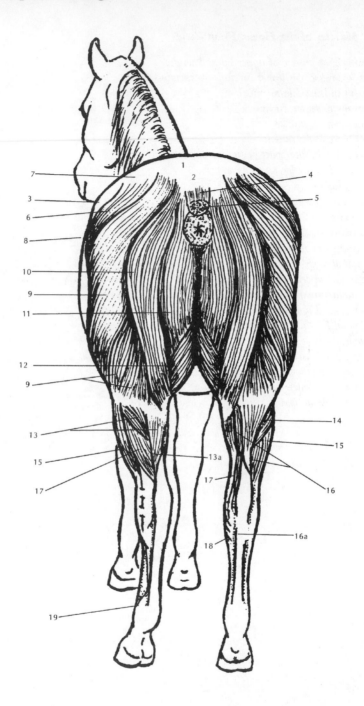

1.15 Muscles of the Horse, Rear View

(1) point of croup
(2) dock of tail
(3) point of hip or haunch (tuber coxae)
(4) levator muscles of tail
(5) depressor muscles of tail
(6) superficial gluteal muscles
(7) gluteal fascia
(8) tensor muscle of lateral femoral fascia
(9) biceps femoris muscle
(10) semitendinosus muscle
(11) semimembranosus muscle
(12) gracilis muscle
(13, 13a) gastrocnemius muscle and tendon
(14) soleus muscle
(15) lateral digital extensor muscle
(16, 16a) superficial digital flexor muscle and tendon
(17) deep digital flexor muscle
(18) inner or medial tendon of the cranial tibial muscle
(19) suspensory ligament

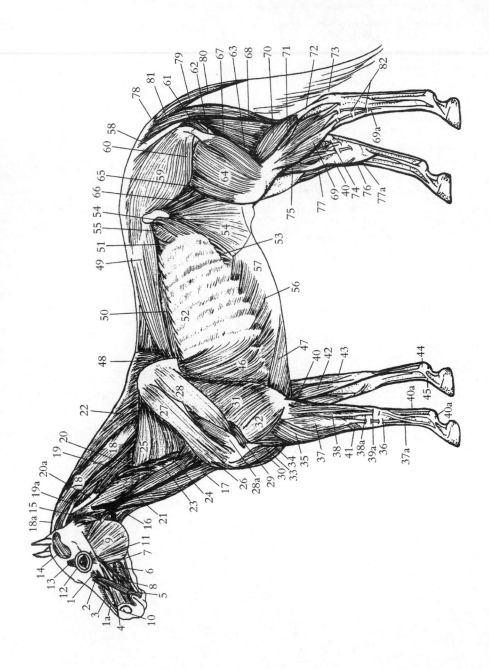

1.16 Deeper Muscles of the Horse

(1, 1a) levator muscle of upper lip and its tendon
(2) levator muscle of upper lip and nostril wing
(3) dorsal part of lateral nasal muscle
(4) lateral nostril dilator muscle
(5) orbicular muscle of the mouth
(6) buccinator muscle
(7) depressor muscle of lower lip
(8) zygomatic muscle
(9) masseter muscle
(10) transverse nasal muscle
(11) depressor muscle of lower eyelid
(12) orbicular muscle of the eye
(13) corrugator supercilii muscle
(14) temporal muscle
(15) occipitomandibular muscle (jugulo-mandibular)
(16) sternothyrohyoid and omohyoid muscles
(17) sternomandibular part of sternocephalic muscle
(18, 18a) complexus muscle and tendon (part of semispinalis capitis muscle)
(19, 19a) longissimus capitis muscle and tendon
(20, 20a) longissimus atlantis muscle and tendon
(21) rectus capitis ventralis muscle

(22) rhomboideus muscle
(23) scalene muscle
(24) intertransverse muscle
(25) cervical part of ventral serrate muscle
(26) cranial deep pectoral muscle (the anterior part of the deep pectoral)
(27) supraspinatus muscle
(28, 28a) infraspinatus muscle and tendon
(29) teres minor muscle
(30) cranial superficial pectoral muscle (anterior or clavicular part of superficial pectoral)
(31) long head of triceps muscle
(32) lateral head of triceps muscle
(33) biceps brachii muscle
(34) brachialis muscle
(35) radial carpal extensor muscle
(36) radial carpal extensor tendon
(37, 37a) common digital extensor muscle and tendon
(38, 38a) lateral digital extensor muscle and tendon
(39, 39a) lateral carpal flexor muscle and its two tendons, long and short
(40, 40a) deep digital flexor muscle and tendon

(41) oblique carpal extensor muscle
(42) medial carpal flexor muscle
(43) middle carpal flexor muscle
(44) suspensory ligament (superior sesamoidean ligament derived from interosseous muscle)
(45) suspensory ligament, extensor branch, attaching to the common digital extensor tendon
(46) thoracic part of ventral serrate muscle
(47) caudal deep pectoral muscle (posterior part of deep pectoral)
(48) spinalis dorsi muscle (musculus spinalis and semispinalis thoracis and cervicis)
(49) longissimus dorsi muscle (musculus longissimus thoracis and lumborum)
(50) iliocostalis dorsi muscle (musculus ilio-costalis thoracis and lumborum)
(51) retractor costae muscle
(52) external intercostal muscles
(53) internal intercostal muscles
(54) internal abdominal oblique muscle
(55) transverse abdominal muscle
(56) external abdominal oblique muscle

(continued)

1.16 Deeper Muscles of the Horse (continued)

(57) aponeurosis (flattened tendon)
(58) sacrosciatic ligament
(59) medial gluteal muscle
(60) deep gluteal muscle
(61) gemellus muscle
(62) quadratus femoris muscle
(63) adductor femoris muscle
(64) lateral vastus muscle (part of quadriceps muscle)
(65) rectus femoris muscle (part of quadriceps muscle)

(66) iliac muscle
(67) semimembranosus muscle (part of the hamstring group of muscles)
(68) semitendinosus muscle (part of the hamstring group of muscles)
(69, 69a) long digital extensor muscle and tendon
(70) lateral head of gastrocnemius
(71) soleus muscle
(72) Achilles tendon (tendon for gastrocnemius and soleus muscles)
(73) superficial digital flexor tendon

(74) accessory or tarsal tendon
(75) popliteal muscle
(76) saphenous vein
(77, 77a) peroneus tertius muscle and its tendon
(78) short tail levator muscles
(79) long tail levator muscles
(80) tail depressor muscle
(81) coccygeus muscle
(82) annular ligament

and deep massage. These techniques will promote blood circulation, bringing new oxygen and nutrients to affect healing and to break down scar tissue within the muscle fibers.

As a result of heavy training and exercise, a stress point may develop close to the origin tendon of the muscle. A *stress point* is a small spasm in the muscle fiber. Keep the horse free of stress points by using the stress point technique in chapter 5. (Chapter 10 describes the stress points specific to each body part and chapter 15 describes the stress points specific to each discipline.) Another side effect of an intense training program and vigorous exercise is the formation of trigger points. A *trigger point* is a combination of lactic acid build-up and motor nerve ending irritation, mostly in the fleshy part (belly) of the muscle. The term "trigger point" derives from the fact that when pressure is applied to a particular point, a pain signal will be sent to other parts of the body. Trigger points can be found in any muscle of the body. Keep your horse free of trigger points by using the trigger point technique in chapter 5.

Study all the charts and learn about all aspects of the horse's body. Understanding the interrelation of all the various systems will contribute greatly to your expertise in assessing the various problems you may encounter and wish to treat with massage.

A solid understanding of equine anatomy will assist your ability to properly massage each body part of your horse. Knowing all the muscles, the joints they influence, and the bones involved will give you a more assertive approach in your massage care. You will be amazed at how much information you can learn from this chapter. This knowledge will give you confidence in your practice.

2

THE HORSE AND MASSAGE THERAPY

Most horses, like humans, enjoy massage therapy when it is done with skilled hands and a good understanding of anatomy.

If you are interested in knowing how your horse will feel during and after his massage, it would be helpful for you to have a therapeutic massage yourself. You would realize how good it feels when skilled hands release your muscle tension. Feeling someone manipulating your muscles will make it easier for you to "feel-see" with your fingers as you massage your equine friend. You would also appreciate how relaxed your horse can get after such treatment.

During his first massage experience, the horse will be very curious about what is happening to him. He may become defensive. Often feeling nervous or impatient, the horse will move away, perhaps reacting suddenly if the pressure is too aggressive. On the other hand, some horses might be very passive and quiet, as good as gold.

Be aware of the feedback the horse gives you. Learn to recognize the sure signs of apprehension: raising of the head, ears pulled back, eyes widening and becoming intense, skin twitching, tail swishing, swinging of the rear toward you, stamping of feet, breathing short and hard, and biting. Sure signs of relaxation and enjoyment, however, include: eyes half-closed, head down, ears to the side, heavy sighs, relaxing of the lower lip, and nuzzling. Monitor your horse's body language constantly and adjust your work accordingly.

After a few sessions, the horse will accept your efforts without any trouble and start to enjoy massage. Some horses with traumatic histories (abuse, accidents) may be more resentful of massage than others, tensing up all over. Sometimes there can be a fear of being touched, or "touch-shyness," simply because humans have not spent much time bonding with a particular horse. Time, patience, and care will do wonders for a shy horse.

In some cases, touch-shyness in one area of the body (for example, the head or back) can indicate an underlying condition. When dealing with an extreme case of phobia or restlessness, consult your veterinarian or homeopath. A mild tranquilizer might be in order.

Be especially aware of the horse's temperament and character when approaching him; be particularly careful with stallions. Most geldings, mares and foals, however, respond very positively to their first treatment.

Take time to build a rapport with the animal during the first massage. As a rule, use the relaxation routine in chapter 6 prior to giving any massage at any time to any horse. Don't rush! With each session you will build your horse's trust while allaying his instinctive fears.

As the horse relaxes during the session, his head will go down and his breathing will become deeper and slower with occasional sighing. Sighing is a definite indication of tension release. You will feel a strong energy field around the animal as he relaxes. Depending on the nature of the massage you use, the horse might go to sleep or perk up and be ready for exercise. Either way, massage will benefit the horse's overall health.

How the Horse Responds

Like humans, horses have both visual and auditory aspects to their mental makeup. Many factors in the horse's life will influence his psychological and physical behavior. Visual and auditory tendencies will vary in relationship to: age, sex, environment (people, stabling), experiences, and training. Adjust your approach accordingly.

The Visual Horse

A visual horse loves company. Such an animal communicates primarily through motion, expressing his emotions by physical reactions and movements. This type of horse needs to be secure in his visible surroundings. Familiar areas play a strong role in his well-being. Body language signals are important, particularly since horses like to be touched when they *want* to be touched. A horse may even refuse to be touched.

When massaging a visual horse, proceed gently and peacefully. Demonstration through gesture is more important than talking, but it is good to maintain a soft-spoken contact with him as you massage his body. Allow the horse to look around. Work him in a familiar area.

THE AUDITORY HORSE

An auditory horse is more perceptive than a visual horse; he pays attention to sounds. It's important to talk to an auditory horse. This type of horse is less body-expressive than the visual horse but is willing to please. He is curious but more fragile in his self-esteem. The auditory horse always loves to be touched, but also likes serenity and time alone.

The auditory horse can be massaged anywhere; because of his nature, he copes with new environments easily. Throughout the treatment, talk to the animal in a peaceful tone of voice. Avoid high-pitched or loud sounds in his presence. Due to the auditory horse's sensibility, you need to pay extra attention to your approach during your massage (i.e., gentle touch, awareness of horse's feedback).

Keep in mind that both visual and auditory conditions will appear in a horse's make-up during different periods of his life. The one condition may change to the other gradually over a long period of time, or the change may be quite rapid. As part of the relaxation massage routine, the head massage routine in chapter 6 gives you a good opportunity to evaluate the horse you are working on.

DURATION OF A MASSAGE

For your first massage, and especially if it is the animal's first massage, the relaxation massage routine in chapter 6 is highly recommended. It should last between 10 and 20 minutes. Use your own judgment and modify the time in relation to the horse's temperament and the feedback signs he gives you. The first massage is a very special time in which you should really emphasize a soft, mindful, and caring contact to gain the animal's trust.

On your first full-body massage, again proceed gently in a very relaxed manner, avoiding awkward rhythms and deep pressure, until you have gained the horse's confidence. After several sessions you can increase the duration of your massages to 45 or 60 minutes, up to an hour and a half if the animal permits it.

The head massage routine in chapter 6, which complements the relaxation routine, can take anywhere from 10 to 30 minutes. Again, some animals love having their faces touched; some simply do not, but with patience and perseverance you might win them over.

A maintenance massage routine (chapter 6) can be done anytime to keep the animal's muscles fit; it should last 30 or 40 minutes in the early practices, and increased to 60 or 90 minutes later on. A recuperation routine (chapter 6) should be used after the horse has exercised in order to prevent stiffness or tying up. The routine should last between 20 and 30 minutes.

It is not unusual to spend an hour and a half on a thorough maintenance routine with a horse accustomed to massage. The expression "being massaged to death" is very appealing but not very realistic; most horses will become nervous, almost agitated, after an hour-long massage. But some animals can easily take a two-hour, gentle, in-depth maintenance massage. This may sound exhausting for the masseur or masseuse, but with practice and the use of efficient techniques mentioned later (chapter 5), he or she will quickly develop good endurance.

The connection you have with the horse is important. When massaging a strange horse for the first time, do not expect too much. But after 5 to 10 massage sessions, most horses will love to be massaged; they will lower their heads and go into relaxation very quickly. That's their way of showing you that they appreciate your work!

When dealing with an injury, consult with your veterinarian before any massage is considered. Depending on the case, once the injury is past the acute stage, a massage treatment should last from 20 to a maximum of 60 minutes, including hydrotherapy and stretching time where applicable. The severity of the case and the degree of inflammation symptoms (heat and swelling) present will dictate the nature and course of treatment. Chapter 5 presents several massage techniques that are commonly used for injury treatment. Always keep in mind that injured tissues are extremely painful; you must not overwork them. Keep your treatment time short at the beginning. As the inflammation decreases, you can proportionally increase the duration of your massage sessions.

When working on any one specific area—for example, the hindquarters or back—do not work for more than 10 to 15 minutes; otherwise you could overwork the tissues. This could result in inflammation and irritation of the tissues.

For the same reason, do not spend more than 5 to 10 minutes on a small area such as the poll or stifle. Judge the situation carefully. Consider the state of the tissues and the horse's tolerance at the time of treatment. And always relieve any inflammation by following the massage with lots of drainage and cold hydrotherapy (chapter 4).

Plan and evaluate your treatment mentally before you start, keeping track of time as you move around the body. With practice, this will become second nature to you.

WHEN TO MASSAGE YOUR HORSE

Basically, any time is a good time to massage your horse, but you want to choose the moment when your horse will be most receptive. Depending on your goals and the situation at hand, you need to find the optimum time in order to achieve the best results.

The most effective way to use massage therapy is to integrate the massage movements into your everyday way of working with your animal. For example, you can massage right after grooming, after exercise, or when putting your horse away for the night. You can massage for a few minutes over a small area, such as the back, right after unsaddling. You can choose a morning or evening schedule for a thorough, full-body session. You are the judge; common sense is the rule. If you try to work an animal during feeding time, well, good luck.

In any case always observe these guidelines:

❖ Always do a "health" check to ensure that there are no prevailing contraindications prior to massaging the animal (page 47).

❖ Develop a routine and base your work on it. A repetitive pattern ensures confidence and relaxation (chapter 6).

When you want to deliver a good massage, it is best to wait for the horse's "moment." Evaluating your horse's temperament will help you discover his "best time." If your animal is a "morning horse," work in the morning; if an "afternoon horse," work in the afternoon; if a "night horse," work in the late evening. If your animal seems to have an auditory–dominant nature, he will probably prefer a massage when everything is quiet, usually in the evening or perhaps during the day when the other horses are out. As mentioned earlier, if your animal is more visual, he will prefer a massage in familiar surroundings; within normal limits, noise will have little effect on him.

The type of training and lifestyle your horse is used to will also play a role in determining good times for massage; i.e., maintenance massage before exercise, recuperation routine after exercise, relaxing massage before and after traveling or when restless or in pain.

Keep in mind outside influences: an approaching electrical storm, strong winds, or abnormal activities going on in the barn (construction, competition, seminars, arrival of a new horse, and so on). A horse can be restless during feeding time, if he has worms, if he's colicky, during a hot summer season, when in a heavy training schedule with very rich feed, during competition, during travel, and the like.

The relaxation routine in chapter 6 can be done at any time; it is always used to start a full-body massage. This routine works wonders in switching a horse's mood, especially if he is depressed, naughty, mischievous, or simply tense.

The maintenance routine in chapter 6 is best done when the horse is warm after some exercise, in either the morning or evening. A simple walk or a little longeing will be enough to warm up the horse. If the horse cannot be warmed by exercise, cover him with a blanket or use hot and cold hydrotherapy (also known as a "vascular flush") to produce increased circulation (chapter 4).

The recuperation routine in chapter 6 is always done after heavy training. This routine helps the horse recover faster and can help prevent tying up.

Injury treatment should be worked into a schedule followed by stretching exercises or a rest period, depending on how well the horse is recovering.

How to Approach the Horse You Want to Massage

Your first contact, the actual first few minutes with the horse, is crucial. The situation requires awareness, some common sense, and a lot of horse sense. If you approach the horse with an understanding of his nature and immediately make him feel secure, he will trust you very quickly.

It is recommended that you observe a horse briefly before actually approaching him. Try to determine which dominance he is displaying in his character—visual or auditory. A visual horse loves company and will be much easier to approach. An auditory horse is very perceptive, pays more attention to noises, and will be more difficult to reach.

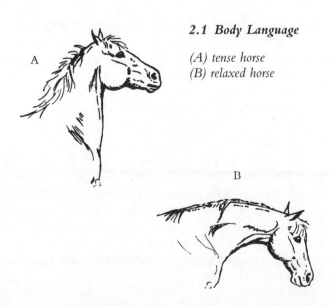

2.1 Body Language

(A) tense horse
(B) relaxed horse

A

B

Remember that some animals have been physically abused. They will be more suspicious of you as you begin work. Some horses might even try to get you with a quick bite or a springy cow-kick. Be alert. Keep assessing the feedback signs he gives you.

First of all, ensure that you are calm and relaxed. Do not start when you are stressed, anxious, tired, or fearful. Your feelings will be communicated to the animal through your touch, so be relaxed and have a positive attitude. In other words, the way you are is the way the horse will be. (Riders, you have heard that one before!)

Speak softly and kindly to the horse as you approach him more to one side. Do not stand in front of him. Keep your hands low (at waist level) and fully opened. Give your horse time to acknowledge you before you touch him. The horse's response will be to bring his head toward you and nuzzle you; this is how a horse shakes your hand. Meanwhile, evaluate his breathing rhythm and adapt your breathing to the horse's. This action will allow you to observe his inner state, whether calm or restless.

Once the horse has acknowledged you, quietly raise your right hand—your natural giving hand—to his nose, and lightly massage the face. Keep talking to the animal, furthering your bonding with the softness of your voice. Gently bring your left hand to the horse's attention, then start touching the neck lightly at the poll. If the horse does not like this, bring your hand down to the withers.

The first hand contact needs to be very warm, thoughtful, rich in feeling and vibration. Thus this contact will have a strong, positive impact on the horse. Take your time. There is no need to rush. A few minutes are all it takes to establish this crucial first impression.

Then proceed with your massage. As mentioned above, the relaxation routine is the best way to start any massage session, especially when you are breaking the ice for the first time. Always start with a very gentle, light touch, going deeper progressively. Start with 2 to 5 pounds of pressure, moving up to 15, but no more than 20 pounds in the first session. Increase your touch gradually. To familiarize yourself with the pounds of pressure, use a bathroom or kitchen scale to appreciate how quickly pressure builds. For more detail on pressure gauges, see chapter 3, page 57.

Keep up verbal contact as you progress in the sessions and look for signs of feedback (ears twitching, changes in breathing rhythm, eyes closed or bulging, body movements, moving into you or away, stamping of feet, switching of the standing leg, swishing of the tail, twitching of skin, noises, etc.)

Memorize the four "T's": temperature, texture, tension, and tenderness (see the following section).

What you learn through your fingertips is very important; make sure you remain sensitive to them and what they communicate.

Take note of your observations and record them after the treatment. If someone is available to take notes as you work, so much the better. A record of your efforts will help ensure that you perform well (chapter 16).

Always think of your horse as a very picky, demanding client who is always checking on you. You want to give him the best of your massage abilities.

CONTRAINDICATIONS TO MASSAGING A HORSE

The term *contraindication* is used to describe specific situations in which you should not massage a horse and in which you should seek the advice of your veterinarian.

Do not massage when the horse's *temperature* is over 102° Fahrenheit (F) or 39° Celsius (C). A horse's normal temperature is 100°F, 38°C. A mild fever is present at 102°F, 39°C. A moderate fever is present at 104.5°F, 40°C. A high fever is present at 106°F, 41°C. An increase in temperature occurs during serious illnesses; feverish conditions call for complete rest. Massage will only render the situation worse by increasing blood circulation, which is already rampant. Cover your horse with a blanket to keep him warm and to avoid a chill. Check with your vet.

The laying on of hands over the forehead, at the poll, and over the sacrum area will soothe the horse, bringing relief to the central nervous system. Use the right hand on the sacrum, the left on the poll. A cold towel over the sacrum and along the spine will feel good to the horse. During high fever a complete rubdown with a cold towel will decrease the body temperature and cool the animal. Follow by blanketing to avoid a chill.

When there is an open wound (broken skin) or healing wound (bleeding) anywhere on the body, avoid that particular area, although you may massage the rest of the body to help with excess swelling and to release compensatory tension.

When there is *acute trauma* (a torn muscle or an area with internal bleeding, such as an acute hematoma), use ice for the first few hours. Massage can be resumed in the chronic stage (past 72 hours).

When severe forms of functional nervous disease (tetanus) are present, do not massage the horse. The nerve stimulation would drive him insane. Even the laying on of hands would be risky, although it could help.

Acute nerve problems or nerve irritation (*neuralgia*) in a particular area (following a wound or a bad stretch) is a contraindication to massage. The laying on of hands might soothe. Use cold hydrotherapy to numb the nerve endings before and after the laying on of hands.

During colitis, diarrhea, pregnancy, or hernias, use just a light stroking on the abdomen and only if the horse does not mind.

Acute rheumatism and arthritis are too painful to permit massage. Massage would worsen the inflammation. Instead, use cold hydrotherapy locally. Once the acute stage is relieved, resume your treatment. Chronic stages of rheumatism and arthritis require different treatment. Light massage over the areas affected would relax the compensatory tension from the muscles supporting those structures. Do not work deeply around the joints.

Calcification around joints or within soft tissues should not be massaged; it would only increase the inflammation in these areas. Check with your veterinarian for possible surgical removal.

An inflammatory condition such as phlebitis would be worsened by direct massage. Use cold hydrotherapy and check with your veterinarian.

If cancerous tumors and cysts are present, don't massage. Massage could spread them. Avoid the affected areas, but you may massage the rest of the body. Check with your vet.

Massage is absolutely contraindicated in the following conditions, since it would contribute to their spread:

- Skin problems of fungal origin, such as ringworm
- Infectious conditions of fistulous origin, such as poll–evil or fistulous withers
- Infectious diseases, such as strangles, tetanus, and pneumonia
- Acute stages of viral diseases, such as equine influenza or herpes

Be careful when dealing with what appears to be an abnormal situation. If in doubt, contact a veterinarian. Otherwise, use massage cautiously. When massage is contraindicated, the laying on of hands will often bring soothing energy to an irritated area, relieving the pain. Hydrotherapy (chapter 4) will also relieve the inflammation and pain considerably, assisting recovery and definitively comforting your animal.

Knowing how to safely approach an animal for massage is part of the secret to success. Your patience, perseverance, good humor, kindness, knowledge, and skills will reduce the psychological and physical barriers between the horse and you, leading to better communication with the animal.

Some Massage Do's and Don'ts

The atmosphere in which you work will directly influence the efficacy of the massage. What follows are some suggestions for making massage treatment safe for both you and your horse.

Do's

✔ Do evaluate the horse's health by checking his vital signs (pulse, temperature, eyes, breathing, etc.). Be sure there are no contraindications.

✔ Do work in a large space, free from obstacles. Remove distracting objects such as boxes, shovels, blankets, and ropes.

✔ Do keep small pets away.

✔ Do avoid small stalls. Use the barn aisle or an arena, or work outside if weather permits, preferably in the shade. Windy conditions disturb horses.

✔ Do maintain a soothing atmosphere: not too much traffic, not too many noises. Eventually you may play peaceful, quiet music.

✔ Do have somebody hold the horse by the halter or the lead rope.

✔ Do secure your horse between cross-ties if no one else is around, although cross-ties will restrict head motion and interfere with relaxation. It is preferable to allow the horse complete freedom of head movement since this promotes better relaxation and permits more feedback signals.

✔ Do clean your horse before starting a massage.

✔ Do begin massage with a very light pressure and progress to deeper strokes.

✔ Do keep your fingernails short, and avoid wearing jewelry.

✔ Do keep talking to the animal throughout the treatment.

✔ Do pay attention to feedback signs from the ears, eyes, feet, tail, etc.

✔ Do keep records of your observations and the types of treatment you give.

✔ Do establish a treatment and exercise schedule for the following weeks, or until recovery.

Don'ts

✘ Don't disregard the physiological signs of contraindications.

✘ Don't work in a narrow space. This is dangerous if the horse suddenly moves or panics due to outside influences (loud noises, falling objects, storm, etc.).

✗ Don't stand between a horse and a wall as you work because you can be squeezed.

✗ Don't allow loud music, commotion, or smoking, especially when dealing with an auditory animal.

✗ Don't allow cats, dogs, or other pets to wander around your work area. Prevent that intrusion before starting treatment.

✗ Don't work a dirty horse—one with mud or manure on his body.

✗ Don't work hastily, too quickly, or too forcefully.

✗ Don't wear jewelry, have long fingernails, or wear heavy perfume.

✗ Don't stop speaking to the horse; he needs praise and reassurance.

✗ Don't talk loudly or shout.

✗ Don't talk to somebody else while working. It will affect your concentration and the quality of your work. The horse will definitely feel the difference.

✗ Don't use heavy pressure to begin with.

✗ Don't ignore the horse's body language.

✗ Don't be angry or in a bad mood when working on the horse.

✗ Don't think negatively.

SAFETY TIPS

When working closely with horses, follow these safety guidelines:

❖ Wear large-size clothes to give yourself freedom of movement.

❖ Wear strong boots. You could be stepped on.

❖ In cold weather, keep your fingers warm by wearing leather riding gloves while giving a massage. The leather is thin enough so that you do not lose "touch" quality. If you only want to warm up your animal with some wringings, shakings, or tapotements as described in chapter 3, you can wear warm mittens, but it is better to work with bare hands. Some people like to wear gloves at all times to protect their skin. This is fine so long as your gloves are thin enough to allow you to feel the quality of your touch.

Understanding how to properly approach your horse for massage will secure best results. Recognizing the different contraindications will allow you to better care for your horse. Observing the Do's and Don'ts of this practice will maximize your efficiency. This overall knowledge will give you confidence in your practice.

3

PRINCIPLES AND CONCEPTS OF MASSAGE

When massage is employed with knowledge and skill, it not only treats specific health problems in horses but also improves their general health. Massage has a positive influence on the physical and psychological well-being of horses, regardless of age. The caring feeling transmitted to a horse through the soothing contact of massage will contribute to the relaxation of the nervous system and assist in relieving stress.

After massage treatment, the "feel-good" sensation derived erases much nervous tension and anxiety. That sensation will convey a sense of satisfaction and reconnection with life that subconsciously promotes recovery and improvement.

During the first massage, your horse might wonder what you are doing. After a few sessions, however, he will show signs of enjoyment through his body language. Even when a horse is experiencing a painful condition, massage can have a pain-relieving effect on him. Although unproven through scientific research, it is theorized that massage inhibits pain by stimulating the release of *endorphins* (opiate-like enzymes produced in the brain) to reduce the awareness of pain.

DEVELOPING MASSAGE SKILLS

PROPER APPROACH

How you approach your horse is most important—for example, being calm, being aware of his personality, and so on. This was discussed in detail in chapter 2. You may want to review that information. A full understanding of this subject will ensure good mental and physical contact during a massage treatment.

PROPER POSTURE

Good posture is essential to giving a good massage.

Good posture helps you save your energy by avoiding unnecessary movement and fatigue. Good posture is the sum of the mechanical efficiency of the body. With good posture, you will feel well grounded in your work and more centered. You will feel your own body's energy field as well as your horse's energy field, which will permit a better exchange between you.

To maintain good posture:

- ❖ Stand with your back straight, but not rigid or stiff. Your shoulders should be loose and mobile.
- ❖ Relax and breathe slowly and deeply. Adapt your breathing rhythm to that of the horse.
- ❖ Keep your head in line with your spine. (Imagine a cord pulling you up lightly from the top of your head.)
- ❖ Tuck in your chin slightly.
- ❖ Look forward.
- ❖ Drop your shoulders. Do not tense your neck.
- ❖ Stretch out your arms, then let the elbows flex a little. You will now be at the right distance from the horse.
- ❖ Develop a feeling of working from your elbows, not just your hands and wrists. This action will save energy and prevent soreness. Furthermore, it will give you more strength because you will feel more connected to your whole body.

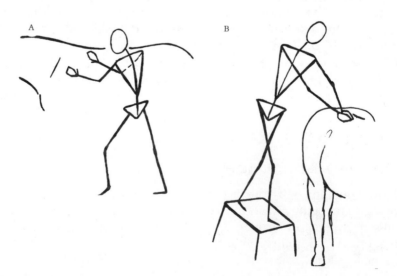

3.1 Proper Posture

(A) regular stand   *(B) using a stool*

❖ Use your body weight when doing large movements (for example, effleurage), to prevent serious fatigue.

❖ Bend your legs slightly at the knee, keeping your feet apart at shoulder width, similar to the stance in Tai Chi.

❖ Be light on your feet. Use your body weight in your movements. This agility will also help prevent accidents should the horse move unexpectedly.

❖ Work from your pelvis when exerting pressure; this action will help you exert more power.

Always be aware of your posture during massage. If you do, you will maximize your energy and the quality of your treatment. With practice, good posture will come to you automatically.

For proper posture to become second nature to you, practice mental reinforcement at the beginning of or during a treatment with a "posture check":

❖ Head up, chin in, look forward

❖ Back straight, not stiff, breathing relaxed

❖ Neck relaxed, shoulders loose, elbows flexed

❖ Knees slightly flexed, feet apart at shoulder width

❖ Moving and flowing from the pelvis

With your arms and hands relaxed, this posture will allow you to perform massage smoothly, avoiding tension in the chest, shoulders, and back. Remember to take deep breaths regularly to keep yourself relaxed.

Use your body weight to regulate the amount of pressure applied. Avoid unnecessary movements of the body; they will fatigue you and may annoy the horse. In her video *Centered Riding,* Sally Swift demonstrates how good posture will ensure connection with the vital energy that life offers you at all times.

Good posture will ensure an energy flow from your hands to the horse and back to you, benefiting both you and the horse. Stand fairly close to your horse to reinforce this energy exchange. In some cases, such as working on trigger points, you may consider leaning against the animal if he allows you to. It is important to give the horse a feeling of closeness to increase his relaxation and to ensure benefit from your treatment. But exercise judgment. Closeness reinforces the feeling of care that occurs naturally when giving a massage, but if the horse objects to your proximity, you should always be ready to move away.

3.2 Proper Posture: *Back straight, elbows and knees flexed.*

3.3 Proper Posture: *Using body weight for added strength.*

SENSITIVITY OF THE HANDS

A good touch provides a soothing and comforting feeling during your treatment. The palms of your hands and your fingertips will give you accurate feedback on the physiological state of the various parts you are working on. Learning to trust your hands is not easy, however. You must concentrate so as to detect subtle changes in the body on which you are working. The quality of your work depends strongly on the sensitivity of your hands.

In the early stages of practice, a good way to develop your perceptions is to work with your eyes closed. This will help you focus on your fingertips, developing your tactility and enhancing your touch. This manual participation in massage is doubly beneficial to you. First, massage stimulates the circulation of blood to your hands and fingertips, nourishing them and preventing blood and lymph congestion. Second, since the nerves in the fingertips are directly connected to the brain, the use of the hands tends to promote a feeling of psychological ease. The Chinese habit of turning walnuts around and around in the hand springs from a knowledge of the salutary effect of manual activity. By putting the fingertips to extensive use, massage promotes emotional stability and physical health as it stimulates the blood flow to the hand.

THE FOUR T'S

The sensations you perceive during massage—temperature, texture, tension, tenderness—are referred to as the "four T's."

TEMPERATURE

The normal body temperature of a horse is 38° Celsius (99 to 100.5° Fahrenheit). Any changes in the temperature of the horse's skin suggest that certain problems exist. For example, an area that is abnormally cool to the touch (due to lack of blood circulation in that area) compared to the rest of the body may indicate such problems as muscle contraction or deep chronic tension. An area that is hot to the touch indicates the presence of an inflammation and is a sure sign of an underlying problem (such as microspasm, stress points, trigger points, or traumas).

TEXTURE

By *texture* I mean the density and elasticity of the skin and the muscular fibers. By practicing on healthy animals, you will quickly develop a sense for what normal, healthy tissues feel like. Tissues that appear either too soft or too puffy indicate the presence of swelling (edema), a sign of sluggish blood and/or lymph circulation, or of an underlying inflammatory condition.

TENDERNESS

By tenderness of the structures (muscles, tendons, ligaments, joints), I mean the degree to which the animal responds to your touch. If he is highly sensitive, it is a sure sign of an underlying problem (nerve endings are irritated or perhaps damaged). The horse's reaction to your touch is proportional to how severe and how stressful the condition is.

TENSION

Muscle tension is the result of a heavy workload or too much exercise. Sometimes muscle tension can result from scar tissue buildup after trauma. Too much tightness means less blood circulation, fewer nutrients, and less oxygen. Tension will increase toxin buildup, creating an underlying inflammation. Trigger points and stress points might result. It is normal to expect some high muscle tone immediately after exercise. But to find tension in the muscles after a good rest is a sure sign that it is a compensatory response to some other problem. Too much tension in a muscle might be a sign of scar tissue developing as a result of an inflammation.

Thus, when you start a massage, always remember to use your fingers as sensors to get feedback (the four T's) on the particular condition you are working on. Your fingers should become an extension of your brain. Use them as probes, quickly feeling and assessing what they touch, knowing almost instinctively how to adjust the pressure and to use the right massage move. You will be amazed to find how fast this heightened perception will develop for you.

PRESSURE, CONTACT, AND RHYTHM

The key to a successful massage is in the heightened perception of your fingers and the mastering of pressure, contact, and rhythm.

PRESSURE

To appreciate how much pressure you are applying in a massage, experiment by pressing on a bathroom or kitchen scale. You will be amazed to find how quickly pressure builds up. Practice by simultaneously or alternately using one thumb, two thumbs, the fingers of one hand, the fingers of two hands, the palm of the hand, two palms, one fist, two fists, your elbow, etc. Practice the various massage moves on the scale with and without using your whole body weight. Be creative! This exercise will help you realize how little you must exert in order to reach deep into the muscle structure. In massage we have to be very careful about applying too much pressure because we inadvertently can bruise the muscle fibers. Obviously, a bruise can't be seen under the horse's coat. A bruise will be indicated by a slight hardening of the tissues— caused by the blood's stagnation—and the tenderness of the tissues that you will feel on palpation several hours after treatment.

Also use a scale to practice evaluating a 5- or 10-pound pressure, then 15 or 20 pounds, up to 30 or 35 pounds. Repeat the exercise until you feel what it takes for you to reach any desired level of pressure.

Degree of Pressure	Actual Force
finger–stroking touch	0.1 to 1 pound
light touch	2 to 3 pounds
regular touch	3 to 5 pounds
firm touch	8 to 10 pounds, 12 for a heavy horse
heavy pressure	starts at 15 pounds

More than 25 pounds can bruise fibers in the thin muscle layers of the average horse. If the horse has been well warmed up, he will take heavy pressure much more easily during the treatment. Thicker muscle layers can take up to 30 or 35 pounds of pressure.

When working on scar tissue or on ligaments, use up to 35 pounds of pressure, but again be very careful at that particular stage of your treatment.

The best pressure is one sufficient to cause a sensation midway between pleasure and pain. A good masseur or masseuse can apply pressure that produces deep bodily effects without discomfort. When getting into the deeper aspects of your work, closely observe the animal's feedback signs, especially the eyes.

Choosing the right degree of pressure will depend mostly upon the symptoms shown by the horse and by your goals for that massage treatment. Your posture should always be such that you use your body weight at all times; if necessary, you can ease up on the pressure immediately. Using your body weight will prevent fatigue.

Never jab your fingers into the animal's flesh. Instead, apply firm pressure with the soft bulbs of the fingers, the thumbs, or the palms of your hands as if you were resting all your body weight on them.

Always begin with a light pressure and progress to heavier pressure. Start with light strokings; follow with effleurages; then build up to wringings, kneadings, or compressions, all interspersed with effleurages (every 20 to 30 seconds) before using pressures above the 15-pound mark. Do not get carried away while working over stress or trigger points or on scar tissue. Very heavy pressure will trigger soreness in the muscles, especially the next day. Use the four T's. Always pay attention to the feedback signs of the animal, and "listen" to your fingers. Pain and discomfort should always be regarded as a warning signal. Be attentive, constantly adjusting the pressure of your massage. It's better to give several light treatments than one too-heavy treatment.

Because your thumbs, fingers, and palms are in constant contact during massage, they need careful attention. Whether employing the thumbs or the fingers, always press downward firmly using the bulbs of the fingers, not just the tips. When pressing forward with the tips you can tire or even injure your hands; don't do it! (Overuse of finger joints can result in many problems, including premature arthritis.) Years of correct massage action have given me well-developed, silky-smooth thumbs—the kind essential to this profession. Correct massage practice can do the same for everyone.

CONTACT

To get the best contact with the horse, keep your hands flexible, molding them to his body parts. A mindful contact will be strongly perceived by the animal, strengthening his trust in your work. Much information passes through your hands, both to you and to the animal. You should feel a lot of warmth—lots of energy—flowing through your hands during a massage. This deeper sense of contact will give you much feedback on what is happening with the animal as you are progressing with your massage.

Always weave each stroke into another, thus giving a feeling of continuity. Never remove your hands completely before the end of a massage move, not even when going around the horse to go on the other side. If you do not weave your moves one into another, if you often lose hand contact during the massage, you will create a disruptive feeling that prevents the horse from relaxing (you would feel the same if you were being massaged in that manner). Keeping hand contact makes a big difference in ensuring connection and comfort. Your proper posture will ensure that you work smoothly, passing on a feeling of general relaxation to the animal.

RHYTHM

In this context, rhythm refers to the frequency with which you apply your movements. Rhythm plays a strong role in the effectiveness of your massage.

A gentle, almost slow rhythm of 1 stroke per second is used most frequently. Use a soothing rhythm to start your session, to weave your moves into one another, and to finish your work. A soothing rhythm works wonders in relaxing the horse's nervous system, yet this soft approach allows you to work deeply if necessary.

A faster rhythm stimulates the animal. It is used to perk up the horse before riding or exercising, to stimulate circulation before deep treatment, or simply to warm up your animal when he is chilled. Be aware: Too brisk a rhythm could quickly irritate the horse, causing him to react against this type of massage. (How to choose specific rhythms will be discussed in chapters 5 and 6.) Develop your sense of rhythm by counting in your head, by listening to music, or by singing.

With practice you will develop a true appreciation of the feedback your fingers give you and you will know exactly how to achieve the right pressure by adjusting your contact and rhythm. Solid knowledge of the structure you are working on and of your massage techniques, plus a strong dose of common sense, will be all that you need to keep pressure, contact, and rhythm in harmony.

THE MAIN EFFECTS OF MASSAGE

THE MECHANICAL EFFECT

The mechanical effect is the actual physical contact caused by pressure on the body. Therefore the mechanical effect is directly proportional to pressure. The force you exert in the massage movements will stretch the tissues and drive the fluids (arterial, venous, and lymphatic) in the direction of the movements. Light pressure will gently start things moving, whereas heavier pressure will affect more efficiently the circulation of fluid in the area being worked on. The positive effects of increased fluid circulation are:

- ❖ Better tissue oxygenation
- ❖ Good metabolism
- ❖ Removal of carbon dioxide
- ❖ Lowered blood pressure

Deep mechanical pressure will also contribute to the release of endorphins. *Endorphins* are secreted in the brain and help the body diminish the awareness of pain. Although unproven by scientific research, it is thought that massage inhibits pain by stimulating the release of endorphins.

The mechanical pressure of specific massage moves will stretch and soften the tissues. This stretching and softening will help release muscle tension, contractures, trigger points, stress points, and spasms, eventually breaking down collagen fibers (scar tissue).

Note: On a human, mechanical pressure on the abdomen will affect the digestive organs and stimulate digestion. But on a horse, you should be very cautious when working on this area; it's very sensitive and the horse is very protective. Be aware!

Mechanical pressure also produces an effect on the nervous system. Depending on the type of application, it will either stimulate or soothe muscles. For example, slow, rhythmic, light-to-medium pressure will soothe and relax very efficiently, whereas faster rhythm with medium-to-heavy pressure will stimulate very quickly.

PURE NERVOUS REFLEX EFFECT

The pure nervous reflex effect, as the name suggests, influences only the nervous system. This effect is achieved with a very light touch. Exert almost no pressure; rather, contact the skin lightly to touch the cutaneous sensory nerve endings.

Stroking, light effleurage, and wide and very gentle kneadings are mostly used to elicit this effect. Gentle stimulation of the skin sends relaxing impulses to the brain. The motor nerves then "let go" of the tension. For this type of massage, use a slow, gentle, soothing and nourishing rhythm of 1 stroke per second on average.

Pure nervous reflex does not increase the secretion of glands, cause a chemical response, or have a mechanical impact on circulation of fluids, but it will soothe and relax a horse that is in a state of general tension, anxiety, shock, or pain. (See the relaxation massage routine in chapter 6.)

MASSAGE MOVES

There are eight essential classes of massage moves (stroking, effleurage, petrissage, shaking, vibration, friction, nerve manipulation, and tapotements), and a multitude of combinations.

Each individual class has several moves and each move can be performed in either a soothing or stimulating manner, depending upon pressure and rhythm. Some of the movements appear very similar, but they all offer specifics you need to be aware of. This knowledge will help you become expert in choosing the right massage moves. With practice these movements will become second nature to you.

STROKING

Stroking is used for its soothing, relaxing, calming effect (pure nervous reflex effect) on the body, directly affecting the central nervous system. It is the main move used in the relaxation massage routine. When the horse is very nervous, stroking his back and legs will soothe and "ground" him.

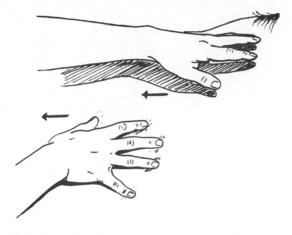

3.4 Stroking Movement

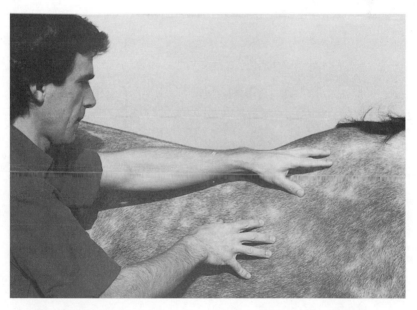

3.5 Stroking Massage Movement

You always start or finish a massage routine or massage treatment by applying several strokings over the body part that has
been worked on. Also use strokings to weave together various
massage techniques or when moving from one area of the body
to another.

Stroking movements are performed in a relaxed, superficial manner with the tips of the fingers or the palms of the hands. When
stroking, use very light pressure, from 0.1 to 1 pound of pressure—
2 pounds maximum when working on a heavy coat. Stroking can

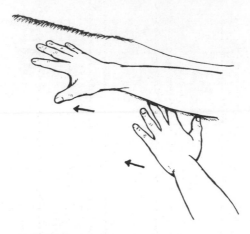

3.6 Effleurage Movement

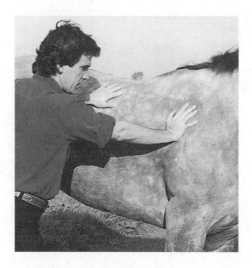

3.7 Effleurage Massage Movement

be done in any direction, but preferably along the length of the muscles, or following the direction in which the hair lies.

Done in slow motion, stroking gives a very soothing, relaxing sensation, producing an almost sedative effect. Done fast, stroking will have a stimulating, almost exciting, effect on the animal's nervous system.

EFFLEURAGE

Effleurage is the move you will use the most. Effleurage is used as every second move (every 20 to 30 seconds) during any massage work to emphasize proper drainage. It is also used after strokings to start or weave between movements during any massage routine or technique. To assist the natural flow of the venous blood circulation, always perform effleurage toward the heart.

Effleurage is a gliding movement done with the fingers and palm. During a one-handed effleurage stroke, the thumb never leads the hand but rather follows the fingers. The hand should be well-molded and in full contact with the body part being massaged. You can use one or both hands, simultaneously or alternately, in an even, gliding movement. The pressure is usually even throughout the entire stroke, except when going over bony processes such as the scapular ridge, point of the hip, point of elbow, or hock.

Effleurage has a mechanical, draining effect on body fluids such as blood and lymph. This draining effect is proportional to the pressure applied and the rhythm of the movement.

When performed in a superficial manner with a light pressure (2 or 3 pounds) and a slow rhythm (an average of 1 stroke per second, 2 seconds for long strokes over big muscles), effleurage will have a very soothing effect and boost circulation as well. This massage move is a very good one to start or finish a massage. When effleurage is done with a faster rhythm (2 to 3 strokes per second), it is more stimulating. It can be used in this way during treatment on small areas to drain swelling without hurting the structure. But do not use this combination over a large area. The fast rhythm often causes nerve irritation and makes the horse nervous.

When effleurage is applied in a deep manner with heavy pressure (10 or 15 pounds) and in a slow rhythm, it stimulates the circulation of blood and lymph. Yet the slow rhythm still soothes the nervous system. This combination is used to drain large areas between sequences of massage moves after heavy training. (See the maintenance massage routine and recuperation routine in chapter 6.)

When doing effleurage on a narrow area (the lower legs, for example), use mostly the palmar region of the fingers instead of the whole hand. Adjust the pressure according to the structure being worked on. Work lightly over thin muscle layers and bony structures but more heavily over thick muscle groups.

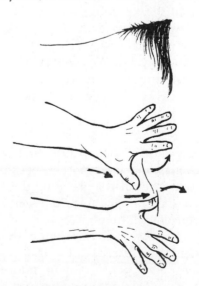

3.8 Petrissage: Kneading Movement

3.9 Double Thumb Kneading Movement

PETRISSAGE

Petrissage is the foundation movement of massage. It comprises kneading, compression, muscle squeezing, picking up, wringing up, and skin rolling. All these moves are mechanical and soothing, but if done quickly they will become stimulating. Petrissage manipulations alternate pressure and relaxation.

In the kneading, compression, and muscle squeezing massage moves, the tissues are pressed against the underlying structure. In the wringing-up, picking-up, and skin-rolling massage moves, the tissues are lifted away from the underlying structure. Used constantly in sport massage, these moves work on muscle tension, muscle knots, congestion, and small spasms.

Kneading

Kneading is done in a rhythmic, circular motion (small half-circles overlapping one another, pushing outwards) the same way you would knead dough, using the thumbs or the palmar surface of the index finger, middle finger, and ring finger. Contact is maintained at all times.

The tissues are intermittently compressed against the underlying bone structure. To relax a horse, the rhythm should be 1 movement per second; to induce stimulation, increase the rate to around 2 or 3 movements per second. Kneading has a pumping

3.10 Petrissage: Compression Movement

(A) palmar compression
(B) fist compression

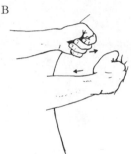

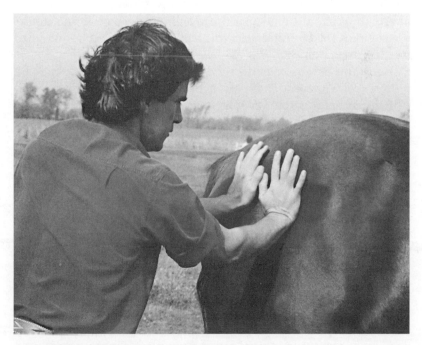

3.11 *Palmar Compression Movement*

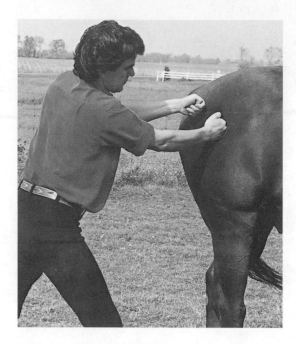

3.12 Fist Compression Movement

effect that boosts circulation and improves oxygenation. It also affects the various bundles of muscle fibers, separating and draining them. Kneading will help you feel scar tissue patches or small spasms (stress points).

Kneading is usually performed with two hands but it may be performed with one hand when the area being treated is small (the flexor tendon, for example). You can try other combinations, using only two fingers or a thumb and finger. When dealing with large areas (the hindquarters, for example), use the palms of your hands in combination with your body weight (proper posture). It is a very efficient technique.

When kneading, gauge your pressure. Start at 2 or 3 pounds. Increase to between 10 and 15 pounds when working the big muscle groups. Use up to 20 pounds when working on heavy horses. Intersperse your kneadings with a good deal of effleurages every couple of minutes.

Compression

Compression movements are made with the palm of the hand or with a lightly clenched fist, alternating each hand rhythmically and applying pressure directly to the muscle. Compression is used over large, bulky muscle areas, such as the hindquarters or the

shoulders if well muscled, working from your elbows and applying your body weight. The method is similar to that of kneading
but without the gliding movement over the muscles. The rhythm
should be 1 compression every second. Any faster would be highly
stimulating, almost irritating to most animals. Do not use compression on bony or thinly muscled areas.

Compression complements kneading; it is used to save time and
reduce fatigue when working on large muscle groups. Compression
produces the same pumping effect and has the same benefits as
kneading. Be careful not to over compress the muscles. Gauge
your pressure at between 20 and 30 pounds maximum. It is better to repeat the exercise several times and secure the desired effect
rather than go too fast or too heavily, which will result in irritated
or bruised fibers.

Muscle Squeezing

Muscle squeezing is mostly used to decongest and relax tense
muscles, principally along the crest of the neck and on the legs
and tail. The movement is made between extended fingers and the
heel of the hand, keeping the entire palm surface in full contact
with the body part worked on. Take care not to pull the muscle
away from its bony support; merely grasp and gently squeeze it.

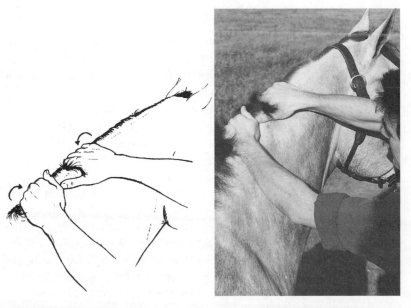

3.13 Petrissage: Muscle
  Squeezing Movement

3.14 Double Hand Muscle
  Squeezing Movement

Muscle squeezing accomplishes several things:

❖ The horse responds to the deeply felt touch by relaxing the muscle

❖ It gives you feedback about the tension in the muscle fibers

❖ It increases circulation

Since we only want to relax and decongest, it is not necessary to exert a lot of strength in this move. When muscle squeezing, always start gently with 5 to 10 pounds of pressure. You can use 15 pounds of pressure if dealing with bulkier muscle groups of heavier horses (thicker neck, legs, or pectoral muscles). If there is tenderness in the muscle, squeeze very gently.

Using muscle squeezing in a soothing, slow rhythm (1 squeeze every second) has a strong calming effect on the nervous system. It is used for this purpose in the relaxing massage routine, over the crest of the neck.

When done in a brisk manner (2 to 3 squeezes per second), muscle squeezing has a very stimulating effect both on the circulation and on the nervous system. The fast pace invigorates the animal. It is a very useful move to warm up such leg muscles as the triceps, the flexors, and extensors during cold weather.

Picking Up

Picking up is a movement done with the palms of both hands, fingers extended. Pressure will be concentrated on the heels of the hands. Grasp the body part between both hands, start to squeeze it gently, and simultaneously lift the muscle away from the bone structure at right angles. Squeeze and let go. Without losing contact, grasp again and repeat the movement. Pressure should be adjusted to the size of the muscle and its level of tension-tenderness (10 to 15 and eventually up to 20 pounds with each hand).

As you lift the muscle, feel for the elasticity of the fibers. Let them go when you reach the maximum stretching point. Don't overdo it. This manipulation will contribute mostly to toning the muscle as well as increasing circulation.

Picking up is used mostly on the upper forelegs and hind legs; it is good on the stifle and on the crest of the neck as well.

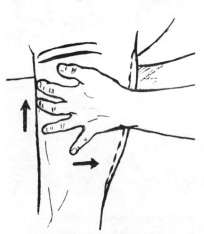

3.15 Petrissage: Picking-up Movement

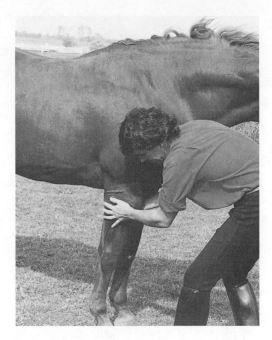

3.16 Picking-up Movement

Done in a very gentle manner, picking up could be included in a relaxing routine when massaging the legs or the neck. But normally it is used in sports massage, in short therapeutic treatments, or in a warm-up routine prior to exercise. If the muscles treated show acute signs of inflammation, do not use this movement. It is too aggressive for this condition.

Wringing

Wringing is a great move to use on the horse's back, shoulders, and hindquarters. This movement efficiently increases circulation and also is very useful in fighting inflammation over the muscles of the back. It can be used before saddling your horse, but mostly should be used after removing the saddle. Horses love it then!

Wringing is done with the palmar surface of the hand, thumbs extended at a 45-degree angle from the hand. Apply both hands flat on the body part; then start wringing the muscle side to side, almost in the same way you would wring a wet cloth. The muscle is lightly and gently lifted, then wrung side to side.

Wringing is a very efficient way to stimulate circulation and warm up muscles in a short time. This movement can be applied anywhere on the horse's body. Use an average pressure, starting at about 2 pounds and building to 15 pounds, depending on the

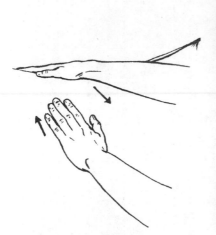

3.17 Petrissage: Wringing Movement

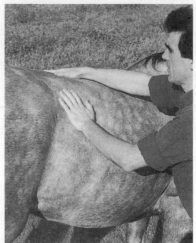

3.18 Wringing Movement

muscle mass worked on. Remain light when going over bony areas such as the spine, scapula, or point of the hip. Your rhythm should be smooth, and average 1 stroke per second or less. A faster rhythm (2 strokes per second) will be very stimulating and may be irritating to the horse.

Skin Rolling

Skin rolling is a very soothing manipulation that is used mostly to:

* ❖ Maintain a healthy and shining coat
* ❖ Prevent the formation of excess adhesions
* ❖ Maintain elasticity of the skin

With thumbs on one side and fingers on the other, grasp and lift the skin. Using either one or both hands (preferably both), push the thumbs forward, rolling the skin toward the fingers. The fingers draw the skin toward the thumbs, lifting, stretching, and squeezing the tissues effectively.

Skin rolling is a gliding movement that should be performed in a slow, soothing manner to avoid irritating the skin, especially over areas where the underlying tissues are close to the bone. The angle of direction may be varied and repeated to ensure maximum effect. This is a great technique to enhance circulation. Use only 2 or 3 pounds of pressure—maximum!

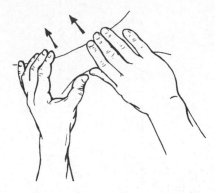

3.19 Petrissage: Skin Rolling Movement

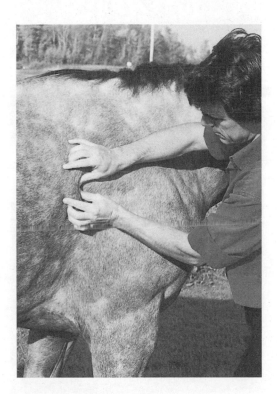

3.20 Skin Rolling Movement

VIBRATION

Vibration is mostly used to have an effect on the deeper structures (muscles or joints) that are below the superficial tissues. This quivering type of movement is done with the hand. It has a soothing effect and can be used alone or as part of another routine.

3.21 Vibration Movement

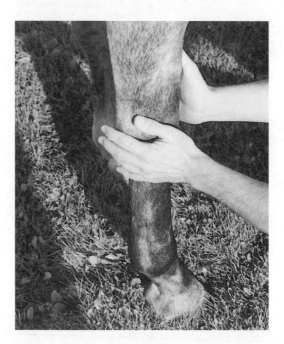

3.22 Vibration Massage Movement

At the start, use no pressure other than the weight of your hand on the part to be vibrated (1 pound). Progressively increase your pressure by a few pounds to the point of stretching the structure you are treating. Start the vibration movements from the elbow and let them progress through your wrist to your hand; this is known as a "flat hand vibration."

Another variation, the "point vibration," is done with the thumb or the fingertips only, giving you more accuracy for small, specific areas. Done gently, with 1 or 2 pounds of pressure vibrations have a mechanical, soothing effect with a strong nervous reflex effect.

When employed more heavily, with 2 to 5 pounds of pressure and at a faster, more aggressive rhythm, vibrations are a mechanically stimulating move and less of a nervous reflex.

This manipulation is very useful in relaxing the nervous system. Use the flat-hand vibration move in a gentle manner (light pressure) over the sacrum for a couple of minutes when starting the relaxation routine. It is very efficient in eliciting the parasympathetic nervous response, reaching the central nervous system (brain) quickly. However, I do not recommend using this move directly over the head (skull).

Apply vibration to joints and around bony prominences. This will soothe swollen joints, whether caused by acute trauma or chronic injury. Vibrations are also good for inflamed rheumatism or arthritis where regular massage is contraindicated.

Use vibrations near well-healed scar tissue in order to reduce adhesions. Depending on the area, apply no more than 5 to 10 pounds of pressure until the animal's maximum tolerance is reached.

Start with a small vibratory movement, maintaining it for a few seconds. Then gradually release and move to another position. Start again and repeat over the whole area you want to treat. Intersperse effleurage and stroking frequently with this move to drain the tissues and relax the animal.

A full treatment using this movement alone should not exceed 3 minutes over a small area or 5 minutes over a larger one. Determine the need relative to the degree of inflammation present.

SHAKING

Shaking is a very strong mechanical movement used frequently in sports massage to increase circulation. Shaking is performed with either the fingertips or the whole hand in full contact with the body part.

When done in a gentle manner (1 stroke per second), it is soothing. When applied briskly (2 or 3 strokes per second), it is one of the most stimulating massage moves.

Pressure should be kept between 3 and 5 pounds. The skin can move with your hands over the body parts. When using heavier pressure and a faster rhythm, the hands glide over the skin. As you

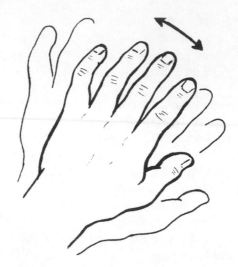

3.23 Shaking Movement

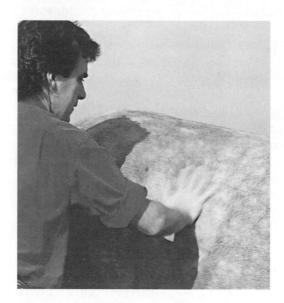

3.24 Shaking Massage Movement

work in this manner, pay attention to feedback signs from your horse. Take care not to irritate the nerve endings of the skin, especially if an inflammation is present. Adjust your rhythm and pressure accordingly. Always ease off a little when going over bony processes such as the point of the hip or the scapular spine.

FRICTION

This movement is mostly used in sports therapy to break down adhesions and scar tissue (fibrosis) over muscular fibers, tendons, ligaments, fascia, joint capsules, and bones. Always warm up the area thoroughly with effleurages, wringings, and kneadings before proceeding to frictions.

Frictions consist of small, deep, circular movements applied across the length of the muscle or up and down over a patch of fibrous tissue. Use the tip of your thumb or fingers when using this movement on small, local areas. Use both hands over large areas.

Friction can be done gently or strongly, depending on your aim. Both styles are mechanically stimulating to the body, causing increased blood circulation. Keep in mind the degree of tissue inflammation, the dimension of the adhesions, and their location in relation to other structures (bones, joints, or veins).

To break down fibrous adhesions you need to use a fair amount of pressure, starting at around 10 to 15 pounds of pressure, progressively building up to 30 pounds; adjust accordingly depending on your aim. Always warm up the area thoroughly before starting, and drain the area well when finished.

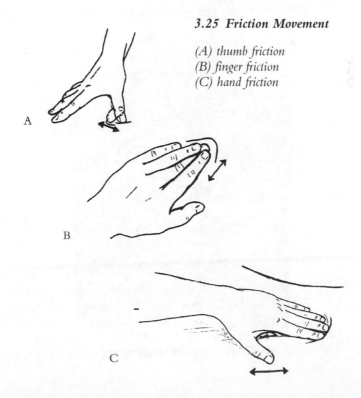

3.25 Friction Movement

(A) thumb friction
(B) finger friction
(C) hand friction

A

B

C

Do not use friction on one specific area for too long; 2 to 3 minutes maximum is enough if no inflammation is present. It is better to reduce scar formation over the course of several massages than to take the risk of worsening the area and creating more inflammation. It is very important to intersperse your work with copious effleurage drainage every 20 or 30 seconds, and some wringing to keep the tissues warm.

When working a patch of scar tissue, start from the periphery and work toward the center of the scar with moderate pressure (8 to 12 pounds) to loosen the fibers. Drain thoroughly with effleurages. Then use friction across the whole fibrous patch, going sideways or up and down (depending on the nature of the scar formation) in a circular fashion, using a much heavier pressure (15 to 25 pounds). Assess the feedback signs of the horse. Remember to drain generously with effleurages every 20 or 30 seconds.

As you use friction to relieve new adhesions or to break down old fibrous masses, it is good to ice before and after treatment. This will ensure the numbing of the nerve endings and will minimize discomfort. Simply apply a cold pack or use the ice massage technique described in chapter 4.

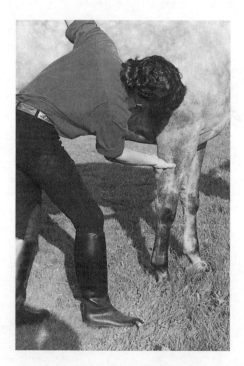

3.26 Thumb Friction Movement

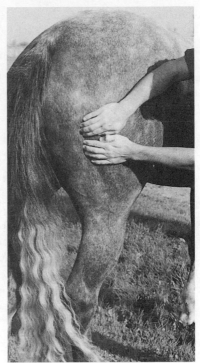

3.27 Finger Friction Movement   *3.28 Hand Friction Movement*

NERVE MANIPULATION

Nerve manipulation consists of stroking, pressure, friction, and stretching. Owing to the nature of the nerve tissues and their function, be very gentle and careful in your work.

All these movements are mostly concerned with nerve maintenance and therapy. All are mechanically stimulating to the nerves except for the nerve stroking manipulation, which is a pure nervous reflex movement.

Your initial contact over the course of the nerve should be very light; use almost no pressure until you feel that the horse has accepted your work. Remember that an irritated or damaged nerve is extremely sensitive. Then you can progressively adapt your pressure. Even during the course of the treatment, however, too heavy a pressure or movements that are performed too quickly can trigger a very abrupt, almost panicky reaction from the animal. Be mindful of this. Here, these massage moves are presented in the order that they should be used to treat a nerve condition such as *neuralgia*, which is the aching of a nerve after a strain.

Nerve Stroking

Employed along the course of a nerve, nerve stroking uses the same stroking massage move presented earlier; it will relax and give a grounding feeling to the animal. Again, no pressure is used beyond the weight of the fingertips over the skin. Because it would be irritating to the nerve, do not apply nerve stroking too long.

Since this is the first movement you will use in this treatment, be extremely cautious during the initial contact. Depending on the degree of inflammation and pain, the horse could be very jumpy.

You might consider cooling down the area before treating it. Apply a cold cloth or hose it down. Do not apply ice directly over the course of the nerve. This would be very irritating, especially over the areas where the skin is very thin and the nerve is right underneath (the inside of the legs, for example). At the end of a nerve treatment, you can apply nerve stroking as a finishing touch to soothe and relax.

Nerve Pressure

Nerve pressure consists of small pressure points applied along the course of the nerve to restore feeling along the horse's limbs. This renewed awareness will promote new nerve growth.

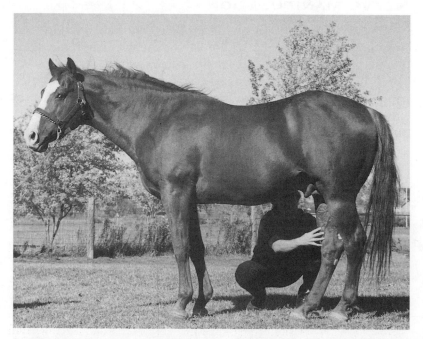

3.29 Nerve Stroking Movement

3.30 Nerve Pressure Point Movement

Always use a light pressure, starting at 1 pound and progressively increasing to 2 or 3 pounds maximum. If the nerve course shows some inflammation, it would be beneficial to cool the area first (see cold hydrotherapy application, chapter 4). Use only very light pressure points afterwards (1 to 2 pounds), progressively increasing as the structure improves. Again, be very gentle and aware of the progress of your treatment. And be alert when using this massage move because the horse might abruptly move his leg in response to the pressure.

Nerve Friction

To perform nerve friction, use the friction massage move described earlier. Apply it along the course of a nerve to stimulate regeneration and new growth. Only apply nerve friction once the area is well warmed up through your massage treatment so your horse is well aware of your working that area.

When a nerve has been elongated (overstretched during a bad fall, for example), apply a light friction along the whole course of the nerve. This will strongly promote the regeneration of the nerve tissues. Do not proceed if the nerve shows strong signs of inflammation. Wait for the inflammation to go down. Use cold hydrotherapy, gentle stretching, and rest.

When a nerve has been totally severed (as with a bad cut, for example), you only need to work the few inches above the section that was injured. This action will strongly promote new nerve growth. Below the trauma, the distal section that was cut off will degenerate. It cannot be saved.

3.31 Nerve Friction Movement

When using nerve friction, always be very gentle at the start, applying only 1 or 2 pounds of pressure. This move can be quite painful at times and your animal might react strongly. Apply cold hydrotherapy before and after treatment to numb the area. (For more information on Hydrotherapy, see chapter 4.) When dealing with a serious nerve problem (trauma, cut), consult your veterinarian before applying this move.

Use this massage therapy only in the chronic stage (past 72 hours) of an injury. Do not apply if the nerve is inflamed (symptoms of heat, extreme sensitivity).

Nerve Stretching

Nerve stretching is basically a regular stretch of the limb that will affect the course of the injured nerve (see chapter 8). This stretch is done much more cautiously than others, starting with a very small stretch and progressively getting deeper over the course of several sessions.

Remember that nerves—especially injured nerves—ache easily. Never use the nerve stretch during the acute stage (first 24 hours) of an injury; stretching should only be used in the chronic stage (past 72 hours) of recovery. (For more information on injury recovery stages, see chapter 4.) If the nerve is inflamed, use cold applications to reduce the inflammation.

TAPOTEMENTS

Tapotement massage consists of a series of soft blows to the body, done rhythmically. Clapping, cupping, hacking, beating, and pounding are all tapotements. All these movements are mechanical and stimulating. Hands usually work alternately in a light and springy manner. The rhythm of application varies according to pressure. Light clapping, cupping, and hacking are done at approximately 2 to 3 beats per second for starters, then up to 6 beats per second when the horse is warmed up. Heavier beating and pounding are performed more slowly, at 2 to 3 beats per second. The moves are mostly used to increase circulation and to energize the body; they are used frequently in therapeutic massage treatments, sports massage sessions, and in warm-up routines.

Done on their own, tapotements are very effective for warming up muscle groups just prior to exercise. Your horse might take some time to adapt to tapotements, but he will soon learn to like them. Start with a very light pressure and increase it progressively. The application of tapotements should last a few minutes: 1 or 2 minutes over small areas and up to 3 minutes when working large parts. A strong, soothing feeling of relaxation will follow such an application. Try it on yourself and you will see. Always finish with some effleurages and strokings.

Clapping

Clapping is done with the palm of the hand, the hand flat and the fingers stretched as though applauding.

Use only 2 or 3 pounds of pressure to start, building to 5 or 10 pounds of pressure. Use only on muscle groups, not on bony structures, except over the ribcage. Keep the pressure light over thin muscles (scapular muscles, for example).

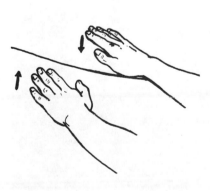

3.32 Tapotement: Clapping Movement

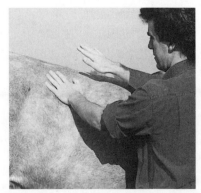

3.33 Clapping Movement

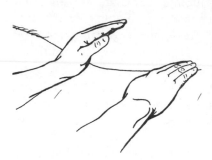

**3.34 Tapotement: Cupping
Movement**

3.35 Cupping Movement

Cupping

Cupping is done with the palm of the hand cupped as though holding water.

Use 5 to 10 pounds of pressure. This is a softer version of clapping that is used over the rib cage and around bony structures (scapula, withers, hip, stifle, etc.) or over curved muscle areas (front chest, rump).

Hacking

Hacking is done in a springing manner with the flat side of the hand, the fingers spread out in a flexible, non-rigid manner.

Use 5 to 10 pounds of pressure, and up to 15 pounds when working over big, bulky muscles. Hacking penetrates deeper into

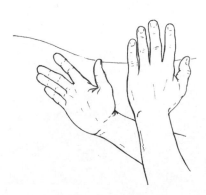

**3.36 Tapotement: Hacking
Movement**

3.37 Hacking Movement

the muscle structure and yet is very gentle. It is a favorite move to treat the back muscles or the thicker muscle of the hindquarters.

Beating

Beating is done with a relaxed closed fist, hitting the muscle groups with the flat side of the hand.

Pressure can be 10 to 15 pounds and up to 20 pounds over big muscle groups. Only use this move after you have already done several clapping, cupping, and hacking moves, and only over fleshy parts. A strong stimulation of fluid circulation will immediately follow this application.

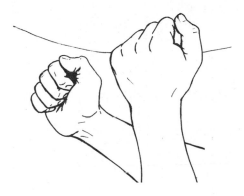

3.38 Tapotement: Beating (Medium Pressure) and Pounding (Heavy Pressure) Movements

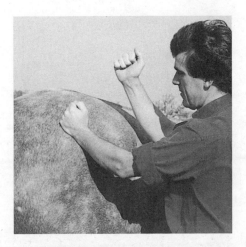

3.39 Beating or Pounding Movement

Pounding

Pounding is a harder version of the beating move. The fist is clenched tight. Use a pressure of between 15 and 25 pounds. This move is rarely used except for deep stimulation of big muscle groups like those of the hindquarters.

THE LAYING ON OF HANDS

The laying on of hands has great therapeutic value in soothing acute wounds, inflammation, nerve irritation, and stress of a mechanical or nervous origin even though it is not technically a classical massage movement. The technique is used where regular massage cannot be used; it is a great addition to regular treatment routines that furthers the soothing effect.

Put your hands gently over the area of concern and mindfully feel the energy, the vibration of that part. Use very little pressure (0.5 pound) for this simple hand contact. Be thoughtful of the moment, of the animal, of yourself as you do this. The feeling of closeness that will quickly develop between you and the animal is a sure sign of the effectiveness of this procedure. A warm feeling will develop between your hands. As the nervous stress connected to that particular problem releases, you will feel a heat wave coming out of the part treated. That heat wave will be proportional to the stress recorded and the pain involved. The laying on of hands will soothe the area and induce relaxation on both

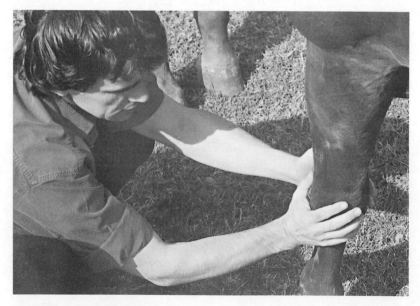

3.40 Laying on of Hands

the physiological and the nervous levels. A great feeling of relief will follow such procedure.

When massage is contraindicated, the laying on of hands will often bring soothing energy to an irritated area, relieving pain. Cold hydrotherapy (such as a cold wet towel; see chapter 4) applied to the animal's treated body part will also relieve inflammation and pain considerably.

BASIC MASSAGE MOVEMENTS

Massage is classified into three basic groups: Soothing, stimulating, and producing a pure nervous reflex.

SOOTHING MASSAGE MOVEMENTS

A soothing massage can inhibit nerve impulses to the muscles, which results in relaxation. The soothing massage moves are:

- ❖ Slow stroking
- ❖ Gentle effleurage
- ❖ Fine vibration
- ❖ Fine shaking
- ❖ Gentle petrissage with kneading, muscle squeezing, wringing, and eventually gentle compressions—all done with very light pressure and in a peaceful rhythm

STIMULATING MASSAGE MOVEMENTS

A stimulating massage produces a nerve-exciting reflex in the muscles. This reflex stimulates muscle tone (light contraction, causing an increase in blood and lymph circulation with resultant increased oxygenation, etc.).

Rhythm and pressure play important roles in the degree of stimulation you want to induce. Working in a hasty manner with abrupt changes of movement will irritate your animal very quickly. Therefore, always start gently and build up your pressure and rhythm accordingly.

Pressure need not be heavy. On a healthy structure, 10 to 20 pounds is plenty. The mechanical repetition of the movements will secure the desired effects. Always start lightly and monitor the feedback signs of your animal, adjusting proportionally.

In time and with practice you will develop a sense of all these nuances. You should always stay on the safe side by starting gently. As your horse becomes accustomed to massage, he will allow you to work deeper, especially if he is well warmed up.

Always remember to ensure thorough drainage (via effleurage) after using stimulating moves.

The stimulating moves are:

- ❖ Fast stroking
- ❖ Firm to vigorous effleurage
- ❖ Petrissage with firm kneadings, compressions, wringing, picking-up moves, and skin rolling
- ❖ Coarse vibrations
- ❖ Coarse shaking
- ❖ Frictions, fine and coarse
- ❖ Nerve manipulation with nerve pressure, nerve friction, and nerve stretching
- ❖ Tapotements with clapping, cupping, hacking, beating, and pounding

PURE NERVOUS REFLEX MOVEMENTS

Pure nervous reflex massage movements result in a lessening of nervous tension, stress and anxiety, and promote strong relaxation.

The pure nervous reflex moves are:

- ❖ Stroking
- ❖ Fine vibrations
- ❖ Nerve stroking
- ❖ Laying on of hands

Regular practice of massage on your horse will quickly develop your ability to know the approach necessary for each type of massage. You will be amazed at how much information you can learn through your fingertips, and this will give you confidence. Remember, practice makes perfect. And even more, quality practice makes perfect.

4

HYDROTHERAPY

In this book, the term *hydrotherapy* is used to mean water treatment applied externally to the horse's body. If used before and after massage, hydrotherapy will increase the effectiveness of massage treatment.

Hydrotherapy comes in a number of forms, depending on the temperature of the water, the method of application, the duration of treatment, and so on.

Water applications can produce both a temporary and a longer-lasting effect. For example, cold water first constricts the blood vessels and numbs the nerve endings; then it triggers a longer-lasting dilation of the vessels. Hot water first dilates the blood vessels and soothes the nerve endings; then it causes a longer-lasting relaxation of the tissues.

The following chart classifies water by temperature.

WATER TEMPERATURE	
Cold	40 to 60°F (4.4 to 15.5° C)
Cool	65 to 75°F (18.3 to 23.8°C)
Tepid	85 to 95°F (29.4 to 35°C)
Warm	90 to 100°F (32.2 to 37.7°C)
Hot	100 to 110°F (37.7 to 43.3°C)

WARNING: For hot applications, the temperature should be 41 to 53.6°F (5 to 12°C) above normal body temperature, which is about 100.4°F (38°C). Between 109.4 and 122°F (43 to 50°C) should be safe. **Above 122°F (50°C), you risk burning the skin.** Use a thermometer to be sure.

Heat and cold are used to relieve pain in acute or chronic conditions and in inflammatory disorders in both humans and animals. Heat and cold are peerless as methods that are effective, safe, easy to apply, free from side effects, and cost-effective.

DURATION OF TREATMENT

The more extreme the temperature, the shorter the duration of the application. The more moderate the temperature, the more prolonged the application.

Because they affect the cutaneous nerve endings, both heat and cold decrease pain and muscle tension. They do this through opposite physical effects and therefore are used at different stages of an injury's development.

Length of Duration	Actual Time
short duration	15 to 60 seconds for initial application of heat or cold, especially on sensitive areas
average duration	2 minutes for hot applications
prolonged duration	3 to 10 minutes for warm and cold applications
very prolonged duration	10 to 30 minutes for tepid or cool applications and poultices

STAGES OF RECOVERY

Typically in therapy, there are three stages in the recovery process of an injury: acute, subacute, and chronic. These definitions are not exact; there are in-between stages as well.

THE ACUTE STAGE

The first 24 hours following an injury is the acute stage. Use cold immediately. This will stop hemorrhaging in the damaged tissues and will contribute to reducing any swelling before you commence treatment. You can apply cold as ice (in solid form or crushed with some water in a plastic bag) or as cold running water. After you have performed your massage (swelling technique, chapter 5) you should apply more cold.

THE SUBACUTE STAGE

Between 24 and 72 hours after an injury is the subacute stage. By then the injury has usually stabilized. Use the *vascular flush,* which is the alternation of cold and hot applications for several minutes each. Right after massage, you might apply some cold to soothe tender tissues.

THE IN-BETWEEN STAGES

When closer to the acute condition (first 24 to 48 hours), first apply cold for 3 minutes, then apply hot for 2 minutes. Repeat this cycle 3 times, up to 4 or 5 times per day. *Always finish with cold for 2 minutes.* Follow with a light effleurage toward the heart or simply use stroking if the body part appears too sensitive.

When closer to the chronic stage (48 to 72 hours), first apply hot for 3 minutes, then apply cold for 2 minutes. Repeat 3 times, up to 4 or 5 times per day. *Always finish with cold for 2 minutes.* Follow with a light effleurage toward the heart or use light stroking if the body part appears too sensitive.

THE CHRONIC STAGE

Beyond 72 hours is the chronic stage. Use heat to loosen the tissues and to increase blood circulation. After massage, you might apply some cold to soothe the tender tissues, especially if you have worked deeply.

When an old chronic injury flares up, soreness with some degree of inflammation and swelling might occur at the site. In this case, use cold hydrotherapy to relieve the edema and numb the irritated nerve endings. This action will take the inflammation down and allow you to work more easily. You might use a vascular flush as well, finishing with cold for 2 minutes. Consider the situation carefully. If you choose to use cold water over a large area (for example, to deal with inflammation of the back), do not apply it if the horse is cold or chilled. Warm up the animal first by walking or longeing him. However, if a cold water treatment is to be used over a local area (for example, in the case of tendonitis), the warming up of that area can simply be achieved by massage (wringings and effleurages).

COLD

Cold is widely used in emergencies right after trauma to stop any bleeding and to prevent excessive swelling. Cold can also be applied during the flare-up of old chronic injuries to reduce inflammation and pain.

EFFECTS OF COLD

Cold water application first chills the skin, which causes constriction of the capillaries. This constriction drives the blood to the interior of the body, thus reducing circulation and preventing swelling in the trauma area. Cold also decreases pain by numbing the sensory nerve endings.

After the cold is withdrawn, there comes a secondary reaction. The capillaries expand, allowing blood to return to the body's surface. This reaction is the body's defense mechanism to warm the entire body. If the treatment is applied to the entire body, circulation will be stimulated all over as well.

This stimulation will raise the body's temperature and blood pressure, contract muscles, strengthen heart action, stimulate the nervous system, stimulate the metabolism, and slow and deepen breathing.

Prolonged cool applications produce effects similar to cold, but these are not as marked and the reaction is therefore less pronounced.

APPLICATION OF COLD

Cold is used most often in the acute stage, immediately following trauma or surgery. Ice packs and other cold applications may be used for contusions and sprains during the first 24 hours. Cold reduces hemorrhaging and swelling in the damaged fibers. It also contributes to controlling pain by activating the production of endorphins.

In treating acute problems be careful not to lower the body temperature too much by excessive cold or prolonged water treatment. A "cold reaction" might follow. Gently stimulate circulation with some effleurages, wringings, shakings, or light friction massage.

4.1 Ice Massage Technique: *Peeling the rim of the foam or paper cup for the ice massage application.*

Cold is also used in chronic cases to decrease pain in very tender sores or to reduce swelling in a chronically inflamed area (caused by tendonitis, bursitis, or arthritis). By absorbing heat from the irritated area, cold lowers the metabolic rate, thereby keeping the inflammation down. It also reduces the incidence of muscle spasms and reduces nerve irritation by slowing down the velocity of nerve conduction. All of this breaks the pain-spasm-pain cycle. Cold is used extensively in the control of inflamed tendons and joint structures.

Cold water should be used to relieve pain from burns. Immediately immerse the burned area in very cold or ice water, or spray cold water over the area until the animal is pain-free. Check with your veterinarian if the burn is serious.

Cold Devices and Techniques

Several cooling devices are used in cold therapy:

- ❖ Specially designed, Velcro-equipped leg wraps containing chemical ice bags. These leg wraps are easy to assemble and are very convenient to use when traveling.
- ❖ Specially designed leg boots that can be filled with cold water.
- ❖ The most widely known, and very practical, application is cold water hosing (spraying or bathing).
- ❖ Buckets of cold water are very practical and popular for horses to stand in when treating the lower leg. To remove toxins from the skin and keep swellings down, some people add cider vinegar and sea salt to the water. You can also consider sponging the upper aspect of the leg if necessary.
- ❖ Crushed ice and water in a towel-wrapped plastic bag applied to the skin and held with a bandage is both practical and inexpensive.
- ❖ Poultices are very effective in relieving tendon inflammation. They are semisolid mixtures of clay in cotton cloth that are applied cold to the body part.
- ❖ A cotton towel wrung out in cold water and kept in a refrigerator or freezer can be wrapped around a leg or joint to fight inflammation. Hold it in place with a leg wrap or pin.
- ❖ A cold towel or cold mitten applied with large friction movements over the whole body will produce a stimulating, tonic effect.
- ❖ Sponging with cool water is a quick way to cool off a horse during exercise.
- ❖ Some facilities are equipped with pools for water exercises, but these are not always easy to access.

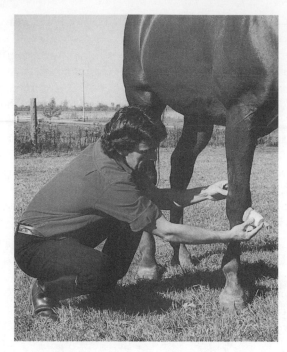

4.2 Ice Massage Technique: *Applied here on the knee.*

THE ICE CUP MASSAGE

Take a 4 to 8 ounce paper or foam cup, fill it with water and freeze it. Hold the cup by the bottom, peel the rim away and, using circular motions, apply the ice to massage the coat. The rhythm should not be too slow or too fast: approximately 4 seconds per 5-inch circle. The pressure should be light (1 or 2 pounds). The application should last for 2 to 5 minutes maximum. Observe the structure, the degree of swelling, and the inflammation present in, and tenderness of, the tissues. Be careful not to cause ice burns. Follow with a light massage (strokings, effleurages, gentle kneadings) or wrap the area with some cloth to generate warmth quickly. This technique is very useful when dealing with any swelling and inflammation.

DURATION OF COLD APPLICATION

Cold used in an emergency (acute stage) should be applied for a prolonged (3 to 10 minutes) to a very prolonged (10 to 30 minutes) duration, depending on the size and nature of the injury. Cold used in chronic cases should be applied for a prolonged duration (3 to 10 minutes) and up to 15 minutes, according to the size of the swelling.

Direct application of ice, such as an ice massage, should be of prolonged duration (3 to 10 minutes).

When using cold on an open, bleeding wound, do not apply it for more than 10 to 15 minutes because it will interfere with coagulation.

Use a short (15 to 60 seconds) up to an average (2 or 3 minutes) application for the very sensitive body parts such as the face or groin.

Cold hydrotherapy applications are very effective. Make sure you have some ice cups and wet towels in your freezer ready for use. It pays to be prepared for emergencies! Include this procedure in your preventive therapy, before and after your massages; it will make your work easier and more effective.

HEAT

Heat is invaluable in therapy. Heat is used at every level in medical practice—not only in hydrotherapy, but with ultrasound, lasers, heat lamps, and so on.

In combination with massage therapy, heat greatly helps in the recovery stages of injuries as well as in maintenance and preventive programs.

EFFECTS OF HEAT

Primarily, heat decreases pain by soothing the sensory nerve endings. It causes dilation, resulting in improved circulation and thus bringing more oxygen and nutrients to tissues. Heat loosens the fibers of muscles, tendons, and ligaments; dislodges toxins; and prepares the area for a good massage. Moist heat is more effective than dry heat because it penetrates more deeply into the body.

Secondarily, heat brings a general feeling of relaxation to the muscle fibers, tendons, and ligaments. It raises the body temperature, stimulates metabolism, and lowers blood pressure.

APPLICATION OF HEAT

Heat is used mostly in subacute or chronic stages of post-traumatic recovery. It can lessen the aches of old wounds, ease low-grade inflammations, and relieve stiffness in older animals. Used widely in deep massage treatments, heat loosens muscle fibers and other fibrous tissues prior to the employment of friction moves.

Heat may be used to control pain in acute injuries. If heat is used on contusions, sprains, and other acute injuries, it should be as hot as can be tolerated, usually above 118°F (48°C).

At higher temperatures, heat works as effectively as ice packs because of its great ability to stop bleeding in tissues.

Heat Devices and Techniques

❖ A hot-water bottle is very effective if it can be applied properly. Unless you can take the time to hold it on the horse, it is impractical.

❖ A heat lamp is efficient, but requires a special installation.

❖ An electrical heating pad is effective, but the cord presents a danger because the horse's feet could become entangled in it.

❖ Hydrocollator packs are probably the most convenient. These packs contain mud and are preheated in hot-water containers. Wrap them in a towel before you apply them. Be careful that the temperature is not so high that it burns the horse's skin (no more than 53.6°F [12°C], above normal body temperature).

❖ Hot towels are convenient to use, but need to be replaced frequently. As mentioned above, wet or moist heat is generally more effective than dry heat because it penetrates deeper into the muscles. When applying hot towels, cover them up with plastic so the horse produces more body heat.

❖ Poultices produce moist heat from a semisolid mixture of various substances (clay, flax seed, or mustard) that is applied to the body while hot.

❖ Hot-water hosing is very practical.

❖ Some facilities are equipped with warm-water whirlpools, which are excellent for therapeutic exercises and training, but are not easy to access.

❖ Counterirritant liniments produce heat effectively.

Duration of Heat Application

Prolonged to very prolonged applications are the rule for temperatures under 110°F (48°C). The usual amount of time for a heat application is 10 to 20 minutes; because of the risk of overheating, do not apply heat for longer than 30 minutes at one time.

Extremely hot applications (over 110°F [48°C]) should be used very carefully and for only about 5 to 15 seconds. When hot applications are used to stop hemorrhaging, a short to average duration—1 or 2 minutes—is enough to do the job.

Too much heat applied too long can irritate nerve endings and result in *neuralgia*, a dull to severe ache in the nerve endings. If you suspect this has happened, use cool cloths to numb those nerve endings and bring back normal sensations.

Warning: The temperature of heat should be 41 to 53.6°F (5 to 12°C) above normal body temperature, which is about 100.4°F (38°C). Between 109.4 and 122°F (43 to 50°C) should be safe. Above 122°F (50°C), you risk burning the skin. Use a thermometer to be sure.

Heat is not as accessible as cold but it is very useful in recovery and in maintenance programs.

POULTICES

A poultice is usually an application of moist heat produced by a semisolid mixture of various substances and applied to the body while hot. A poultice is a very effective way to treat arthritis, rheumatism, and other inflammations.

To make a poultice, first spread the chosen mixture on a piece of cotton cloth large enough to cover the entire area to be treated. Second, gently apply the cloth with the mixture side directly in contact with the body. Third, cover the poultice with an extra piece of flannel to hold in the warmth. To get more of a drawing-out effect, apply flexible plastic (i.e., a plastic bag) on top of the flannel piece covering the poultice. This will keep moisture and heat close to the body and enhance the desired effect.

When applying a poultice to the leg, use a leg wrap to secure the poultice. When applying a poultice to another body part, improvise, or hold it in place with your hand.

Allow the poultice to remain on for 15 to 30 minutes, depending on the part of the body being treated. For young, growing animals (foals and yearlings), 10 minutes is sufficient. When using clay poultices to reduce tendon inflammation, however, leave them on for 8 to 12 hours or overnight.

If there appears to be any tenderness or skin eruption, do not apply the poultice directly on the skin. If the skin is broken, put a layer of clean cotton cloth between the poultice and the skin.

COMMON POULTICE MIXTURES

Clay poultice is very effective in treating arthritis and inflammations. Use a well-known brand of clay (either white, gray, or green clay) such as Vogel or other popular commercial brand, because these clays are "clean," meaning their contents are known. If you consider using a clay found on your farm or in a local river bed, be aware of its chemical makeup before applying it.

Onion, cabbage, and cottage cheese are very good at drawing toxins out of dirty wounds and especially out of boils. You can use each ingredient separately or mixed together (1/3 of each). Chop the onion and cabbage in fine, small pieces. Mix well with enough cottage cheese to produce a semi-solid paste. Apply in the same manner as the other poultices.

Mustard is the most successful and the most popular treatment for joint pain, rheumatism, and neuralgia. Mustard has a strong analgesic effect and brings blood to the surface, thus increasing circulation. The chief medicinal property of mustard is its natural and penetrative volatile oil, which has a pungent odor. This volatile oil is released when mustard powder is mixed with water, provided the latter is not too hot.

Dry mustard, such as Colman's or Keen's, must never be mixed with very hot water because that would destroy the volatile oil. Thus when a very hot mustard poultice is needed, the mustard must be mixed first with cold or lukewarm water and allowed to stand for a few minutes, after which hot water is added.

Make a paste of equal parts of flour and mustard. For sensitive skin, use up to 4 parts flour to 1 part mustard. Spread the mixture on a cotton cloth and apply. Cover with a piece of flannel to retain warmth. When applying the poultice on a leg, secure it with a leg wrap, otherwise improvise or hold by hand for 15 to 30 minutes.

A mixture of equal parts of bran and sea salt, 2/3 cider vinegar and 1/3 water (enough to make a paste) is also commonly used to relieve inflammation. Apply in the same way as a mustard poultice.

The use of water applications and poultices will greatly enhance your work and bring a lot of comfort to your horse. Even when massage is contraindicated, hydrotherapy applications can help your horse. They are an inexpensive and quick form of therapy.

5

MASSAGE TECHNIQUES

The massage techniques in this chapter have been developed to further your knowledge and to provide you with guidelines for the best course of treatment for muscle problems. These techniques will prevent aggravation of those problems, speed up the healing process, and ensure proper recovery.

Massage therapy has developed several techniques of deep massage to eliminate muscle tightening, which causes muscle resistance to natural motion (e.g., shorter stride, restricted neck movement, etc.). Tightening can lead to the build up of stress points (small spasms), trigger points (lactic acid buildup), and poor circulation, which in turn will cause pain and potential lameness to the horse.

By massage techniques, I mean specific massage moves arranged in a pattern and done in an orderly fashion to secure a desired effect. These techniques can be applied to any body part and at any given time after proper warm-up of the area to be worked on, unless massage is contraindicated (see chapter 2).

The techniques are:

- ❖ The thumb technique for a variety of effects
- ❖ The elbow technique for deeper treatments
- ❖ The swelling technique to deal with edema
- ❖ The trigger point technique to deal with lactic acid buildup
- ❖ The neuromuscular technique to deal with weak/strong muscles
- ❖ The stress point technique to deal with small spasms
- ❖ The origin–insertion technique to deal with chronic muscle contractures, full spasms, or weak muscles
- ❖ The SEW/WES approach to ensure adequate warm up before a treatment and adequate drainage following a treatment

97

These techniques can be used separately or in any combination to ensure efficient overall treatment and positive results. Although the swelling and spasm techniques are used in emergencies, all the others are used in maintenance and preventive routines according to the horse's training schedule.

Here, more than anywhere else, the four T's apply—tension, texture, tenderness, and temperature (see chapter 3). Every stroke will give you feedback on the condition under your fingers. So "listen" to your fingers and adjust accordingly.

THE THUMB TECHNIQUE

The thumb technique plays a very important role in massage movements, in palpations, and in assessing the structures to be treated. Due to its shape, strength, and versatility, the thumb is a key player in most of your massage moves. It is your most valuable tool for deep work (friction of adhesions).

The thumb should be held at a 90-degree angle when working. You can use the tip of the thumb like a probe, or you can use the tip's medial or lateral aspects to make contact with angled surfaces.

The thumb technique is very useful when performing specific, localized work. Never use the thumb without warming up the area to be treated (strokings, effleurages, kneadings, etc.). For more general, less localized or less specific work, you can use the broad surface of the thumb. The thumb's extreme flexibility allows you to modify the direction of your movement and the force used.

5.1 Thumb Technique

(A) thumb
(B) reinforced index finger

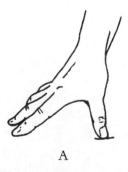

A   B

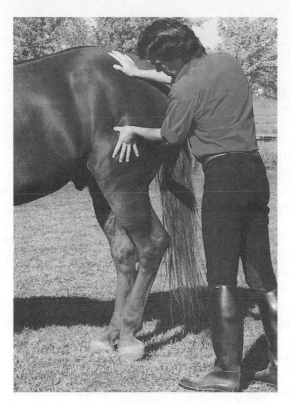

5.2 Thumb Technique

Thus a wide range of therapeutic effects is possible. You can use the thumb for drainage of small or localized areas, to stretch fibers, to friction scar tissue, to release trigger points, and to make investigative palpations and assessments. The thumb is not to be used mechanically across the tissues; it is to be applied intelligently with knowledge of the structures being treated.

Because of its highly developed sensory nerve endings, your thumb sends messages directly to your brain. If you close your eyes during thumb palpation, or indeed during any other work, you will feel minute changes in the tissues.

To maximize your strength when using the thumb during frictions or when applying deep pressure, use your body weight. You should feel the force going in a straight line from the shoulder through the elbow, the thumb, and to the target. Allow the elbow or the wrist to bend only a few degrees. Proper posture will facilitate your work and save your energy. The level of pressure used with the thumb depends on the condition of the tissues being treated and the location of the treatment. Use your judgment, but remember that pressure above 25 pounds may bruise the muscles.

If your thumb is not strong enough, you can resort to using your index finger, reinforced with your thumb and middle finger (see figure 5.1[B]) in a similar fashion.

THE ELBOW TECHNIQUE

The elbow technique can be used in two different ways. One way is to use the elbow and the forearm to stroke large muscle groups, like an effleurage, to stimulate circulation and thus warm up the area before deeper work. This allows more efficient coverage of larger surfaces and it delivers a nice soothing feeling to the horse. When using the elbow technique to stroke, give the horse an idea of what you are doing without shocking him: make your first pass extremely gentle (2 or 3 pounds of pressure). Then work progressively deeper with each pass: 5, 8, 10, 15, and 20 pounds of pressure—but no more. This technique is very mechanical; it will trigger a massive reaction, stimulating circulation and loosening muscle fibers, tendons, and ligaments. Your elbow is a large, strong bone; use it wisely and carefully. Pay attention to the animal's feedback signs. It is recommended that you thoroughly warm up all areas before starting deeper work.

The other way to use the elbow technique is to use the tip of the elbow to apply heavy pressure over stress points or trigger points on large muscle groups—for example, the hindquarters or back muscles. Use your fingers or thumbs to detect stress points or

5.3 Elbow Technique

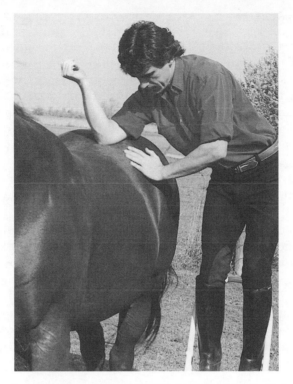

5.4 Elbow Technique: *Using a stool to position yourself better*

trigger points, then carefully place the tip of your elbow right over the target and gently apply pressure starting at around 10 pounds. Then build up the pressure using your body weight. Do not exceed 25 to 30 pounds, depending on the location and the size of the muscle groups. The tip of your elbow and its sharpness reach very deeply into the tissues. Hold the point between 20 to 60 seconds (on average) until you feel the release. Occasionally it takes 2 or 3 minutes for chronic points to release, but no more. Intersperse with lots of effleurages to drain the area every 20 or 30 seconds. Be careful not to overwork the tissues in one treatment.

In either application you must position yourself properly. Stand on a stool so that you stand directly above the area to be worked on. In this way, you will be able to apply your body weight effectively, thus conserving your energy while you work. Leave enough space between you and the horse so you can move if you need to glide your elbow. To ensure your comfort and safety, make sure the stool is strong and wide enough.

With practice, you will become adept at this very effective technique and will use it often. It saves much work on the thumbs, especially with animals that have a lot of muscle mass.

THE SWELLING TECHNIQUE

A swelling results from trauma—such as a strain, sprain, wound, kick, inflammation from overwork, or the flare-up of an old injury—because an increased amount of fluid (lymph or blood) comes to the affected area. An excess of fluid increases tension in the skin and renders it very sensitive to touch. The temperature of the swollen area will be higher than normal relative to the degree of inflammation. Use a very light pressure, 1 to 3 pounds, to avoid mechanical stress on the skin and deeper tissues.

Before applying the swelling technique described below, first apply hydrotherapy (chapter 4): cold in acute cases, vascular flush (hot/cold) in subacute cases, and hot in chronic cases.

When the case calls for cold hydrotherapy, the ice cup massage is a terrific, practical technique to use with swellings. Choose the most practical device (hose, ice cup) available to you and apply it before your massage treatment to induce vasoconstriction and numbing of the nerve endings.

Also, at the end of your massage treatment, apply cold hydrotherapy to reduce nerve irritation and cause vasoconstriction to aid the drainage effect. The cold application's secondary effect will contribute to the overall circulation of fluids in the treated area.

The swelling technique starts with some light stroking moves over the body to relax the animal and help him accept your working close to the problem site. Then apply light strokings over the swollen area to soothe the irritated nerve endings. Your rhythm should be at a relaxed pace of 1 move per second. When the initial tenderness seems to be relieved, you can use a fine vibration movement to stimulate the circulation. Then resume the light strokings. Weave your strokes into very light effleurages (2 or 3 pounds of pressure maximum) around the periphery of the swollen area, draining toward the heart. This will help stimulate circulation and begin the drainage process. Keep a relaxed pace of 1 move per second.

Next, proceed with a very gentle double-thumb kneading massage at the edge of the swelling, going clockwise around the damaged area and draining excess fluid toward the outside of the swollen area.

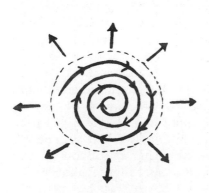

5.5 Schematic Diagram of Swelling Technique

Always start on the outside, not at the center. Use 3 to 5 pounds of pressure or less if the skin is very tight or tender. Even when light pressure is used, the mechanical effect will be sufficient to induce drainage rapidly. Once you have completed the circumference of the swollen area, use light but thorough effleurage, draining away from the periphery of the trauma and always moving toward the heart.

Repeat the kneading technique, progressing in a spiral fashion toward the center of the problem area, alternating with effleurages at the completion of each kneading movement around the circumference of the area.

When there is a considerable decrease in the swelling, use more effleurage, progressively with more pressure but never in a heavy manner. You might slightly increase the rhythm of your moves. Estimate the degree of inflammation and tenderness and adjust your pressure and pace.

DURATION OF APPLICATION

Over a small area 2 or 3 inches in diameter, the application should not last more than 5 minutes in order to avoid irritating the skin.

Over a larger area, 10 to 15 inches in diameter, the application should not last more than 10 minutes.

If the swollen area is very large (an entire leg or hindquarter), do not exceed 20 minutes. Use palmar kneading instead of thumb kneading to cover more area, but do not use heavy pressure. Remember that the tissues are very tender and a gentle pressure is enough to cause a mechanical rerouting of the excess fluid. Always keep a relaxed rhythm of 1 move per second.

Evaluate the condition—the degree of swelling, inflammation, and tenderness. It is best to do several small treatments over the course of 1 or 2 days and thus achieve a steady rate of recovery. By attempting large treatments in a short period you take the risk of aggravating the inflammation and delaying the healing process.

When dealing with the swelling of the lower leg, first gently but thoroughly massage the upper leg to stimulate circulation. Ice massage does wonders for lower leg edema. When dealing with the foreleg, you can use one hand to flex the knee to raise the lower leg to a 90-degree angle, and work the tendon thoroughly with the other hand, using mostly effleurage moves. Here your overall treatment should not exceed 20 to 25 minutes.

Follow this swelling technique with a cold hydrotherapy application (chapter 4) to reduce nerve irritation and to cause vasoconstriction to further the drainage effect. The secondary lasting vasodilation effect of the cold application will affect circulation.

FREQUENCY OF TREATMENT

The degree of inflammation present in the tissues will determine the frequency of your treatments. If the inflammation is very severe in a small area, apply the swelling technique only once or twice a day. If it is in a large area, apply just once a day. However, you can apply cold hydrotherapy several times a day (up to 10 times) for 10 minutes at a time.

If the inflammation is moderate, the swelling technique can be repeated 2 or 3 times a day, with a minimum of 6 hours between treatments. When dealing with a larger area such as a leg, you may work this technique twice daily. As the swelling goes down and the tissues become less tender, you can use more pressure and more effleurages.

Be gentle and very careful in the acute stage, becoming more invasive gradually as the site of swelling gets better. Remember to use hydrotherapy before, after, and in between the treatments to reduce inflammation.

In the case of a flare-up of an old injury, relieving the swelling might take twice as many treatments as in an acute injury, due to the chronic nature of the inflammation. If tenderness is present in the tissue, the use of cold hydrotherapy might be more beneficial than heat. But if the nerves do not appear to be irritated, use heat or vascular flush (see chapter 4). Once the swelling is definitely gone, resume regular massage practice.

THE TRIGGER POINT TECHNIQUE

The trigger point technique is used to release and drain trigger points.

This condition occurs mostly in response to muscle tension (overuse) or nervous stress; it is sometimes the result of poor circulation. The *hypertonicity* (strong/well-used) or *hypotonicity* (weak/unused) of the muscle fibers causes a decrease in blood circulation and thus a decrease in oxygen, resulting in a build up of toxins and nerve irritation. Muscular tension is mostly due to overwork with not enough stretching or rest. Too much fatigue, nervous stress, restlessness, and boredom can trigger the same muscular tension.

When the triggered pain is of low intensity, it is called a *silent trigger point*; when the triggered pain is strong and very sensitive to touch, it is termed an *active trigger point*. Occasionally, one trigger point will affect more than one area; these are called *spillover areas*.

Trigger points vary in size and can feel like nodules. Whatever the size, they are usually very tender, give easily under pressure, and release fairly quickly. Hot hydrotherapy application over the

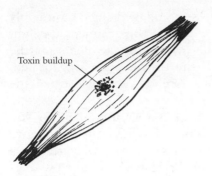

Toxin buildup

5.6 Schematic Diagram of a
Trigger Point, Trigger Point
Technique: Toxin buildup in
the belly of the muscle, resulting
in a trigger point.

specific area will contribute greatly to the effectiveness of your
trigger point technique. It will loosen the tissue fibers and boost
circulation over the area. Use hot packs, hot towels, or electric
pads (see chapter 4).

After thoroughly warming up and loosening the area with massage moves (strokings, wringings, kneadings, all interspersed with
effleurages every 20 seconds), you should apply a light pressure at
the location of maximum tenderness, or directly over the nodule
that your fingers have detected, and hold until the muscle relaxes.
The release process might take just a few seconds for recently
formed trigger points, or up to 2 or 3 minutes for more chronic
trigger points. Intersperse your work with effleurages every 30
seconds.

Your initial touch will likely be very painful to the horse. But
after 20 to 30 seconds, the tenderness will decrease tremendously.
When dealing with a silent trigger point you might consider raising your pressure up to 15 or 20 pounds, depending on the muscular mass you are working on and the horse's reaction. For an acute
trigger point, you should hold a light pressure (2 to 5 pounds) for
most of the application, only raising the pressure slightly to 10 or 15
pounds maximum at the end when you feel the trigger point
releasing. When it may appear dangerous to apply strong pressure
because of the underlying structure (the brachiocephalic muscle of
the neck, for example), you may squeeze or pinch that trigger point
between your thumb and index finger. Use the same pressure and
duration as you would in any other situation.

Do not use more pressure than necessary; trigger points can be
over treated. The ideal pressure is the one that gives a sensation
somewhere between pleasure and pain. Evaluate the pressure
applied relative to your horse's feedback; watch his eyes. You may
apply a continuous or varying pressure. If the pressure is too heavy,
the horse will certainly let you know. Play it safe. Some old,
chronic trigger points may need up to 3 minutes before completely releasing.

Once released, trigger point areas should be drained thoroughly with plenty of effleurages. Then, to further the treatment, use light frictions along the length of the whole muscle fiber—or the whole muscle bundle—in which the trigger point was located. This, with the effleurage, will increase the effectiveness of the drainage.

Drainage after trigger point release is very important. As you break down a long-standing buildup of toxins, you must move those toxins into the bloodstream in order to avoid creating a worse condition. Drainage will also bring fresh blood, new oxygen, and nutrients to greatly assist the healing process.

The area where the trigger point (or points) was located might be very sore for a few hours or even a day or so. In that case wait a day or two before working it again. In the meantime, apply effleurages, wringings, and gentle finger frictions or large kneadings daily if possible to increase circulation and assist recovery. If some degree of inflammation is present, use cold hydrotherapy after the treatment to soothe the nerve endings and stimulate circulation.

The trigger point technique is used very often as part of the maintenance routine (chapter 6) and in sports massage treatments. You can consider using the trigger point technique as a preventive measure, particularly if the symptoms have just developed during exercise. Just ensure sufficient drainage before, and especially after, treatment.

Lightly exercising your horse (longeing, walk/trot) immediately after this type of work is recommended; it will allow the muscles to recover their full power and function as they were meant to.

THE NEUROMUSCULAR TECHNIQUE

The neuromuscular technique is used to treat hypotonic or hypertonic muscles. As the word "neuromuscular" suggests, the neuromuscular technique works on the sensory nerve cells located in a muscle. There are two types of muscular sensory nerve cells: the Golgi tendon sensory nerve cells and the muscle spindle sensory nerve cells. Both act as reporting stations, providing the central nervous system with information regarding the position of the muscle at any given moment (*proprioception*) and how much of a workload is being developed by this muscle.

Start your technique with light stroking for several seconds to relax and comfort your animal. Weave your moves into effleurages, wringings, and kneadings to stimulate circulation and warm up the area.

THE GOLGI

The Golgi tendon receptors are located in both tendons, origin and insertion, of a muscle. The *origin tendon* is the muscle part that anchors to the most stable, least movable bone, whereas the *insertion tendon* attaches the muscle to the movable part, so that during contraction the insertion is brought closer to the origin. The origin tendon is usually stronger and bigger than the insertion tendon because its anchor attachment sustains greater stress, which is responsible for most of the problems found close to the origin tendons. The Golgi tendon sensory receptors indicate how hard the muscle is working. If the sensory nerves detect an overload, they will stop the muscle's activity to prevent damage.

The Golgi tendon sensory nerve cell can be activated manually by massage manipulations, which will either tone or relax the muscle. You have to know the muscle structure well in order to use this technique effectively. After thoroughly warming up the muscle with massage moves, use your thumbs to apply vigorous kneadings (10 to 15 pounds of pressure) on the tendons. For big or deep-seated muscles, you might consider using the elbow technique (up to 20 pounds of pressure). If a strong inflammation is present in the muscle fibers, use cold hydrotherapy (chapter 4) before applying the technique, and then use lighter pressure (5 to 8 pounds) in your kneadings. When finished, drain thoroughly and reapply cold hydrotherapy.

To tone up a weak muscle, apply pressure on the tendon, firmly stretching the tendons toward the center of the muscle. This action will stretch the sensory nerve cell and send impulses to the central nervous system. The central nervous system will respond by improving the muscle tone. It is better to work both tendons simultaneously, but working them alternately will also do.

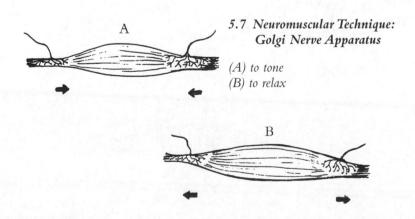

5.7 Neuromuscular Technique: Golgi Nerve Apparatus

(A) to tone
(B) to relax

To relax a hypertonic (overused) muscle, use the same technique; only reverse the direction of your pressure. Pressure is firmly applied on the tendons, toward the bone and away from the muscle belly. This move will produce a reflex action that will relax the muscle.

THE MUSCLE SPINDLE

Very sensitive and complex, the muscle spindle sensory nerve cell coils around the muscle fiber. It sends feedback information to the central nervous system, reporting on the relative length of the fibers and any changes to it. It adjusts the length of the muscle in which it lies, setting the tone by increasing or decreasing it. If the muscle is abruptly elongated, the muscle spindle nerve cell will discharge signals immediately to the brain and contribute to an instant muscle fiber contraction, thus preventing a muscle tear. This nervous reflex reaction happens very quickly.

The muscle spindle sensory nerve cell can be activated manually by massage. First use your thumbs or fingertips to apply gentle frictions (5 pounds of pressure) along the course of the muscle fibers to loosen the whole muscle bundle, reset the sensory nerve fibers, and contribute to the muscle's readjustment.

Then, to tone the muscle, apply with your thumb or fingertips a firm pressure (10 to 15 pounds) over the center of the muscle belly and stretch the fibers toward the muscle ends. This action will stretch the nerve cell and produce a "tonifying" reflex in the muscle. Also, firmly frictioning the whole muscle bundle will produce a similar effect, activating and resetting the muscle spindle

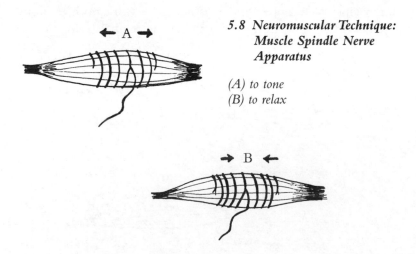

5.8 Neuromuscular Technique: Muscle Spindle Nerve Apparatus

(A) to tone
(B) to relax

nerve cells. If the muscle appears inflamed, reduce your pressure to a gentle friction (5 to 8 pounds).

To relax the muscle, you need only reverse the technique. With your thumb or fingertips, apply firm pressure (10 to 15 pounds) over the muscle belly, pressing toward the center and shortening the muscle spindle sensory nerve cells. A reflex action will occur, releasing muscle tension. This technique is very effective in relieving hypertonic fibers, spasms, or cramps.

The muscle spindle and the Golgi tendon sensory nerve cells harmoniously work together to provide constant information to the central nervous system. Fatigue, stress, work overload, and boredom will acutely and possibly chronically affect those structures. Whenever you are massaging a muscle, work both types of sensory nerve cells. This will produce a strong reflex action from the central nervous system. Use a firm pressure (between 8 to 15 pounds, proportional to inflammation if any) because nerve cells are easily irritated. Work each muscle for 2 or 3 minutes at a time, interspersing effleurages every 20 or 30 seconds, but do not overdo the treatment. Evaluate the degree of inflammation. It is always better to work several short sessions than to overwork and further damage the tissues in one long session. Remember to use hydrotherapy to assist the efficiency of your treatment.

STRESS POINTS

Many horses experience muscle tightness, resulting in reduced muscle action. Stress points are microspasms involving only a few fibers out of a whole bundle. However, these microspasm stress points can turn into full-blown muscle spasms. If a stress point is not inflamed, it is called a *"dormant"* stress point. If a stress point is inflamed, it called an *"active"* stress point, which will display more tenderness and will eventually produce heat and swelling.

HOW STRESS POINTS FORM

Stress points form as a result of great mechanical stress, causing micro-tearing of the muscle fibers. Heavy training, repetitive actions, weight overload, and strenuous effort are all examples of great mechanical stress.

Stress points also develop as a response to a trauma, such as a kick, a bump, or a fall, or as a result of overstretching. If a horse has been injured, during the recovery stage the muscular compensation will trigger formation of other stress points within the compensatory muscles. For example, a horse with a sore knee will develop compensatory stress points in the shoulder muscles, as well as in the muscle attaching the scapula to the rest of the body.

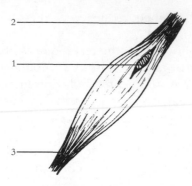

5.9 Schematic Diagram of a Stress Point, Stress Point Technique

(1) stress point, usually found next to the origin tendon
(2) origin tendon
(3) insertion tendon

We need to remember that inflammation—the body's natural healing response to any trauma—can lead to a vicious cycle of pain, tension, inflammation, and more pain. Inflammation could therefore produce more stress points. A bad case of "cold back", an inflammation of the horse's back muscles, is a good example of this phenomenon. Keep the inflammation under control by using hydrotherapy (chapter 4) to cool the area and maintain the inflammation at a "healthy" level. Use lots of effleurages to ensure proper drainage of the area; otherwise the cycle of pain will never end.

WHERE STRESS POINTS FORM

Stress points can be found anywhere in the muscular structure of the horse. Due to the nature of the horse's locomotor system, there are some well-known key areas of the skeleton and related specific muscle groups where stress points can usually be found.

Stress points will most often develop at a muscle's origin tendon, which is the tendon that anchors the muscle to the stable, non-movable body part during a concentric contraction. The origin tendon tends to be quite strong and of good size because it is the anchor attachment for the muscle, and therefore sustains great mechanical strain. The other tendon, the insertion tendon, attaches the muscle to the movable part. This tendon is not as strong or as large as the origin tendon, but will sometimes show stress, especially during *isometric contraction* (to stabilize the body) and *eccentric contraction* (when absorbing great tension during landing, for example).

The horse, like a human, works all of his body at once. Muscle tightening does not remain localized. As one muscle group tightens up, the antagonist group must compensate for the loss of movement and therefore receives extra stress. You will find several stress points during a treatment. Some are related, some are not.

HOW STRESS POINTS FEEL

A stress point feels like a spot of hardened, rigid tissue about the size of the end of your little finger. It might be slightly swollen and will feel tender to the horse when touched. Also, a tight line of muscle fibers (the muscle bundle associated with the stress point) will be felt across the muscle.

During an acute stage or an inflammation flare-up, stress points will show up very quickly and be easy to detect because of heat and swelling. If the stress point area appears inflamed, use cold hydrotherapy (chapter 4) to numb the nerve endings prior to your treatment. Apply the swelling technique if necessary and follow with the stress point technique (page 112). When inflammation is present, work very lightly, progressing gently into deeper massage over a few sessions.

During chronic stages, the stress points will be more difficult to detect because the symptoms of heat and swelling are less evident. But with practice, you will develop a feel for stress points and will recognize them easily. If no inflammation is present, you might consider using heat or vascular flush (chapter 4) over the area to loosen the fibers prior to your treatment.

WHEN STRESS POINTS FORM

Stress points can form at any time, especially when the animal is under a lot of strain (heavy workload) or fatigued by intense training, or when there is chronic pain from an old injury or chronic condition such as arthritis or rheumatism. Older horses show arthritic deterioration in leg joints; the resulting pain causes muscle tension. This muscle tension triggers more arthritic degeneration in the joints. Massage can help break this cycle of muscle tension and stress point buildup as well as relieving pain and stiffness in the associated muscles. Remember, stress points will sometimes appear in response to a direct trauma.

HOW HORSES RESPOND TO STRESS POINT WORK

The animal's response to your work will vary greatly according to the degree of inflammation present. With stress points, the pain reaction you get in relation to your pressure indicates the severity of the stress. To assess the stress point, start with light pressure and then increase gradually.

In human massage therapy, pain caused by a stress point is usually not as sharp as that of a trigger point, but it can be severe on occasion, especially during acute inflammation. The initial contact on the stress point may elicit some tenderness, but soon after a feeling of relief will replace the original discomfort.

When a stress point is *dormant* (inactive), firm pressure (8 to 12 pounds) applied to it will cause a skin-twitching reaction; after a couple of minutes, a general release of the muscle will follow. Horses often seem to enjoy this form of work.

When a stress point is *active* (inflamed), the reaction will be more pronounced. As you apply medium pressure (5 to 8 pounds) to an active stress point, you will notice excessive skin twitching and flinching; the animal will pull away from the pressure. If the reaction is sharp or if the adjacent muscles are showing excessive tightness, you may suspect that the muscle might be close to full spasm. Be very gentle and methodical in your approach.

THE STRESS POINT TECHNIQUE

The stress point technique consists of two stages. The first deals with the Golgi apparatus nerve cell, the other deals with the muscle spindle nerve cell. (See pages 107–108 for an explanation of these nerve cells.) As you locate a stress point, identify the muscle it belongs to.

First Stage

A thorough massage of the origin tendon (with pressure applied toward the bone) will stretch the sensory nerve endings (Golgi nerve cells) located in the tendons. While being stretched, the Golgi nerve cell will send nerve impulses to the brain and cause a reflex action. This will relax the corresponding motor nerve responsible for the stress point. The nervous reflex might take a few seconds to a few minutes to occur. Small stress points might release very quickly or might take several minutes. Do not overwork them.

If the stress point area appears inflamed, use cold hydrotherapy to numb the nerve endings. Otherwise, if the area does not appear inflamed, consider using heat or vascular flush over the area to loosen the fibers (see chapter 4).

Start your technique with light strokings for a few seconds to relax and comfort your animal. Then weave your moves into effleurage or wringings to increase circulation and warm up the area. Proceed with some thorough kneading moves over the tendon where you found the stress point. Then with your thumb or fingertips apply gentle pressure (2 or 3 pounds) to establish the initial contact and evaluate the degree of inflammation. Progressively increase your pressure to 5 pounds, then up to 10 to 15 pounds as the release occurs. Depending on the location of the stress points, you may use the elbow technique (page 100) to work over large muscle groups, increasing your pressure to 20 or 25 pounds.

These moves will work the fibers against the bone, increasing the blood flow to the area. Watch your animal's reaction as you proceed and adjust your pressure accordingly. Hold the pressure until you feel the stress point let go. Follow with lots of effleurages to thoroughly drain the area. If after a minute no release has happened, progressively release your pressure, intersperse with a few effleurages, and repeat the procedure of applying pressure to the stress point until it releases.

Second Stage

The second stage of this technique consists of working the muscle spindle nerve cells. By gently frictioning the muscle spindle you will reset nerve awareness and fully relax the muscle. This will loosen the tight fibers, increase circulation through the muscle, restore freedom of motion to the fibers, and decrease painful symptoms.

Move your thumb or fingertips very gently across the grain of the muscle, perpendicular to the fibers, all along its course. Use a medium pressure of 8 to 12 pounds. Eventually, you may do this to the whole muscle bundle. This action will loosen the muscle spindle nerve cells. Intersperse your gentle frictions with effleurages every 20 to 30 seconds to drain the area.

Be aware that if you friction over the muscle spindle too vigorously or with too much pressure, it will stretch the muscle spindle and cause the muscle to react by contracting (this feature is used to strengthen weak muscles; see neuromuscular technique, page 106). Be gentle during this phase of the technique.

Follow up with thorough drainage (wringings, effleurages) to bring in new blood, nutrients, and oxygen and to remove toxins from the site. The muscle will feel better immediately. The horse should be lightly exercised for 5 to 10 minutes (longeing, walk/trot) immediately after the treatment.

When the horse is warm, use stretching exercises to further the release of the affected muscle groups (see chapter 8).

If you do not see any improvement after working on a stress point for 3 to 5 minutes, stop. Overworking the tissues will aggravate the inflammation. Especially in chronic tension cases, it sometimes takes several treatments to relieve a stress point. After all, these kinds of stress points have been there for a while; it may take up to five treatments to bid them adieu! If inflammation is present, use hydrotherapy after your treatment to cool the nerve endings and elicit vasodilation. Keep records of your work and of the results produced (see chapter 16).

The stress point technique is very efficient when properly applied. If underworked, a stress point will still present the same symptoms with little or no improvement. Overworking a stress point is more dramatic, resulting in stronger inflammation (heat, swelling, pain). In that case, immediately apply some cold hydrotherapy to relieve the symptoms. Give the animal a couple of days of rest before further massage in that area.

Regular practice will allow you to experiment and gain expertise.

THE ORIGIN-INSERTION TECHNIQUE

The origin–insertion technique, which is derived from the neuro-muscular technique, is applied on both tendons and will assist in releasing muscle contractures (hypertonicity) and muscle spasms, or when dealing with muscle weakness (hypotonicity).

The term "origin-insertion" refers to the origin and the insertion tendons of a muscle. The origin tendon anchors to the most stable, least movable bone, whereas the insertion tendon attaches the muscle to the movable part, so that during contraction the insertion is brought closer to the origin. The origin tendon is usually stronger and bigger than the insertion tendon because its anchor attachment sustains greater stress. Stress is responsible for most of the problems found close to origin tendons.

Contracture can be found anywhere in the belly of the muscle. It is a hypertonic state in which muscle fibers cannot let go of their contractile power. Due to high stress, pain, and inflammation, many motor nerve impulses cause the muscle fibers to contract indefinitely. Contractures are responsible for the decrease of muscle action, which results in *congestion* (lack of fluid circulation in the muscle fibers) and in a restricted movement (shorter stride).

By thoroughly massaging the origin and insertion tendons, we stretch the sensory nerve endings, which send relaxation impulses to the brain. In response, the corresponding motor nerve signal causing the muscle to remain contracted will cease, releasing the spasm. This release might occur quickly, depending on the stress level, the severity of the spasm, and whether the spasm is associated with a trauma or a wound. Sometimes a spasm will let go several hours after the treatment.

Your knowledge of the muscle group you are working on, where muscles attach and their direction, is most important to the effectiveness of the treatment.

5.10 Origin-Insertion Technique: *Here done on the longissimus dorsi muscle.*

After you locate the problem and ascertain which muscle you need to work, start by lightly stroking the area to soothe and comfort the horse. Then use light effleurages, wringings, and kneadings to stimulate circulation and warm up the area.

To release a spasm or a contracture, begin by using a gentle but firm double-thumb kneading over the origin tendon, pressing it against the bone (away from the belly of the muscle). Apply pressure at approximately 5 to 10 pounds (15 to 20 on large muscle groups) for approximately 2 or 3 minutes. Intersperse with some effleurage every 30 seconds. Then repeat the same procedure on the insertion tendon.

Next, use thorough effleurage to drain the entire muscle area. Using your fingertips, friction the whole muscle lightly across the fibers. Repeat these moves 2 or 3 times and follow with a thorough drainage.

Depending on the severity and degree of inflammation present in the tissue, the origin-insertion technique should not continue more than 10 minutes. Avoid overworking; it will only aggravate the situation. It is better to repeat the treatment several times over a few days than risk irritating the nerve endings or worsening the inflammation in the muscle fibers on the first treatment.

In most acute stages, the contracture or spasm will release shortly after the first treatment—within 30 minutes or a couple of hours. If the contracture is in a chronic stage, it might take several treatments to produce a positive result.

In the case of a torn muscle, the origin–insertion technique is contraindicated in the acute stage.

When using this origin–insertion technique to strengthen a healthy muscle, you must reverse the direction of your pressure by pressing over the tendon area (see neuromuscular technique, page 106) toward the belly of the muscle. In this case you may apply the technique for about 5 to 10 minutes at a time, proportional to the muscle size. Repeating the treatment several times over a few days will show tremendous improvements.

In all cases, follow with a stretch but only if there are no torn muscle fibers!

Cold hydrotherapy is beneficial before and after treatment. Cold hydrotherapy reduces nerve irritation and cools down the inflammation. The vasoconstriction followed by the vasodilation reaction will flush the toxins from the muscle and provide new nutrients and oxygen. Heat would be more appropriate to deal with a weak muscle.

The origin–insertion technique is used a lot in maintenance and preventative massages to stimulate and strengthen weak muscles. The technique also reduces hypertonic muscles and fine-tunes muscle groups under constant stress.

THE SEW/WES APPROACH TECHNIQUE

The SEW/WES approach technique is very important in massage work. It gives you the proper approach for warming-up and for draining any area you wish to work on. The title of this technique is made up of two acronyms. The acronym SEW stands for Stroking, Effleurage, and Wringing, while the acronym WES stands for Wringing, Effleurage, and Stroking.

The SEW approach is used to start and progressively warm up any area you are to massage. Always start with very light and gentle strokings (0.1 to 0.5 pound of pressure) over the area you will be massaging. Then follow with two to three effleurage passes (2 to 3 pounds of pressure) to thoroughly cover the entire area draining towards the heart. Now apply gentle wringing (2 passes back and forth, using 3 pounds of pressure) over the whole area. Follow with a set of effleurages and continue with either kneading, and/or gentle friction depending on the nature of your goal. Remember to intersperse with effleurages every 20 seconds.

The WES approach is used when you are finished with the deeper aspect of the massage. This approach will allow you to properly and progressively move out of the area you worked on, ensuring proper drainage. After the last set of effleurages following your deeper massage work, apply a gentle but firm set of wringing over the entire area worked on (2 passes, back and forth, using up to 5 pounds of pressure). Follow with extra effleurages, twice as many as usual (4 to 6 passes) to thoroughly drain the tissues you have massaged. With each effleurage pass you should release your pressure a little, starting around 5 pounds and ending with 2 pounds. Then finish with a light stroking, covering the entire area. The last bit of stroking in the WES approach can become the opening stoking of the SEW approach to the area you will massage next.

The various techniques presented here will sharpen your skills and ensure the best work possible to assist the horse in his recovery or maintenance program. They will make your work more specialized, more effective, and much more fun.

6

A massage routine is a series of massage moves or techniques arranged in a specific order to achieve the best results in the shortest time. For example, there are relaxation, maintenance, and recuperation routines, all designed to address particular situations in the most effective way possible. These routines can contribute to the maintenance and preventive care of your animal while simultaneously giving you feedback on his general health; all these factors affect training and performance.

Thus when a horse is restless, scared, or upset, especially after a long trailer trip, a relaxation routine will ease him fairly quickly. A maintenance routine will keep the muscular structure free from trigger and stress points while improving your horse's performance. When your horse has been training heavily, a recuperation routine will help shorten the recovery time and prevent the tightening up and stiffening of the locomotor structures. Warm-up and cool-down routines will assist the animal just before and after riding. The "trouble spot" routine will help prevent muscular problems in the heavily exercised horse.

To ensure proper maintenance, most routines should be applied on a regular basis. Such a schedule will give you frequent feedback on the physical and emotional well-being of your animal while developing his confidence during your work. This confidence will cause him to become deeply relaxed and to trust you more and more, responding fully to your treatments.

The relaxation routine can be applied at any time. It is mainly used to make initial contact with the animal, before and after traveling, when putting him to rest, before a show, after a fright, and so on. When done in a shorter version, the relaxation routine can be used to start any form of massage treatment. The head massage routine can be done any time to ease the horse's tension and can be incorporated into the relaxation routine as well, especially during a first-time massage session.

If the horse is in an average training program, the maintenance routines should be done regularly, once or twice a week. If the horse is participating in a competitive, more demanding program, maintenance routines should be used on a daily basis.

The recuperation routine should be given after every heavy training session. When a heavy training program ends, apply this routine daily for a few days until the transition to a slower-paced program is complete.

To ensure the effectiveness of any massage routine it is best if you can work the horse in a special location with a quiet atmosphere, free from distraction and noise. You can work the horse in his stall, but sometimes it is better to take him somewhere else, like a quiet aisle, another barn, or outdoors if weather permits. Avoid windy conditions as they make the horse nervous.

With practice you will become familiar with the routines outlined in this chapter. The types of movement, the rhythm, and the pressure are particular to each routine; they are selected and put in a particular order to ensure specific results. Always start working with a gentle approach, progressively increasing your pressure and rhythm when needed.

You will be able to add your own touches and eventually create your own routines according to your aims and the conditions you are treating. Trust your own judgment and be creative. But for safe and effective work in the beginning, follow the guidelines given here.

These routines are designed for healthy animals. If abnormal problems or symptoms arise, check with a veterinarian before proceeding.

RELAXATION ROUTINES

Horses, like humans, experience different kinds of stress, ranging from the physical (exercise, training schedules, workload) to the emotional (boredom, anxiety, fear).

When a horse is stressed his body will show tension, but the original stress itself is in the brain. The purpose of the relaxation routine is to relieve this stress in a quick and efficient way. To do this, you need to massage very specific areas of the anatomy so as to influence the brain directly or indirectly.

Two routines will relax your animal: the relaxation massage routine and the head massage routine. The second routine complements the first but both can be applied separately. Both routines require very little pressure (2 or 3 pounds maximum) and the rhythm of your movements should be very smooth (1 move per second on average). Performed independently or together, the routines will achieve positive results over the course of one to several treatments. Neither routine will put your horse to sleep, but each will induce relaxation and a strong sense of relief. This relaxation will clear nervous tension and blockages, regenerating the flow of vital energy through the spine to the rest of the body.

Your horse will feel an overall improvement as a result of these treatments. The relaxation routine is very effective in inducing deep relaxation in a short time and is good to use when massaging a horse for the first time. Even strong-willed horses will soften dramatically after several relaxing massage sessions, becoming more enjoyable companions to ride. The head massage routine is a great addition to this work; however, a head-shy horse may need a little more time to get used to how good it feels to have his face touched.

THE RELAXATION MASSAGE ROUTINE

The relaxation massage routine concentrates on the nervous system only, using mostly pure nervous reflex massage moves over the spinal column—the neck, the back, the sacrum, and the tail— to elicit the parasympathetic nervous response (see chapter 1).

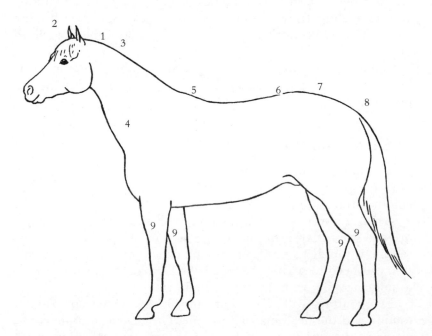

6.1 Relaxation Massage Routine

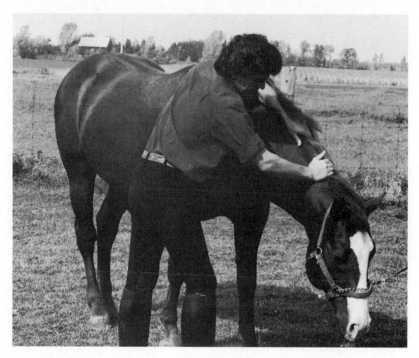

6.2 Lowering the Head: *Relaxation routine.*

Before beginning the routine, it is important to stand beside the horse for a few minutes to establish a rapport. Spend a few moments gently stroking the horse's face and the base of the ears. This version of the relaxation routine does not include working the face because the point is to relax the animal within a short period of time.

Here is the relaxation routine outline (see figure 6.1):

Talk quietly to the horse and gently massage the poll and the upper neck with light muscle squeezings. Lower the horse's head until it is level with the withers, thus helping the animal relax his back muscles. Continue talking in a soft voice to reinforce the relaxing atmosphere. Hold the halter lightly but firmly with the left hand and with the right hand massage the crest of his neck over a couple of inches, starting directly behind the poll with light muscle squeezing, 2 or 3 pounds of pressure at the most. Apply 20 to 30 gentle muscle squeezings to trigger the parasympathetic nervous response.

As the horse relaxes, you can let go of the halter with your left hand and stroke his nose ridge.

Ear Work

Gently pull the ears (point 2; figure 6.1) from the base to the tips, stretching them sideways. Then gently and very lightly rub the tips between your fingers for 1 or 2 minutes. This will soothe the horse. If your horse does not like his ears being worked, don't do it. Spend more time massaging the crest of the neck behind the poll.

Neck Crest Work

With both hands, use the muscle squeezing move along the whole crest of the neck (point 3; figure 6.1) from the base of the skull down to the withers in one pass. Your pressure should be firm but not heavier than 5 to 8 pounds, your rhythm smooth and slow with 1 muscle squeeze per 2 seconds. This particular approach will have a very soothing effect. Most horses lower their heads willingly in this sequence. In that case, you might make a second pass to reinforce this relaxed feeling.

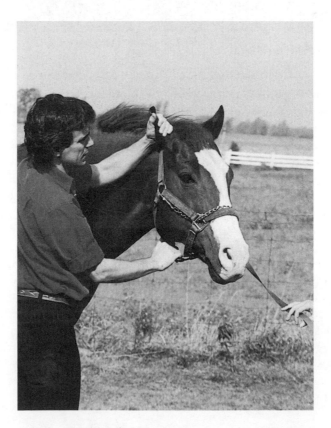

6.3 Ear Work: Relaxation routine.

6.4 Neck Crest Work: *Relaxation routine.*

Neck Rocking

Now use some stroking moves downward in the direction of the hair, very gently over the entire neck (point 4; figure 6.1). Then employ some very gentle neck-rocking movements to further relax the whole neck. To do so, place one hand on the crest and the other on the windpipe for support, then gently rock the top of the neck back and forth. Build up slowly to a rhythm of 1 movement per second. Start at the upper neck and slowly, over 10 to 15 rocking motions, go down to the withers. This will greatly loosen the large muscle group of the neck.

Withers Work

After the neck rocking, stroke the neck towards the body, (point 5; figure 6.1) and start to massage the entire withers area (both sides) with very smooth muscle squeezing. Be gentle. Use 3 to 5 pounds of pressure for approximately 1 minute. Intersperse with light strokings every 30 seconds for 3 to 5 seconds at a time.

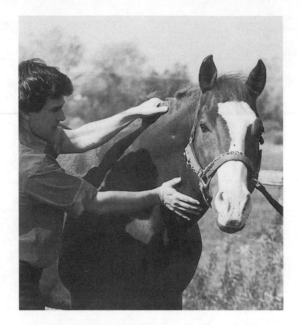

6.5 Neck Rocking Movement: *First part, relaxation routine.*

6.6 Neck Rocking Movement: *Second part, relaxation routine.*

6.7 Withers Work: *Light pressure, relaxation routine.*

Back Work

Follow with 2 to 3 light long strokes over the entire back (point 6; figure 6.1) Keep the pressure very light (at 1 or 2 pounds maximum) and the rhythm very smooth.

6.8 Back Work: *Relaxation routine.*

Sacrum Work

As you finish your back work, place your right hand over the sacrum (point 7; figure 6.1). Hold it there with a light vibration for 10 to 30 seconds. Follow with 3 circular motions clockwise and then 15 to 20 circles counterclockwise.

Tail Work

After the sacrum work, switch your right hand with your left hand to keep contact with the horse. Then with the right hand, use gentle stroking along the rump (point 8; figure 6.1), before starting the next move: the picking up of the tail with your right hand. Grasp the tail a few inches from its base, bringing it upward. Use your left hand as well to stretch the tail into a question mark (see figure 6.11).

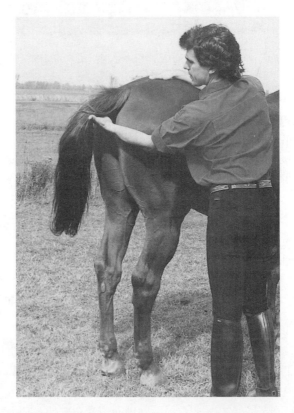

6.9 Picking up the Tail Movement: *From the tail work group of moves, relaxation routine.*

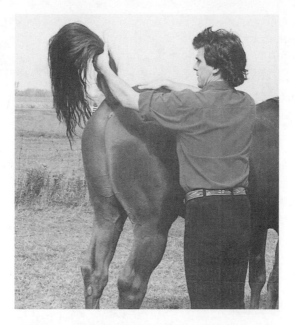

6.10 Raising the Tail Movement: *From the tail work group of moves (stretch the ventral aspect of the tail), relaxation routine.*

6.11 Question Mark Movement: *From the tail work group of moves (stretch the dorsal aspect of the tail), relaxation routine.*

Then gently move the tail in a circle, 3 times clockwise and 3 times counterclockwise. Notice if there is any restriction of movement on either side of the tail. That would be a sign of muscle tension in the tail muscles, and eventually in the hindquarters.

6.12 Clockwise Movement: *From the tail work group of moves, relaxation routine.*

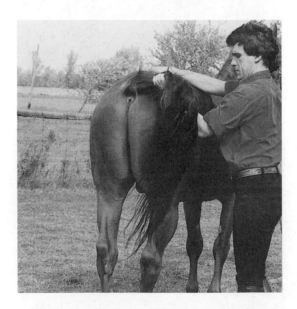

6.13 Counterclockwise Movement: *From the tail work group of moves, relaxation routine.*

At this point, move yourself to the rear of the horse and using only your body weight, pull on his tail very gently. Hold this stretch for approximately 1 or 2 minutes unless the horse shows discomfort. Usually the horse responds positively by pulling against you. Stretching the tail will contribute to and increase the horse's relaxation tremendously.

While stretching the tail, gently work each vertebra with a few muscle squeezings, between the thumb and fingers, from the base of the tail downward; keep stretching the tail with the other hand. Switch hands if you prefer.

Take note of the tail's flexibility and if there are any tender spots or points of possible inflammation. Release the tail-stretch progressively and then stroke the hindquarters and sacrum area for a few seconds.

Warning: If when you start stretching the tail feels "loose" at its attachment site (with half an inch give before the actual stretch starts), stop at once. You could be hurting the horse. The looseness means the horse has a not-uncommon joint problem. If you continue to pull the tail, you could produce a strain. If the horse shows discomfort, inflammation, or other abnormal symptoms on palpation of this area, skip the stretching and check with your veterinarian.

6.14 Stretching the Tail Out: *Carefully and gently working each vertebra with soft muscle squeezing moves, relaxation routine.*

Working the Legs

After the tail work, proceed to a gentle stroking-down of the legs (point 9; figure 6.1). Always maintain hand contact with the horse. Use 5 to 8 strokings on the way down the leg, and 2 or 3 on the way up, and a few more over the upper body as you move from leg to leg. Since you are already at the rear, start with the hind legs; then do the front ones.

Pick up each leg as you would to clean hooves. Safely position yourself relative to the horse. When the leg is flexed, move it gently in a small circle, moving inwards, then forwards, then to the outside, then back. Start again, repeating the movement 2 or 3 times. This action will further the relaxation and the "letting-go" feeling over the legs, the shoulder girdle, and indirectly over the spine. Be gentle.

This relaxation routine should take you from 10 to 15 minutes. You can take longer if you want, but the point of this routine is to initiate the relaxation reflex in a short period. Ten minutes is ideal.

When you use the relaxation routine to start another routine, a shorter version can be used, skipping the muscle squeezings over the crest of the neck, the neck rocking, the withers work, and the leg work at the end. After you complete the muscle squeezing right behind the poll, use strokings down the neck,

6.15 Stroking the Legs Down: *End of relaxation routine.*

over the withers and the back all the way to the sacrum. Then resume the regular routine.

Another variation of this routine is to start by working the withers and using stroking moves to the back and sacrum area, where you apply the sacral work. Then go back up toward the neck using strokings. Then work the neck crest and base of the skull behind the poll. Finish with the tail work and leg grounding. This version is useful when working on a head-shy horse.

We know from experience that the first routine outline works best. It won't take long before the horse associates his relaxation with your work. So with practice, you will be surprised at how quickly your horse will relax.

THE HEAD MASSAGE ROUTINE

The massage of the face, head, and upper neck areas indirectly affects the whole body; it is another great way to relax your horse and is also very soothing if he has sinus problems caused by allergies or a cold. This massage will also tell you about the horse's well-being, whether he is more auditory in orientation, reacting well to your voice, or is visually oriented, responding more to your movements (see chapter 2).

There are several areas on the face and head that will trigger very strong responses. For example:

❖ Massaging the upper lip and gums will elicit the same reflex response as a nose twitch, releasing endorphins into the body.

❖ Massaging the whole lower jaw, cheek, throatlatch, and upper neck will relax the animal tremendously, with a reflex effect on the neck and on through the whole spine.

❖ Massaging around the eyes and over the forehead will relieve tension from around the eye sockets.

❖ Massaging the ears, which are sensitive and always working, is very relaxing to most horses. However, horses are very protective of their ears and some do not like them touched at all; if you find your horse has this reaction, leave the ears until he has become accustomed to the massage routines.

The head massage routine is divided into three phases, each bringing the horse progressively into deeper relaxation and accepting of more detailed work. The sequencing of these routines is important; observe it from the beginning of your practice. Later, you can adjust the sequence to your liking as you develop a feel for your horse and his needs. But before you start, keep these facts in mind to improve your massage routine:

- ❖ When massaging the face and head, you should spend 15 to 20 minutes. Always use a very light touch since you will be massaging over many bones, nerve endings, reflex points, and facial muscles.

- ❖ Massage both sides at the same time to relax the horse gradually.

- ❖ When only using one hand in your massage, maintain constant contact with the horse by putting your other hand over the ridge of the nose.

- ❖ Always assess your horse's feedback signs as well as the feedback given by your fingertips (the four T's listed in chapter 3).

- ❖ Once your horse is used to your work, it is better not to have a halter on him while giving a head massage. Instead, use a very light nose band or put the halter around his neck.

6.16 Head Massage Routine

(A) first phase
(B) second phase
(C) third phase

First Phase

Start on the horse's left side. While quietly talking to the animal, hold the halter with your left hand and start a gentle circular effleurage with the right hand over the left cheek (point 1; figure 6.16), going slowly upwards toward the neck.

Then put your right hand on the neck crest (point 2; figure 6.16) in the area of the first and second cervical vertebrae and hold it there. Place the palm of your left hand on the ridge of the horse's nose (point 3; figure 6.16). Take a couple of minutes to breathe with your horse. Then talk in a soft voice. Since the horse is very protective, this initial contact will help him accept your touch. Keep in mind that the horse's face is a very sensitive area.

Keep your left hand either on the nose ridge or on the halter. Start massaging the upper neck area and the whole poll (point 4; figure 6.16) with your right hand. Do 20 to 30 gentle muscle squeezing movements for about a minute. Then move your right hand to the back of the ears and use light effleurages and gentle petrissage moves, such as light kneadings, around the base of the ears, and gentle muscle squeezing of the ear (point 5; figure 6.16) between your thumb and index finger. Most horses love this, and yours should lower his head in response. If he does not like his ears touched, skip this part.

Then bring both hands to the muzzle (point 6; figure 6.16) and start some light, gentle circular effleurages going from the nose ridge to the sides and all the way up to the ears. Work both sides

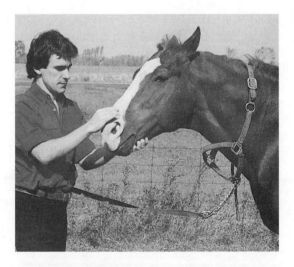

*6.17 **Working the Muzzle:** First pass, head massage routine.*

6.18 Working the Base of Ears: *First pass, head massage routine.*

simultaneously. Observe all reactions. At the base of the ears apply light finger pressure on the temples (point 7; figure 6.16) on each side. Use a light circular motion clockwise to start and counterclockwise afterward, each 3 to 5 circles minimum, more if your horse likes it. This is very soothing; you will notice his eyes will change expression and become "sleepy-looking."

Second Phase

Put the palm of one hand on the muzzle (point 8; figure 6.16) and apply gentle effleurages in a circular motion. Follow with gentle muscle squeezings, working both the lips and the chin thoroughly (point 9; figure 6.16).

Follow with small thumb kneadings from the nose to the forehead (point 10; figure 6.16). Then apply the palm of the hand on the forehead (point 11; figure 6.16) with a light pressure (2 pounds) and gently apply a circular motion, starting clockwise, then counterclockwise, each 2 or 3 circles minimum (more if the horse likes it) while maintaining full hand contact with the forehead.

The position of the eyes and the whorl form a triangle, which is the center of the horse's conscious world. Massaging this triangle will relax the animal greatly.

With your fingertips, apply some very light and small kneadings all around the eyes, draining them with small effleurages away from the eyes laterally. Then, very gently, apply a light pressure point (3 pounds of pressure maximum) half an inch from the corner of the eye for 10 seconds (point 12; figure 6.16), and drain

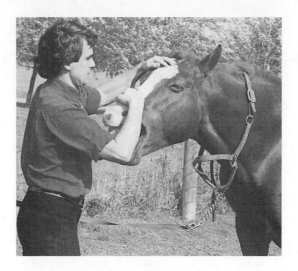

6.19 Working the Forehead: *Second pass, head massage routine.*

6.20 Drainage to the Sides: *Second pass, head massage routine.*

outward (laterally). You might consider using light vibrations from the fingertips while applying this pressure point if the horse does not mind. Repeat below and above the eyes.

Massage the bony depressions above the eye sockets (point 13; figure 6.16) with small, circular fingertip kneadings. Then, using the same move, finish by going from the far corner and under the eyes down to the nostrils (point 14; figure 6.16), repeating 3 times on each side. This will help drain the sinuses further.

Use light thumb kneadings on and in the nostrils. Be gentle because the drainage hole from the eye into the nostrils is a sensitive area. Complete with plenty of effleurage over the entire face of the horse, effleuraging upward toward the poll.

Third Phase

Using your thumbs or fingers as you prefer, gently friction the gums—front, sides, and the bars (point 15; figure 6.16). Then apply effleurages on the nose ridge (point 16; figure 6.16), toward the cheeks. Massage delicately underneath the jaw (point 17; figure 6.16) to assist drainage. Massage the cheeks (point 18; figure 6.16) for a few moments with finger kneadings and effleurages. Since the cheek muscles work a good deal and are thus very well developed, you might feel some tension spots. Release these with some gentle friction and drainage.

Use a lot of effleurages to drain the cheeks toward the ears and neck. Then place one hand on each ear and lightly pull it outward. Repeat 2 or 3 times. Then thoroughly massage the bases of the ears (point 19; figure 6.16) with thumb kneadings and light picking ups. Adjust your pressure to the sensitivity of the animal. Massage the inside of the ears as well; this is a good opportunity to clean out dead skin and inspect the ears for small cuts or insect bites.

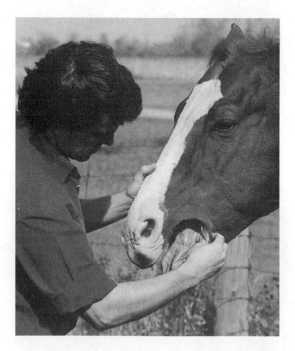

6.21 Working the Mouth: *Gums and bars, third pass, head massage routine.*

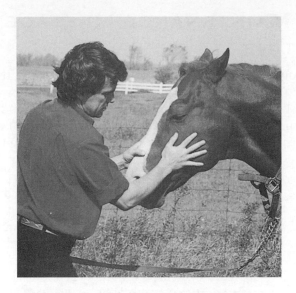

***6.22 Finishing the Facial Work with Lots
of Drainage:*** *Third pass, head massage
routine.*

When a horse swallows, his ears move sideways. This movement
tells us that the structures of this area—the ears, poll, lower jaw,
throatlatch, and upper neck—are all connected. Due to the connection of the deep muscle groups of the spine, tension in these
areas might reflect a hindquarter or a back problem. So take the
ear at the base (point 20; figure 6.16), pull it gently forward toward
yourself and with the other hand open the mouth exactly as you
would to make the horse accept the bit. This action will relax tension in the swallowing mechanism; it will also work well in relaxing the upper neck.

Now put your left hand over the ridge of the nose, with the
thumb and the index finger placed at the corner of each eye
(point 21; figure 6.16), and put your other hand underneath the
jaw as though taking the pulse. Stay in this position for a few minutes, breathing in rhythm with your horse. These are very soothing movements with which to complete the facial routine.

You can complement the relaxation process now by applying
the relaxation routine. You might also consider the reverse, applying the head massage routine after the relaxation routine.

The head massage routine is very specific work; not every horse
will let you work so intimately right away. So do not try this routine on a first massage attempt. In fact, it might take some time
before you can do this work on your animal, but when you do
manage it, you will find you have created a stronger bond between
the two of you.

THE MAINTENANCE MASSAGE ROUTINE

In addition to keeping the musculoskeletal structure fit, the maintenance massage routine also gives you a chance to assess and treat all muscle illnesses—tension, knots, stress points, and trigger points—and to detect any other abnormal symptoms. At any time in the maintenance routine, you can add the use of appropriate techniques (see chapter 5) to deal with a particular situation (swellings, stress points, trigger points, etc.). If any abnormal problems arise, check with your veterinarian before proceeding with your massage.

Connect with the animal for a few seconds by talking quietly and gently massaging the poll and the upper neck with light muscle squeezings (point 1; figure 6.23). Then start at the side of the neck with the SEW approach (see chapter 5): apply gentle strokings, from the poll to the withers. Progress into light effleurages covering the entire neck. Use wringings to stir up circulation. Intersperse with effleurages. Use muscle squeezings along the crest of the spine from the ears all the way to the withers. Then with thumb or finger kneadings, thoroughly work the various neck muscles. Intersperse with effleurages every 30 seconds. Your pressure should be light at the beginning, 2 or 3 pounds, progressing to a firmer touch (10 to 15 pounds of pressure). Your overall rhythm should be smooth, 1 to 2 movements per second. Adjust appropriately.

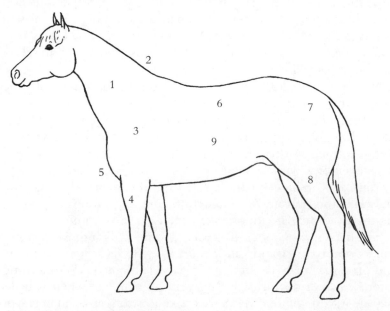

6.23 Maintenance Massage Routine

6.24 Neck Work: With deep double-thumb knead-ing, maintenance routine.

Moving to the withers area (point 2; figure 6.23), use muscle squeezings, gentle frictions, and thumb kneadings to work all the muscle attachments thoroughly, interspersing every 30 seconds with effleurages (5 to 8 pounds of pressure). When dealing with very developed withers, use muscle compressions with the palms of your hands (12 to 15 pounds) to increase circulation and to loosen the fibers through these tight muscles. Follow with effleurages. When done, use the WES approach to thoroughly drain the side of the neck and withers (see chapter 5). Use one pass of wringing followed by plenty of effleurage. Finish with some gentle stroking over the neck.

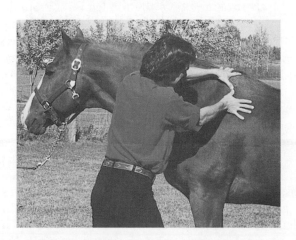

6.25 Withers Work: With deep double-thumb kneading, interspersed with effleurage, mainte-nance routine.

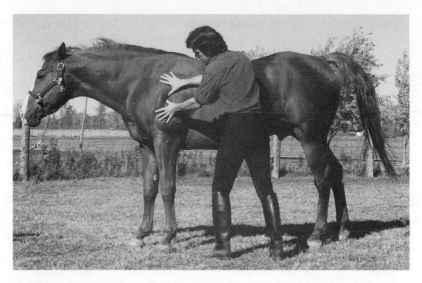

6.26 Shoulder Work: *With deep double-thumb kneading, interspersed with effleurage, maintenance routine.*

Without stopping, proceed to apply the SEW approach over the shoulder area (point 3; figure 6.23). Start with stroking, followed with some effleurages and wringings to warm up the area. Then use light kneadings (thumbs, fingers, or palms) interspersed with large effleurages along the muscle of the scapula. The serratus thoracis muscle often shows tension; use compression moves to loosen the fibers of this muscle, followed with gentle finger frictions. Drain that area thoroughly with the WES approach.

Apply the SEW approach over the leg (point 4; figure 6.23). Begin by gently stroking down the foreleg for a grounding effect. Then, starting at the point of shoulder, use muscle squeezings, picking ups, kneadings, and gentle frictions interspersed with effleurages over the triceps muscle as well as the fleshy part of the flexor and extensor muscle groups, above the knee. Below the knee are only tendons, ligaments, joints, and bones. Gentle muscle squeezings, gentle frictions, and thumb kneadings will loosen the tendons and stimulate circulation all the way down to the hoof; intersperse with effleurages going up the entire leg.

Gently weave your effleurages over to the front of the chest (point 5; figure 6.23). Use large kneadings, muscle squeezings, vibrations, shakings, gentle kneadings, and compressions to massage the pectoral muscles and the point of shoulder. Intersperse with effleurages every 20 to 30 seconds. Be creative. Then apply the WES approach to thoroughly drain the leg and chest. Finally, weave your stroking back over the shoulder all the way to the withers.

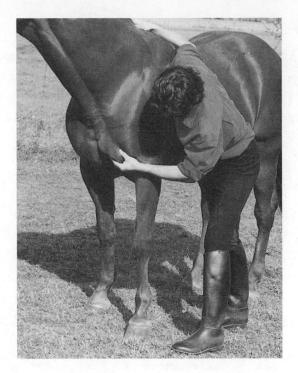

6.27 Chest Work: *With muscle squeezing and thumb kneading, interspersed with effleurage, maintenance routine.*

Warm up the back (point 6; figure 6.23), with the SEW approach. Apply wringings up and down the spine to stimulate circulation. Intersperse with effleurages. Follow with light tapotements on the back muscles to reach deep into the muscle structures along the spine. Intersperse with effleurages every 30 seconds on average. Finger or palmar kneadings and light frictions will help loosen the fibers of the longissimus muscle group of the back. Drain thoroughly with the WES approach.

Moving to the gluteus and hamstring muscles (point 7; figure 6.23), use the SEW approach to warm up the area. Then use compressions interspersed with effleurages. Follow with tapotements and compressions to stir circulation and to loosen the fibers of these large muscle groups. Use thumbs, fingers, or palmar kneadings and gentle finger frictions along the length of the fibers of all the muscle groups of the hindquarters. Intersperse with effleurages toward the stifle. When done use the WES approach.

When applying the SEW approach over the hind leg, stroke down the hind leg (point 8; figure 6.23), and then effleurage upward toward the flank area. Then use gentle picking ups over the gaskin, plus muscle squeezings, kneadings, and gentle frictions,

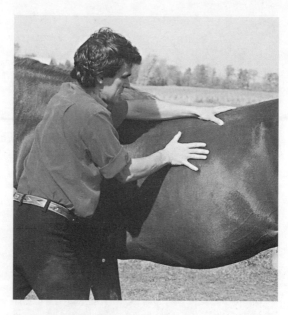

6.28 Back Work: *With deep double-thumb kneading, interspersed with effleurage, maintenance routine.*

6.29 Hindquarter Work: *With deep palmar compression, interspersed with effleurage, maintenance routine.*

all interspersed with effleurages, over the fleshy part of the flexor and extensor muscle group of the hind leg. Drain thoroughly upward, starting from the top of the leg and working your way down. Once at the bottom of the leg, effleurage from the fetlock to the stifle in one long stroke; repeat to cover all aspects of the limb. Below the hock are only tendons, ligaments, joints, and bones. Gentle muscle squeezings, gentle frictions, and thumb kneadings will loosen the tendons and stimulate the blood circulation all the way down to the hoof; intersperse with effleurages going up the entire leg. When done, apply the WES approach to the entire leg,

With strokings, flow back to the thorax area (point 9; figure 6.23). Then use the SEW approach. Use large wringings interspersed with effleurages up and down the thorax 2 or 3 times. Use light kneadings between the ribs and intersperse with effleurages toward the heart. You can use large shakings to stimulate the circulation over the chest area. Do not do this to excess because it might be more stressful than enjoyable to the animal. You can consider using some tapotement moves such as light (3 to 5 pounds of pressure) clapping/cupping and hacking to reach deep stimulation of circulation. Follow with thorough effleurages. The skin rolling move is very efficient in keeping the skin and underlying fasciae loose. When done, apply the WES approach over the entire thorax.

Duplicate this sequence on the other side of the animal. The overall routine can last between 30 and 60 minutes, depending on your goal and the temperament of the horse. Keep it on the short side when in the early stage of massaging your horse. With repetition your horse will become more receptive to your massage work, and once he has become accustomed to it, it will not be unusual to see a maintenance massage routine last for an hour and a half.

The maintenance massage routine will give you feedback on the physiological state of your horse and will help you detect any small problems early and prevent them from becoming more serious. As you find trigger points, stress points, swellings, and inflammations, take notes and apply the appropriate techniques (chapter 5). Always follow with lots of effleurage. The maintenance routine is a wonderful tool for maintaining and increasing the horse's performance. Regular use of the routine, at least once a week, will give you feedback on the quality of your training and will warn you of any potential problems. For highly trained horses, this routine should be applied at least every second day. Due to the frequency of the massage application, you will find that 20- to 30-minute sessions are sufficient to keep your horse in top shape.

THE RECUPERATION ROUTINE

The recuperation routine helps avoid the build-up of lactic acid responsible for the formation of trigger points. This routine is intended to assist the lymphatic circulation (chapter 1) and speed up recovery time. For this purpose we will mostly use lots of effleurages, gentle wringings, and large thumb or finger kneadings, depending on the area you are working on. The recuperation routine is usually applied after heavy exercise but also at any time your horse shows signs of "stocking up" in the lower legs. If the lower legs appear swollen, apply cold hydrotherapy (chapter 4) before your treatment.

Lymph channels run everywhere in the body but are mostly located along the spine and the deep arteries. *Lymph nodes* (glands that act as filters to clean bacteria and unwanted particles) are found along the lymph channels. Lymph nodes are also found in patches at the junction of the limbs and the trunk on the inside of the legs (chapter 1, figure 1.4).

Hydrotherapy is very useful in this routine, as swollen nodes are very sore to the touch. If an inflammation is present, use cold to relieve the irritation. Otherwise, if there is no sign of inflammation, use the vascular flush or heat to relieve congestion and assist with circulation of the lymph fluid (chapter 4).

You must perform the recuperation routine very gently because you are dealing with irritated tissues and inflamed nerve endings. Use mostly effleurage moves lightly over the tender areas with 2 or 3 pounds of pressure, 5 to 10 pounds on thicker muscle groups. When no strong inflammation is present, you may use light vibrations or very gentle shakings over specific lymph node areas; these last two massage moves are very effective in decongesting and in stirring up circulation. Gentle thumb, finger, or palmar kneadings may be used to stir circulation in thick muscle areas.

Use a light (3 to 5 pounds) pressure around the leg joints with small, light, circular effleurages. In a recuperation routine, we drain the lymphatic fluid in the direction of the heart. But we must first decongest swollen and inflamed nodes before bringing more fluid to them. Use cold hydrotherapy to soothe nerve endings and cool off the inflammation. If you have to deal with patches of enlarged lymph nodes, apply the swelling technique (chapter 5) to decongest them. Start at the periphery of the nodes, using light circular effleurage and draining the nodes from the center toward the outside.

RECUPERATION ROUTINE OUTLINE

Connect with the animal for a few seconds by talking quietly and gently massaging the poll and the upper neck with light muscle squeezings.

Begin this routine at the withers (point 1; figure 6.30) on the left side. Use effleurages to drain along the entire spine all the way to the croup. Repeat 2 or 3 times.

Move to position yourself halfway between the fore- and hind legs of your horse (point 2; figure 6.30). Drain the thorax area with effleurages from the spine downwards along the rib cage. Scoop the first half of the rib cage toward the inside of the fore-leg, and the second half of the rib cage toward the inside of the hind leg. Repeat each aspect 2 or 3 times, and then duplicate this work on the other side of the horse.

Work the chest (point 3; figure 6.30) with lots of effleurages and light kneadings, draining downward, along the inside of the foreleg toward the heart.

Use gentle shaking moves on the large shoulder muscles (point 4; figure 6.30). Work the left leg by using effleurages, scooping toward the inside leg. Work progressively down the leg, draining it upwards. Because toxins may be found all the way down to the hoof, thoroughly drain the leg up toward the heart. Duplicate this work on the right leg.

Repeat this procedure on the hind legs. Be gentle when working over the tendons of the lower legs.

When working at the hindquarters of the horse (point 5; figure 6.30), move the tail to the side in order to reach the upper

6.30 Recuperation Massage Routine

attachments of the hamstring muscle groups. Scoop your effleurage movements toward the inside of the leg. In this location, if the patches of lymph nodes appear swollen and inflamed, first apply a cold towel to soothe the nerve endings and follow with a gentle swelling technique (chapter 5). Then proceed with effleurages over the horse's back, scooping downward onto the chest. Massage all the way to the neck (point 6; figure 6.30). Spend some extra time draining the base of the skull and the top of the neck (behind the poll) thoroughly; use gentle muscle squeezings interspersed with effleurages. These moves will help drain the lymph nodes located in the upper neck.

Then move to the head and drain the area under the jaw (point 7; figure 6.30), along the throatlatch and the trachea, back toward the neck. To finish this routine and soothe the horse, use a lot of light strokings over the entire body from neck to tail and down the legs.

Remember that a horse showing stiffness and some lymphatic inflammation will be fairly sensitive. The sensory nerve endings are very tender and will therefore respond quickly to pressure. Be very gentle when you start this routine. Constantly check the feedback signs from the horse as you proceed. Pay close attention

6.31 Thorough Effleurage: *Going up the legs (light to medium pressure), the recuperation routine.*

6.32 Multiple Effleurages: *Light to medium pressure over the whole body, the recuperation routine.*

to what your fingers tell you (the four T's, chapter 3). Your start-ing pressure should be about 1 or 2 pounds. Gently build to between 3 and 5 pounds if the horse appears comfortable.

The recuperation routine should last between 20 and 30 min-utes, and is wrapped up by gently stroking the whole body.

THE WARM-UP ROUTINE

The warm-up routine is designed to stimulate circulation in a short period with the intention of perking up the horse before riding or exercising. The massage will bring more blood, oxygen, and nutrients to the muscle fibers. The routine is not a replace-ment for warm-up exercise, but is nonetheless a valuable start as you are grooming and about to saddle up.

For this routine, use mostly stimulating movements such as shakings, wringings, and tapotements, all interspersed with plenty of effleurages. Perform the routine briskly but not to the point of irritating the horse, at a rhythm of 2 to 3 strokes per second. Your pressure should vary from 5 to 8 pounds at the beginning or when going over bony areas, up to 10 and 20 pounds when going over large muscle groups. Start gently, progressively increasing the rhythm and pressure of your moves. Remember, the intent is not to spend time performing deep massage on specific muscles.

WARM-UP ROUTINE OUTLINE

Connect with the animal for a few seconds by talking quietly and gently massaging the poll and the upper neck with light muscle squeezings.

Beginning on the left side of the neck (point 1; figure 6.33) with light shakings, use a gentle rhythm of 1 stroke per second, slowly increasing the pace to 2 or 3 strokes per second. Then switch to wringings, covering the whole neck all the way down to the left shoulder (point 2; figure 6.33) and upper leg. Thoroughly cover all muscles. Intersperse with effleurages every 20 to 30 seconds and when moving from one body part to another.

Thoroughly massage the upper leg (point 3; figure 6.33), both on the inside and outside. Use shakings, wringings, picking ups, and large kneadings interspersed with effleurages. Drain toward the heart, starting from the upper leg and working down with every move. Once at the bottom of the leg, drain the entire leg with two long effleurage strokes from the fetlock to the shoulder. Keep your pressure moderate (8 to 12 pounds) and your rhythm swift.

Next, massage the chest (point 4; figure 6.33) thoroughly with shakings, muscle squeezings, and kneadings, draining the area with

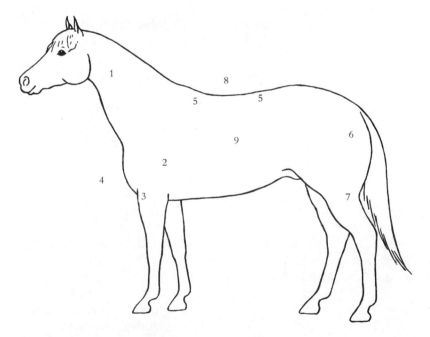

6.33 Warm-Up/Cool-Down Massage Routine

effleurages every 20 or 30 seconds. Then go back over the shoulder with some effleurages or strokings, working your way to the withers (point 5; figure 6.33). From there, apply wringings across the entire back, 2 or 3 times, interspersed with effleurages. Proceed to some tapotements, starting with clappings and then hackings, followed with effleurages. Then work the entire back and rib cage using shakings. Drain toward the heart with effleurages every 20 seconds as you progress. Watch for feedback signs from the horse. You should slow down the pace as you reach the groin area, since it is very sensitive and horses are very protective of it.

Next, go over the large muscle group of the hindquarters (point 6; figure 6.33) and down to the stifle and hock, using shakings, wringings, large palmar kneadings, and compressions, all interspersed with effleurages every 20 or 30 seconds. Work the

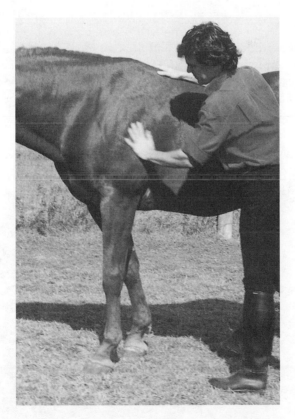

6.34 Fine Shaking: *Performed thoroughly over the whole body, with heavier pressure over large, bulky muscle groups to stir up blood circulation, warm-up routine.*

hind leg (point 7; figure 6.33) in the same way as the foreleg. Start from the top, draining it upward as you work your way to the lower aspect of the limb.

Repeat the entire routine on the right side. When you have completed this, apply a gentle wringing over the back and croup (point 8; figure 6.33), followed by effleurages. Keep the routine to 10 to 15 minutes. Longer sessions of the warm-up routine would irritate the horse. Indeed, the size of the horse is an important factor to consider: the more to massage, the longer the routine.

Immediately before the ride or exercise, apply the shaking move over the legs and the large muscles of the shoulder and hindquarters. This will deliver an extra last-minute touch to perk up your horse.

THE COOL-DOWN ROUTINE

The purpose of the cool-down routine is to loosen the muscles and generate good blood circulation immediately after exercising so as to prevent stiffening and loss of flexibility. This routine should be applied as soon as the walking cool-down period is finished. In application, the cool-down routine is very close to the warm-up routine, but here the emphasis is on drainage and the relaxation of the muscle groups.

6.35 Thorough Effleurage: *Light to medium pressure to assist the circulation and drainage of fluids, cool-down routine.*

COOL-DOWN ROUTINE OUTLINE

Start with generous wringings up and down the entire back (point 8; figure 6.33), 3 to 5 times, interspersed with generous effleurages (15 to 20). Follow with kneadings on the back muscles to relax the tendon attachments along the bones of the spine. Then apply larger shakings with some light hackings over the whole rib cage (point 9; figure 6.33) to clear any lactic acid from the deep muscle layers, followed by effleurages draining toward the heart.

Move on to work the hindquarters (point 6; figure 6.33) with wringings, compressions, and kneadings, all interspersed with effleurages. Work the hind legs (point 7; figure 6.33) with large kneadings and effleurages, beginning at the upper aspect of the leg above the stifle, effleuraging upward. Use 15 to 20 small effleurages until you reach the bottom of the leg, then from the hoof effleurage the whole leg all the way up. Repeat 3 to 4 times to cover all aspects of the leg (inside, outside, front, and back). Do both legs.

Using several effleurages or strokings, move back to the withers (point 5; figure 6.33) where you should apply thorough kneadings over the muscle attachments to relax them. Drain the withers thoroughly with effleurages, then move on to work the shoulders and forelegs (point 2; figure 6.33) with wringings, kneadings, and picking ups (on the leg below the elbow), all interspersed with effleurages every 20 or 30 seconds. Drain the forelegs (point 3; figure 6.33) in the same manner as you drained the hind legs. When finished with the legs, use light compressions, kneadings, and effleurages to work the chest muscles (point 4; figure 6.33). Finish this area with thorough wringings up and down the entire neck (point 1; figure 6.33), followed by large kneadings, and muscle squeezings over the crest of the neck. Follow with lots of effleurages.

Your overall time for this routine should be under 20 minutes. It is a good idea to follow the routine with stretching exercises (chapter 8) to help clear and reset the muscles after the work-out and cool-down routine. If during your work you detect stress or trigger points or other abnormalities, use the appropriate techniques (chapter 5) to remedy the situation.

TROUBLE SPOTS—ROUTINES AND TREATMENTS

See chapter 10 for routines and treatments for specific trouble spots. These routines are a nice complement to a maintenance routine, especially if your horse exercises regularly. A *treatment* is a massage application over a localized body part without delivering a full body routine. Treatments are designed to deal with particular problems such as cold back, neck stiffness, leg soreness, and the corresponding stress points.

With practice you will become familiar with each routine and will discover what works best for your horse in different situations. You will even be able to create your own variations. Do not be afraid to be innovative and to try different approaches. When in doubt about the effect of a specific routine, check with your equine massage therapist.

7

Kinesiology is the study of motion and of the structures that make it possible. To round out your massage skills, it is useful to know something about the kinesiology of the horse. But first, some terminology:

Protraction: The motion of the legs going forward.

Retraction: The motion of the legs going backward.

Adduction: The motion of the legs moving inward.

Abduction: The motion of the legs moving outward.

Isometric contraction: This occurs when a muscle contracts without causing an obvious movement. The best example is when a rider gets on a horse and the horse's body has to adjust in order to remain standing.

Concentric contraction: This occurs when a muscle shortens as it contracts and induces movements in the joints, such as those seen in protraction, retraction, abduction, and adduction.

Agonist: A muscle whose action on a joint is opposed by the action of another muscle, as in a concentric contraction.

Antagonist: A muscle that is opposed to the agonist. It is elongated during the concentric contraction and is often, but not always, responsible for an eccentric contraction.

Eccentric contraction: This takes place when a contracted antagonist releases its contracted state slowly to allow for better muscle control and to permit movement to be slowed down at will. This action contributes to the avoidance of jerky movements, making for elegance and suppleness in the horse's performance. Eccentric contraction also acts as a shock absorber, a very important attribute during landing or any other abrupt movement.

MOTION

A horse's hind legs provide the driving force and the power for the movement of the body. The forelegs are more concerned with direction and shock absorption.

To understand how a horse moves, we need to be aware of the interplay between the bones, joints, ligaments, tendons, and muscle groups that make the movements possible. Muscles are always arranged in opposing groups performing opposite actions; for example, the extensor muscle group of the foreleg extends the hoof during protraction, whereas the flexor muscle group of the foreleg flexes the same hoof during retraction. It is this type of interplay that produces the well-balanced, beautiful motion we love to see in horses.

KINESIOLOGY OF THE FORELEG

Protraction

The muscles involved in concentric contraction (which initiates the forward motion of the foreleg) are (see figure 7.1):

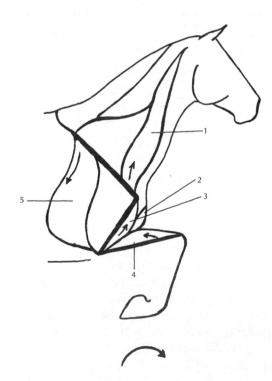

7.1 Foreleg Protraction

1. The brachiocephalic muscle
2. The cranial superficial pectoral muscle
3. The biceps brachii muscle
4. The extensor carpi radialis muscle
5. The thoracic part of the serrate muscle

During protraction, the brachiocephalic muscle (point 1; figure 7.1) pulls the shoulder joint up, initiating forward movement of the foreleg. At the same time, the thoracic aspect of the serrate muscle (point 5; figure 7.1) contracts to assist the rotation of the top of the scapula. The biceps brachii muscle (point 3; figure 7.1) causes flexion of the leg at the elbow. Then the extensor carpi radialis muscle (point 4; figure 7.1) extends the foreleg as the foot comes to the ground. In addition, the supraspinatus muscle, the thoracic part of the trapezius muscle, and the pectoral muscles (point 2; figure 7.1) assist the protraction of the foreleg.

All the muscles involved in the retraction of the foreleg are elongated during the protraction movement and through their eccentric contraction ensure stability and smoothness of action.

Retraction

The muscles involved in concentric contraction (which initiates the backward motion of the forelegs) are (see figure 7.2):

1. The triceps muscle
2. The latissimus dorsi muscle
3. The deep digital flexor muscle
4. The cervical part of the serrate muscle
5. The rhomboid muscle
6. The cervical part of the trapezius muscle
7. The caudal deep pectoral muscle

When the leg is fully protracted, the latissimus dorsi muscle and the triceps muscle (points 2 and 1 respectively; figure 7.2) are the main muscles responsible for bringing the leg backward. The caudal deep pectoral muscles (point 7; figure 7.2) pull backward and toward the center of the horse, contributing to the leg retraction movement and helping prevent the leg from moving sideways. The play between the cervical and the thoracic part of the serrate muscle (point 4; figure 7.2) allows the scapula to move up and forward. The rhomboid muscle and the cervical part of the trapezius muscle (points 5 and 6; figure 7.2) provide extra pull on the top of the scapula. The deep flexor muscles (point 3; figure 7.2) provide extra pull to lift the horse up and forward as the hoof leaves the ground for the next stride.

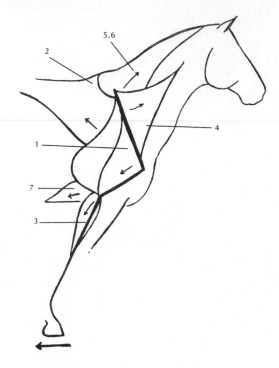

7.2 Foreleg Retraction

All the muscles involved in the protraction of the foreleg are elongated during the retraction movement and through their eccentric contraction ensure stability and smoothness of action.

Abduction

The muscles responsible for the concentric contraction in the abduction of the forelegs are (see figure 7.3):

1. The supraspinatus and infraspinatus muscle
2. The deltoid muscle
3. The rhomboid muscle
4. The trapezius muscle

The elongated muscles in the abduction of the forelimb are:

5. The cranial superficial pectoral muscle
6. The caudal superficial pectoral muscle
7. The caudal deep pectoral muscle
8. The cranial deep pectoral muscle

These muscles attach along the scapula and the bones of the foreleg. Their interplay induces the abduction movement. The

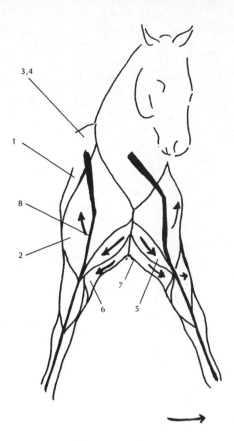

7.3 Foreleg Abduction

deltoid, supraspinatus, and infraspinatus muscles (points 1 and 2; figure 7.3) pull the point of the shoulder laterally, bringing the leg to the outside. The trapezius and rhomboid muscles (points 3 and 4; figure 7.3) assist this movement by pulling on the scapula. The pectoral muscle group (points 5, 6, and 7; figure 7.3) and the biceps brachii, in their eccentric contraction, contribute to stability and smoothness of movement.

Adduction

The muscles responsible for adduction of the forelimb are (see figure 7.4):

1. The cranial superficial pectoral muscle
2. The cranial deep pectoral muscle
3. The caudal superficial pectoral muscle
4. The caudal deep pectoral muscle

The elongated muscles in the adduction of the forelegs are:

5. The subscapularis muscle
6. The supraspinatus and infraspinatus muscle
7. The deltoid muscle
8. The rhomboid muscle
9. The trapezius muscle

These muscles attach to the scapula and along the bones of the foreleg; their interplay induces the adduction movement. The pectoral muscle group (points 1, 2, 3, and 4; figure 7.4) principally causes this motion by pulling the leg medially (inward). The antagonist muscles (points 5, 6, 7, 8 and 9; figure 7.4), by their eccentric contraction, contribute to stability and smoothness of action.

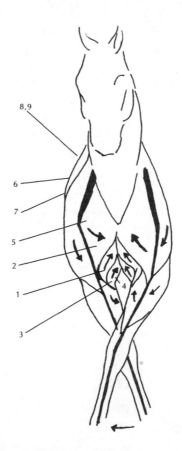

7.4 Foreleg Adduction

KINESIOLOGY OF THE HIND LEG

Protraction

The muscles involved in the concentric contraction (which initiates forward motion of the hind leg) are (see figure 7.5):

1. The iliopsoas muscle
2. The tensor fasciae latae muscle
3. The quadriceps group of muscles (lateral vastus)
4. The biceps femoris muscle
5. The gastrocnemius muscle
6. The long digital extensor muscle

The iliopsoas muscle, made of the iliacus and psoas muscles (point 1 and 2; figure 7.5) initiates the movement by pulling the femur up and forward. This action flexes the hip joint, the stifle joint, and the hock joint. The biceps femoris muscle and the lateral vastus muscle (points 4 and 3 respectively; figure 7.5) assist this action by pulling on the stifle joint and the tibia. The gastrocnemius muscle and the digital extensor muscle (points 5 and 6; figure 7.5) assist in the flexion of the fetlock joint.

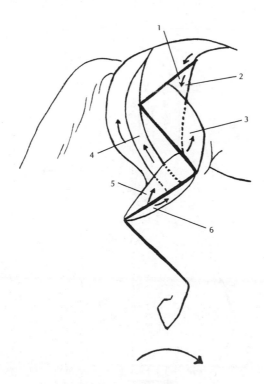

7.5 Hind Leg Protraction

All the muscles involved in the retraction of the hind leg are elongated during the protraction movement and through their eccentric contraction ensure stability and smoothness of action.

Retraction

The muscles involved in the concentric contraction (which initiates backward motion of the hind leg) are (see figure 7.6):

1. The gluteus muscles (especially the medial gluteus)
2. The hamstring group of muscles (the semitendinosus, the semimembranosus, and the biceps femoris)
3. The lateral vastus muscle
4. The biceps femoris muscle
5. The gastrocnemius muscle
6. The deep flexor muscle

The large gluteus medius muscle (point 1; figure 7.6) is attached to the back of the femur; it initiates the retraction movement. The hamstring muscle group (point 2; figure 7.6) is responsible for most of the power of the retraction; the adductor muscles assist in

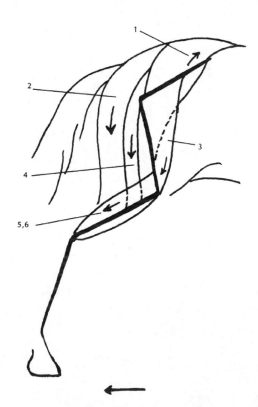

7.6 Hind Leg Retraction

this leg movement. The lateral vastus muscle (point 3; figure 7.6) allows extension of the stifle, which in turn causes the hock and fetlock joints to extend. The biceps femoris, the gastrocnemius, and the deep flexor muscles (points 4, 5, and 6; figure 7.6) assist the flexion of the stifle and the fetlock.

All the muscles involved in the protraction of the hind limb are elongated during retraction and through their eccentric contraction ensure stability and smoothness of action.

Abduction

The muscles involved in the concentric contraction (which initiates abduction motion of the hind leg) are (see figure 7.7):

1. The medial gluteal muscle
2. The deep gluteal muscle
3. The superficial gluteal muscle
4. The biceps femoris muscle
5. The lateral vastus muscle
6. The tensor fasciae latae muscle

The elongated muscles in the abduction of the hind leg are:

7. The great adductor muscle group
8. The iliacus muscle

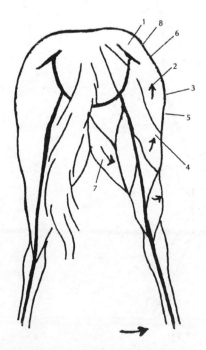

These muscles attach along the bones of the hind leg. Their interplay will cause the abduction movement. The lateral vastus muscle of the quadriceps group (point 5; figure 7.7) pulls the stifle laterally (outward). It is assisted by the biceps femoris and the tensor fasciae latae muscles (points 4 and 6; figure 7.7), which pull on the femur bone laterally (outward). The antagonist muscles (points 7 and 8; figure 7.7), by their eccentric contraction, contribute to the smoothness of action.

7.7 Hind Leg Abduction

Adduction

The muscles involved in the concentric contraction (which initiates adduction motion of the hind leg) are (see figure 7.8):

1. The great adductor muscle group
2. The iliacus muscle

The elongated muscles in the adduction of the hind leg are:

3. The deep gluteal muscle
4. The superficial gluteal and the medial gluteal
5. The biceps femoris muscle
6. The lateral vastus muscle
7. The tensor fasciae latae muscle

These muscles attach along the bones of the hind leg. Their interplay will cause the adduction movement. The great adductor muscle group (point 1; figure 7.8) mostly causes this action by pulling the hind leg medially (inward). The antagonist muscles (points 3, 4, 5, 6, and 7; figure 7.8), by their eccentric contraction, contribute to the smoothness of action.

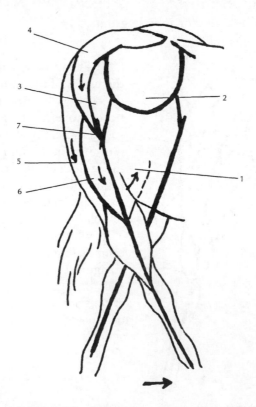

7.8 Hind Leg Adduction

THE VERTEBRAL COLUMN

Besides protecting the spinal cord, the vertebral column provides a frame-like structure composed of strong bones, very thick ligaments, and muscles that bridge the anterior and posterior limbs. Its role is to anchor strong muscle groups as well as to resist the downward effect of the center of gravity in mid-chest. In most equine disciplines, the vertebral column also supports the weight of a rider.

Extension

The agonist muscles responsible for the extension of the column are located above the vertebral column. This extensor muscle group is made of (see figure 7.9):

1. The spinalis dorsi muscle
2. The longissimus dorsi muscle
3. The iliocostalis dorsi muscle

Flexion

The agonist muscles responsible for the flexion of the vertebral column are the abdominal muscle group and the intercostal muscles. The muscles associated with protraction, retraction, abduction, and adduction of the limbs have a secondary function, which is to assist with the flexion of the vertebral column.

Lateral Flexion

Lateral bending is not caused by any specific muscle. In fact, such bending is the result of a unilateral concentric contraction of

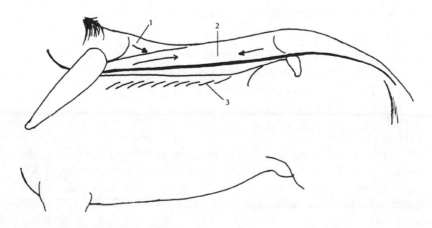

7.9 Back Extension

either the flexor or extensor muscles of the spine. In this movement, the intervertebral muscles play a strong role. Running from one vertebra to the next, the intervertebral muscles are tiny muscles along the side of the vertebral column. The grand oblique muscle of the abdominal group, especially the internal oblique, is also an important player in this particular movement.

THE RIB CAGE

The pectoral muscles and the ventral serrate muscles play an important role in supporting and stabilizing the rib cage, or chest, in relation to the spine. The abdominal muscles assist lateral bending as well as support the rib cage. The intercostal muscles are responsible for the actual movement of the ribs. The diaphragm muscle is responsible for breathing.

THE NECK

Muscles

Because the horse uses his head to counterbalance the weight in the rest of his body, the neck muscles play a very significant role in locomotion. Most obvious at the gallop, but also seen at the trot or walk, the downward swing of the head helps to lift the hind legs off the ground as the horse moves forward.

The neck muscles are:

1. The longissimus nuchae muscle
2. The splenius (capitis and cervicis) muscle
3. The complexus muscle
4. The rhomboid muscle
5. The serrate muscle (cervical part)
6. The trapezius muscle (cervical part)
7. The rectus capitis ventralis muscle
8. The sternocephalicus muscle
9. The sternothyrohyoid and omohyoid muscle
10. The brachiocephalic muscle
11. The scalene muscle
12. The intervertebral muscles

These muscles are attached along the spine from the base of the skull, down the cervical vertebrae to the thoracic vertebrae, and to the upper ribs, and the scapulas. Their interplay will induce several different movements.

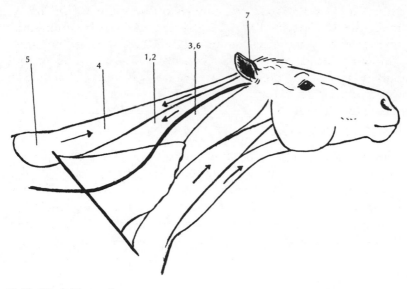

7.10 Neck Extension

Extension of the Neck

The muscles involved in the extension of the neck are (see figure 7.10):

1. The splenius muscle
2. The complexus muscle
3. The longissimus muscle of the neck
4. The trapezius muscle
5. The rhomboid muscle
6. The rectus capitis ventralis muscle
7. The intervertebral muscles

As these muscles contract, they cause the cervical section of the spine to arch in extension, bringing the head upwards.

All the muscles involved in the flexion of the neck are elongated during the extension movement, and through their eccentric contraction ensure stability and smoothness of action.

Flexion

The neck muscles involved in the flexion of the neck are (see figure 7.11):

1. The sternocephalicus muscle
2. The scalene muscle

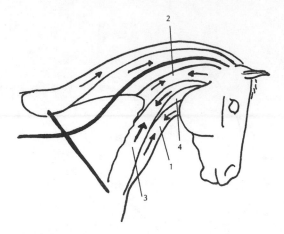

7.11 Neck Flexion

3. The brachiocephalic muscle
4. The sternothyrohyoid and omohyoid muscles

As these muscles contract, they cause the cervical section of the spine to bend forward in flexion, bringing the head downward.

All the muscles involved in the extension of the neck are elongated during the flexion movement, and through their eccentric contraction ensure stability and smoothness of action.

Lateral Flexion

The muscles involved in the lateral flexion of the neck are (see figure 7.12):

1. The rectus capitis muscle
2. The intervertebral muscles
3. The scalene muscle
4. The splenius cervicis muscle
5. The brachiocephalic muscle
6. The sternocephalicus muscle
7. The sternothyrohyoid and omohyoid muscles

The unilateral concentric contraction of these muscles to one side will cause the head and the cervical spinal column to move to the same side.

All the muscles involved on the opposite side of the neck are elongated, and through their eccentric contraction ensure stability and smoothness of action.

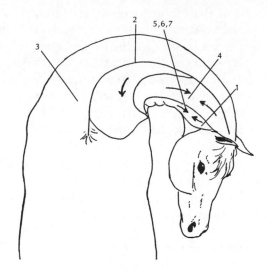

7.12 Lateral Neck Flexion

THE STAY MECHANISM OF THE HORSE

In the wild, horses cannot afford to spend much time lying down. However, they do require adequate rest. Thus nature provides them with a mechanism that allows them to relax and rest while standing. This is known as the "stay" mechanism, which stabilizes both fore- and hind legs. The mechanism consists of ligaments and muscles that "lock" the main joints in the "stay" position.

Both front and hind lower legs have identical mechanisms based on the suspensory ligament and the superficial and deep digital flexor muscles whose tendons possess check ligaments. The rest of the structure is kept in an extended position by a system of muscles (see figure 7.13).

The ventral serrate muscle, both cervical and thoracic parts, mainly connects the foreleg to the body of the animal. The play between the cervical and thoracic parts keeps the scapula at a sloping angle, flexing the shoulder joint. The play between the biceps and the triceps muscles keeps the shoulder in extension. The rest of the leg is well-aligned and the knee joint is prevented from bending forward by the lacertus fibrosus, an inelastic tendon that joins the biceps tendon and the radial carpal extensor muscle and tendon. Tension from the biceps is transmitted through this system to assist knee fixation.

The weight of the hindquarters flexes the stifle and the hock joints. The peroneus tertius muscle counteracts this effect by tensing up. It is assisted in this action by the gastrocnemius muscle, which acts to prevent the flexion of the hock. The gastrocnemius is assisted by the superficial digital flexor muscle. The play between the peroneus tertius muscle and the superficial digital flexor muscle ensures that the stifle and hock joints reciprocate their actions; for example, when the stifle flexes, the hock flexes as well.

At "stay," the stifle joint is fixed by the contraction of the quadriceps muscle and a locking mechanism involving the patella, which comes to hook on top of the enlarged upper end of the inner trochlear ridge of the femur. When locked, the hind legs maintain a steady position with very little effort.

A simple contraction of the quadriceps muscle and of the tensor fasciae latae muscle unlocks the patella, lifting it up and laterally off the ridge, thus freeing the stifle so the horse can move.

Study figure 7.13 to familiarize yourself with the stay mechanism. This way, when massaging or assessing a horse in the stay position, you will know what muscles are involved.

A solid knowledge of the muscles involved in the different movements of the horse will help you to better locate the muscular tension and possible muscle knots in your horse. The information contained in this chapter will also contribute to you better analysis of all the equine gaits. This better understanding of equine kinesiology will give you confidence when assessing the muscular fitness of your horse.

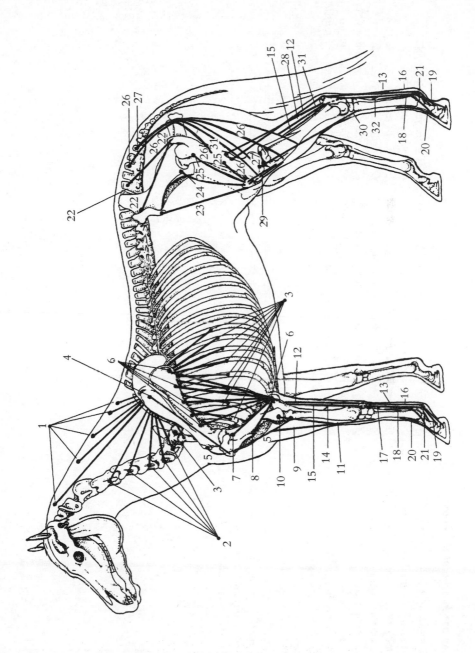

7.13 Stay Mechanism of the Horse

(1) cervical part of rhomboid muscle
(2) cervical part of ventral serrate muscle
(3) thoracic part of ventral serrate muscle
(4) supraspinatus muscle
(5) biceps brachii muscle
(6) long head of triceps
(7) lateral head of triceps muscle
(8) medial head of triceps muscle
(9) lacertus fibrosus
(10) radial carpal extensor muscle
(11) conjoint tendon of radial carpal extensor muscle and lacertus fibrosus
(12) superficial digital flexor muscle
(13) tendon of superficial digital flexor muscle
(14) radial check ligament (superior check ligament)
(15) deep digital flexor tendon
(16) tendon of deep digital flexor muscle
(17) carpal check ligament (inferior check ligament)
(18) suspensory ligament (superior sesamoidean)
(19) distal sesamoidean ligament
(20) tendon of common digital extensor muscle
(21) extensor branch of suspensory ligament attaching to common digital extensor tendon
(22) gluteal muscle
(23) tensor muscle of lateral fascia of thigh (tensor fasciae latae)
(24) rectus femoris muscle
(25) vastus muscle
(26) biceps femoris
(27) semitendinosus muscle
(28) accessory or tarsal tendon from the biceps femoris and semitendinosus muscles of the hamstring group of muscles
(29) straight patellar ligaments
(30) peroneus tertius muscle (tendinous or superficial portion of flexor metatarsi)
(31) gastrocnemius muscles
(32) tarsal check ligament (tendinous head of deep digital flexor)

8

STRETCHING

Horses instinctively know how to stretch; they stretch spontaneously, continually, and naturally, tuning up the muscles they
need to use most. In normal conditions, a horse will not overstretch.

With your knowledge of the bones, muscles, and kinesiology of
the horse, we can now talk about the reasons why stretch moves
should be part of your massage routine. Our stretching routine
will, of course, be timely, gentle, easy, and safe. Regular stretching
will benefit your horse and will give you feedback on his condition. Here are some of the benefits of stretching exercises:

- ❖ Relaxation
- ❖ Reduction of overall muscle tension and stiffness
- ❖ Increased circulation of both blood and lymph fluids
- ❖ Increased oxygenation and nutrition in the tissues
- ❖ Increased elasticity of the muscles, tendons, and ligaments
- ❖ Increased flexibility and range of motion of the joints
- ❖ Improved coordination
- ❖ Reduction of muscle strain and ligament sprain
- ❖ Improvement of the stride length
- ❖ Improved reflex time response

Note: If your horse has had any recent physical problems that
affect the joints and muscles (a fall, direct trauma, kick), or surgery,
consult your veterinarian or equine massage therapist before you
start a stretching program.

171

Reasons for Stretching

Physical

Stretching improves the tone of the muscle fibers and the elasticity of the ligaments and the joint capsules. Stretching reduces muscle tension, and therefore prevents muscle pulls. A strong pre-stretched muscle resists stress better than a strong un-stretched muscle.

Stretching prevents ligament sprain and loosens the joint capsules; it makes the body feel more relaxed. It releases muscle contracture due to old scar tissue, helps relieve muscle pain from chronic tension, and reduces post-exercise soreness.

Better elasticity of the muscles, tendons, and ligaments allows for freer, easier, more controlled, and quicker movements—all resulting in better coordination overall.

Muscle stretching increases circulation, bringing more oxygen and nutrients to the body parts; it prevents inflammation and adhesion (scar tissue) formation, trigger point formation, and stress point buildup.

The physiological benefits of stretching exercises upon the body are immediate. You should apply them regularly with your various massage routines and include them in your massage treatments when applicable.

Cerebral

When we say "cerebral" we refer to the nervous system, which is controlled by the brain and spinal cord. A horse's "body awareness" is, of course, cerebral. One aspect of stretching can be called cerebral since the activity develops body awareness. And as you stretch various body parts, you help your horse focus on them and become mentally "in touch" with them. This process develops the animal's self-awareness, thereby improving his coordination and locomotion. The stretching of muscles sends relaxation impulses via sensory nerves to the central nervous system and it will also decrease tension throughout the body. The animal will relax both physically and mentally, an important factor when dealing with animals that have been in accidents or are frightened or in pain.

Furthermore, stretching will give you feedback on the condition of the muscle groups and ligament structures, particularly regarding their elasticity and tone.

WHEN TO STRETCH

Always stretch when the horse is warm. Muscles, tendons, and ligaments (eventually joint capsules) risk damage if stretched when cold. Stretching a horse after a warm-up period will limit the risk of injury from overstretching. Again, if your animal has had any recent physical problems or surgery, particularly of the joints and muscles, or if he has been inactive or sedentary for some time, consult your veterinarian or massage therapist before starting a stretching program.

Keeping in mind the warning just given, you can stretch your horse at any time. Stretching should be done every day after every training or massage session.

Always warm up before beginning a stretching session. Walk or longe the horse. After warm-up and before heavier physical activity, stretching will trigger benefits such as loosening of the muscle fibers, vasodilation to bring more blood, and greater flexibility of the joints.

If you need only to stretch a specific area during a localized massage treatment, that area can be warmed up with a hot towel (see chapter 4) or simply by massage (effleurages, wringings, compressions, or shakings).

Stretching can be performed as a cool-down immediately after the main exercise or training program. This is actually the best time to stretch because the whole locomotor structure is warm. Stretching will increase circulation, promote relaxation, and cut down on any muscle contracture developed during an intense workout.

HOW TO STRETCH

To attain best results, you need to respect the structures you are working on. To manipulate correctly, it is important to be concerned with the animal's natural body alignment. You should also be concerned with your own alignment and posture in order to work at your best.

Stretching is not a competition; you do not have to push limits or see how far you can stretch each time you do it. The object of stretching is to relax muscle and ligament tension in order to promote freer movement and other benefits. To achieve all this, you need to stretch safely, starting with the easy stretch (see below) and building to a regular, deeper stretch. Never go too far; otherwise the *stretch reflex* (a protective mechanism within the muscle) will cause the muscle to contract in order to prevent its being overstretched and torn. Instead, just hold the stretch in a relaxed manner and for a longer period of time. The horse's flexibility will increase naturally when you start stretching regularly.

STRETCHING SAFELY

The first time you stretch your horse, do it slowly and gently. Give the horse time to adjust his body and mind to the physical and the nervous stress release that stretching initiates. The stretch should be tailored to the animal's particular muscular structure, flexibility, and varying tension levels. Be careful not to overstretch.

When you release a stretch, gently return the hoof to its original position on the ground. Do not let go of the leg halfway down. The horse could snap his hoof on the ground, damaging ligaments and tendons.

Note that many horses show varying degrees of sensitivity to handling. Understand that how you handle your horse from the beginning has a very definite impact on how you will be able to handle him in the future. Learn to make a distinction between a horse's reaction to pain and an objection to being handled.

The Easy Stretch

Always start with the easy stretch, during which you stretch only 75 to 80 percent of the total stretching capability of that particular body part, and hold it for just 10 to 15 seconds. Your horse will enjoy this gentle approach. Be steady in the development of your work. Never work hastily or with jerky movements.

Take hold of your horse's foreleg as you would to clean the hoof and gently guide it through its normal range of motion (forward or backward as needed), bringing it to its natural stretch point. There you should feel a mild tension. Then release your traction slightly. Hold that position for 10 to 15 seconds, during which the tension should subside. Then gently return the leg to the ground. Do not pull excessively on the leg because you risk straining the muscle fibers and tendons by overstretching.

The Development Stretch

Once the horse gets used to the easy stretch, you can work into the development stretch, holding the stretch for 30 seconds or more. Start with the easy stretch. Pass the initial 30 seconds; as the muscle tightness decreases, adjust your traction until you again feel a mild tension. Hold for another 10 to 15 seconds. Repeat 2 to 3 times until you feel you have reached the maximum stretching capacity of the muscle. Do not exceed a total of 2 or 3 minutes on any given stretch. Avoid triggering the stretch reflex caused by overstretching. Be in control.

Spontaneous Stretch

Often during the development stretch and sometimes during the easy stretch, the horse will spontaneously stretch himself fully for a few (5 to 10) seconds. This is a definite sign that the animal is enjoying the stretch and needs it very much. As you hold the limb during such spontaneous release, you can feel all the deep tension coming out as a strong vibration; it is quite an experience. After such a release, there is no need to hold the stretch further. Bring the limb back to its natural position.

Counting

The time-frame in which you stretch a muscle is very important. At first, silently count the seconds for each stretch. This will ensure that you hold tension for the correct length of time. After a while, you will develop a feel for this practice and will subconsciously know without having to count when the animal has reached his full stretching capability.

This practice of mental counting will bring the best results from the stretching technique. If not, let go gently and allow the limb to return to its natural position and repeat this treatment several hours later or the next day. Be aware of the horse's reaction to the stretch before you repeat the exercise. You should also investigate if any undue stress points or trigger points are present; release them with massage.

In summary, first start with the easy stretch for 15 to 30 seconds. Then work into the development stretch. This activity will finely tune the muscles and increase overall flexibility. Do not overstretch; do not make jerky or bouncy movements. Never stretch an acutely (recently) torn muscle. Never twist the joint or force it into an abnormal range of motion. Always stretch the *agonist muscle* (the one responsible for the action) and its *antagonist muscle* (the one that has to let go for the action to happen). In other words, stretch in both directions of a joint's movement. A regular practice of stretching with comfortable and painless movements will help you extend your animal's current limit of flexibility.

Warning: During stretching exercises, your posture is most important. (Position yourself as shown in chapter 3.) Using your body weight properly will contribute greatly to the good development of this technique. As you start stretching the limbs, especially the hind legs, posture is very important to prevent injury to your back. Flex your knees and use your leg muscles to absorb the tension. Keep your back straight and your shoulders relaxed. If the horse retracts a leg abruptly, your posture should allow you to absorb this unexpected jolt. If you are not properly positioned, your lower back will not survive very long! You will be the one who needs the massage and the stretching. Be relaxed as you work. Breathe deeply.

THE STRETCHING ROUTINE

NECK STRETCHES

Neck stretches will affect all aspects of neck muscle action. You can do all of them using a piece of carrot or other treat as incentive. This will make your work much, much easier.

Lateral Stretch: Allow the horse to sniff the "incentive" and guide him toward the withers. As he follows your hand, the resulting movement will stretch both the extensor and flexor muscles of the neck. You can increase the lateral stretch by asking him to stretch further toward the point of the hip. Talk softly to your horse as you get him into the stretch. Do both the right and left sides.

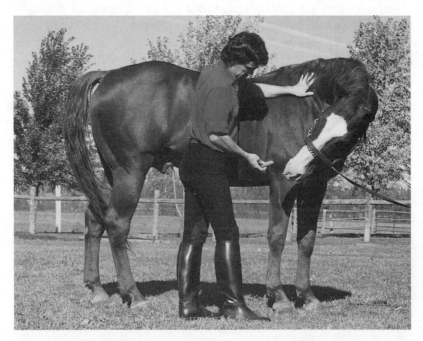

8.1 Lateral Bending of the Neck: *Duplicate on other side; use a food reward to make the work easier.*

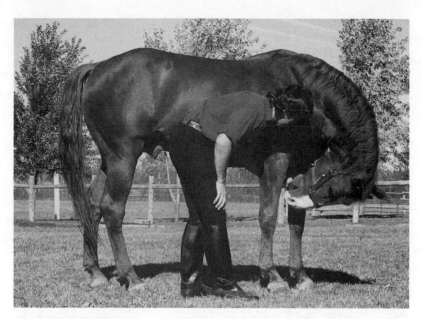

8.2 Neck Flexion: *Again, use a food reward.*

Neck Flexion Stretch: As with the lateral stretch, use an "incentive" to guide your horse's head downward, in between his legs, as close to the ground as possible. While performing this particular stretch, you can add a variation: as you bring the flexion down, move his head to the right or left. The extensor muscles will thus be thoroughly stretched.

Neck Extension Stretch: As with the other neck stretches, use an "incentive" to guide the horse's head upward and out as far as it can go. Do not force this movement. The horse will get into it freely once you show him how. This movement will stretch the neck's flexor muscles.

FORELEG STRETCHES

The Shoulder Extension Stretch: This protraction movement will stretch the muscle involved in the retraction of the foreleg. With a little pinch, pick up the leg above the fetlock joint, take the hoof with one hand and place the other behind the knee.

Gently bring the leg forward and upward. This stretch will affect the muscles of the shoulder, the trapezius muscle, the latissimus dorsi muscle, the serratus thoracis muscle, the deltoid muscle, and the triceps muscles. Once the horse is well into the stretch, maintain the tension with one hand behind the knee and with the other hand extend the hoof. This action will deepen the

8.3 Neck Extension: *Progressively bring the head into this position.*

flexor tendon stretch as well as the suspensory ligament stretch. Be gentle and cautious.

The Shoulder Flexion Stretch: This retraction movement will stretch the muscles involved in the protraction of the foreleg. Pick up the leg with a little pinch above the fetlock joint and with one hand take hold above the hoof. Place the other hand in front and above the knee joint. Gently bring the leg backward until the radius is at a 90-degree angle to the ground. This is a good stretch for the muscles of the chest and the upper leg: the pectoral muscle, the brachiocephalic muscle, the biceps muscle, and the extensor carpi radialis muscles.

The Fetlock Stretch: To complete the stretching movement of the forelimb, bend the leg at the knee and alternately flex and extend the fetlock joint. Secure your grip with one hand, holding the cannon bone firmly, and with the other hand move the hoof. This stretch is good for the structure of the lower leg and ankle, the common digital extensor tendon, the extensor carpi radialis tendon, the lateral digital extensor tendon, and the suspensory ligament. This action positively affects the strong ligament structures of the lower leg.

8.4 Shoulder Extension Stretch: *This protraction stretching movement is good for stretching the flexor muscles of the leg.*

8.5 Shoulder Extension Deep Stretch: *This version is done after the initial stretch and allows for extra stretching of the flexor tendon and the suspensory ligament.*

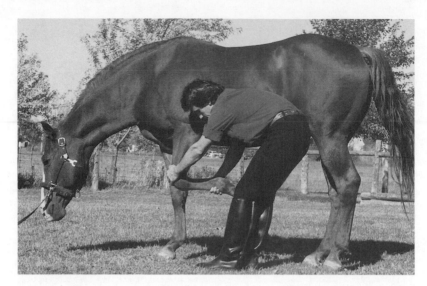

8.6 Shoulder Flexion Stretch: *This retraction stretching movement is good for stretching the foreleg extensor muscles.*

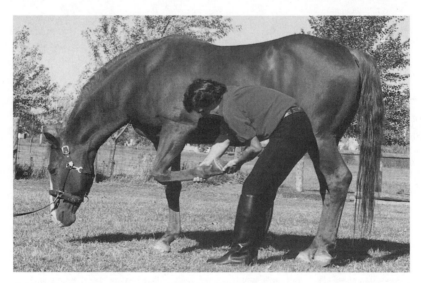

8.7 Shoulder Flexion Deep Stretch: *This version is done after the initial stretch and allows for extra stretching of the extensor tendon and ligament structure of the anterior aspect of the foreleg.*

The Shoulder Rotation: The following variation will help loosen deep muscles such as the pectorals, the serratus cervicis and thoracis, and the intercostal fascia, and will help relax the ligaments of the shoulder girdle structure. Keeping the leg flexed at the knee, secure your grip by holding the knee joint in one hand with the other placed over the fetlock joint. Start initiating a clockwise movement at the knee. First move the leg medially (inward), then forward, laterally (outward), and back. Repeat several times (3 to 5 times), and then switch to a counterclockwise movement. Avoid excessive pressure at the knee joint.

HIND LEG STRETCHES

The Hip Extension Stretch (also known as the Hamstring Stretch): This protraction movement will stretch the muscle involved in the retraction of the hind leg. Pick up the hind leg, grasping it behind the fetlock. Gently move the leg forward in its natural line of movement. While the leg is forward you might consider moving it a little more medially (toward the horse). Do not move the hind leg laterally (outside) because this is not a natural movement; it would affect the joint structure too much. This is a good stretch for the muscles of the hip and thigh: the gluteus, the bicep femoris, and the hamstring muscles (the semitendinosus and the semimembranosus). Be especially careful when doing this stretch because a horse will often forcibly retract his leg, giving you a good jolt. There's also the risk of a ligament injury should the horse snap a hoof on the ground. Be prepared, holding with proper posture.

The Hip Flexion Stretch: This retraction movement will stretch the muscle involved in the flexion of the hip. Pick up the leg and secure your grip by putting one hand above and the other below the fetlock joint. Carefully and very gently bring the hind leg backward. Once the leg is in position, place one hand on the hock to steady the movement for the duration of the stretch. Then stay close to the horse and maintain contact with the leg when bringing the foot back to the ground. This is a good stretch for the muscles involved in leg flexion: the iliacus muscle, the thigh muscles (vastus muscles), the gluteus muscles, the tensor fasciae latae, the long extensor muscles, and the abdominal muscles.

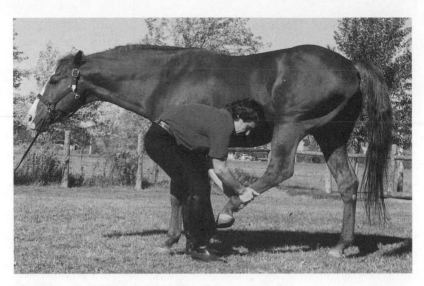

8.8 Hip Extension Stretch: *This protraction stretching movement is good for stretching the flexor muscles of the hind leg.*

8.9 Hip Extension Deep Stretch: *This version is done following the initial stretch and allows for extra stretching of the flexor tendon and the suspensory ligament.*

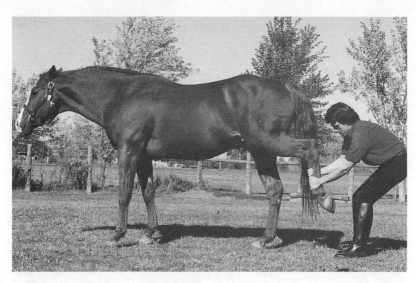

8.10 Hip Flexion Stretch: *This retraction stretching movement is good for stretching the extensor muscles of the hind leg.*

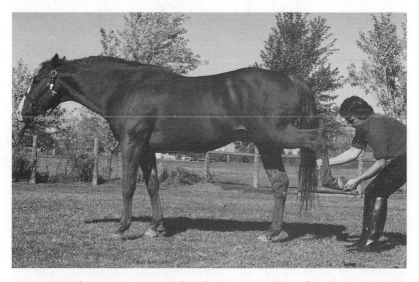

8.11 Hip Flexion Deep Stretch: *This version is done after the initial stretch and allows for extra stretching of the extensor tendon and ligament structures of the anterior aspect of the hind leg.*

The Quadriceps Muscle Stretch: This is another movement to stretch the large quadriceps muscle group of the hind leg and the tensor fasciae latae ligaments. Grasp the rear foot on the opposite side of the horse, and bring the leg under the belly and slightly

8.12 Quadriceps Stretch: *This special stretching movement is good for stretching the quadriceps and gluteus muscle groups.*

toward the opposite front foot. Secure your grip with both hands, holding at the pastern. Be aware of the torque you will produce on the hock and the stifle joint by stretching this way. Do not apply too much pressure. Be gentle, paying attention to your horse's comfort. This is a good movement to stretch the quadriceps, the gluteus, and the hamstring muscles, as well as the tensor fasciae latae ligaments.

BACK MUSCLE STRETCHES

There is no particular stretching movement for the back muscles. But by reflex, you can affect these muscles if you press your thumb into the belly region, right over the attachment tendon of the posterior deep pectoral muscle on the sternum. This will cause the horse to tuck up, thereby rounding his back and stretching these muscles: the longissimus dorsi, the longissimus costarum, and the spinalis dorsi. Tickling the belly will also cause the same reflex. This is one of the easiest stretches.

Another way to affect these muscles is to apply point pressure with your thumbs on both sides of the sacrum (croup), approximately 3 inches from the spine. This will cause a reflex action in the abdominal muscles, which will result in the horse tucking his rump and arching his back, stretching his back muscles.

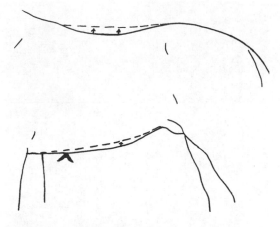

8.13 Back Stretching

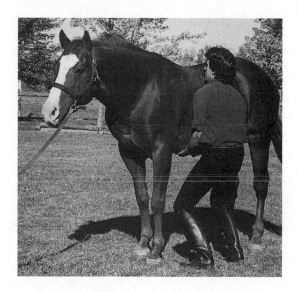

8.14 Back Muscles Stretch

Tail Stretch: Stretching the tail is a great way to produce a feeling of deep relaxation in your horse. This stretch is a major part of the relaxation massage routine (chapter 6).

When approaching the rear, use gentle strokings along the tail bone and down the buttocks before picking up the tail with your right hand. Keep your left hand on the sacrum. Take hold of the tail a few inches from its base and gently move it in a circle, first clockwise 2 or 3 times, then repeat counterclockwise. Take note of any restrictions.

8.15 Tail Stretch

At this point move to the back of the horse and, using your body weight, very gently pull on the tail. Hold this stretch for approximately 1 or 2 minutes unless the horse shows discomfort. Usually the horse, feeling good, responds positively by pulling against your traction.

Using light muscle squeezing moves between the thumb and fingers of your right hand, gently work each vertebra from the base of the tail down. Keep stretching with the left hand. Reverse hands if that suits you better. Make note of the tail's flexibility, looking for sore spots and possible inflammation. Release the stretch progressively and then stroke the hindquarters and sacrum area for a few seconds.

Warning: If when you start stretching the tail it feels "loose" and has a "give" of one quarter to half an inch, stop immediately. The horse has a joint problem, not an uncommon condition. Stretching would trigger pain and could result in a strain of the tail attachment site.

If the horse shows discomfort, inflammation, or abnormal symptoms with palpation of this area prior to stretching, then stretching is contraindicated. Check with your veterinarian.

Regular stretching exercises will contribute greatly to the animal's overall flexibility and fitness. They should be part of his exercise program. Done individually, stretching will assist you in the application and success of your massage treatments. Also, the reaction of your horse to the stretch is a great source of feedback on how he carries himself.

9

CONFORMATION CHECK-UP ROUTINE

In general, the better the conformation, the better the movements. Poor conformation will predispose a horse to injuries.

Before giving a thorough massage to a horse, it is important first to evaluate his conformation, action, and soundness. The ground check routine will accomplish this. Train your eye to assess the horse's posture and body parts in relation to each other: size, proportion, and alignment. Observe the fitness of the muscular structure. Get a general impression of the horse's state of health. Is he alert, with ears moving back and forth? Is his coat glossy and lying flat? Does he have good muscle tone? Appreciate the overall quality of this picture.

GROUND CHECK ROUTINE

Check all body parts with a light palpation (2 to 5 pounds of pressure) from front to back on both sides. The skin should be loose and supple; it should move easily over the underlying structures. Remember the four T's: texture, tension, temperature, and tenderness (chapter 3).

Pay attention to any abnormal swelling, heat, muscle knots, or abnormal reactions. Note that many animals show varying degrees of sensitivity to handling, so make a distinction between a reaction to pain and an objection to being handled.

HEAD AND NECK

❖ The head should be proportional in size to the rest of the horse. The head influences balance. A somewhat oversized head could unbalance the animal, leading you to suspect deep muscle tension in the neck and withers.

187

❖ The neck should be strong and flexible in all directions.

❖ The position of the head at the neck and throatlatch should be well-angled, with a good width between the throatlatch and lower jaw so that no restriction of movement or breathing will occur.

❖ Palpate the underside of the head to check the glands, larynx, and trachea.

❖ Palpate the neck at the first cervical vertebra to check for any obvious misalignment that would cause neck muscle tension on both sides of the neck.

❖ If there is heat over the poll area, suspect poll evil, or it could simply be an inflammation caused by a bang.

❖ The neck should feel solid and have a convex crest line through to the withers.

WITHERS

❖ The withers should be clearly defined and approximately the same height as the high point of the croup.

❖ If the withers are too high or too low, an ill-fitting saddle or harness may cause muscle tenderness. The withers may then become inflamed and eventually transfer muscle tension over the front end as well as over the back muscles.

CHEST, GIRTH, AND RIBS

❖ If the chest is narrow, you might see interference of the legs.

❖ If the chest is too wide, there will be difficulty when galloping (rolling in center).

❖ The girth should be wide and deep, with a well-developed rib cage giving room for the lungs. A horse with good conformation will have a girth measurement greater than his height.

❖ If the rib cage is not flexible, suspect intercostal muscle tension.

❖ Look at the horse's flanks during exhalation. Contraction of the flanks twice every time the horse exhales signifies a possible case of heaves.

SHOULDERS

❖ Well-muscled shoulders with a forward 45-degree slope (ideally) give the horse freedom of movement when he moves. The shoulders also act as shock absorbers.

❖ Shoulders that are too wide will cause poor movement; the condition is known as "loaded shoulders."

❖ If the scapular muscles (supraspinatus and infraspinatus) are under-toned or atrophied compared to the rest of the body, suspect a "sweeney" condition—suprascapular nerve damage.

❖ If the point of the shoulder is inflamed, suspect bicipital bursitis.

FORELEGS

❖ The forelegs should be well muscled, squarely set, and fairly straight from the top of the leg to the hoof. They should not toe in (pigeon-toed) or toe out (splayed feet), or be too close (base narrow) or bowed (base wide). Such defects will affect movement, leading to sore ligaments, tender joints that will eventually swell, and muscle tension throughout the leg and chest.

❖ When viewing the horse from the side, run an imaginary plumb line from the middle of the scapula down past the front of the knee to the back of the foot and the ground. If the conformation is correct, a straight line will run through the middle of the leg, ending up at the heel of the foot. When viewed from the front, the bone of the forearm (radius) and the cannon bone should be in a straight line with the knee centered between them.

❖ The elbows should be clearly defined, standing clear from the ribs.

❖ An inflammation at the point of elbow is called a capped elbow.

❖ If the triceps and the extensor muscles are atrophied, suspect radial nerve paralysis.

❖ Weak forearms show lack of muscle tone and tendon weakness. There is therefore a greater risk of strain.

KNEES

❖ The knees should be broad and flat, showing a clean outline with no bony lumps.

❖ If the knees point in different directions, suspect underlying problems in all parts of the leg.

❖ If the knees are swollen (popped or sore knee), suspect inflammation, the formation of bone spurs, arthritis, or capsulitis.

❖ If when viewed from the side the knee seems to sit behind the straight line (calf-kneed or back at the knee), there is a serious conformation fault. This makes the horse more prone to tendon strain and severe problems in the joint itself.

❖ If when viewed from the side the knee is in front of the center line (buck-kneed or knee-sprung), there is a risk of tenderness at the joint. This is an acceptable condition, not to be considered a serious conformation fault.

CANNON BONES

❖ The cannon bones should be short and strong, with clearly defined tendons behind them.

❖ If there is any inflammation in the upper third, suspect splints (green splints); if in the middle third, suspect sore shins (bucked shins); if in the lower end, suspect epiphysitis and wind puffs.

❖ If the cannon bone is narrower below the knee than at the fetlock joint, there is a risk of weakness in the bone and the tendons (known as "tied in below the knee").

❖ If the tendon at the back of the cannon bone is inflamed, suspect a bowed tendon.

FETLOCKS

❖ The fetlocks should have a clean outline with no bumps or swellings.

❖ If the fetlocks are swollen, suspect wind puff or sesamoiditis.

❖ If there is a bump on the inside, suspect brushing from interference.

❖ Very tender fetlocks may indicate an inflammation of the suspensory ligament, the deep flexor tendon, the sesamoid bones, or the navicular bone.

PASTERNS

❖ The pasterns should slope at an angle of 45 to 50 degrees, the same as the shoulder blade angle. The length of the pastern bones will vary with the breed. However, a pastern bone should be proportional to the rest of the leg without being too long (resulting in strain on ligaments and tendons) or too short (producing a choppy stride that results in much concussion and jarring of the leg structures).

❖ If you feel a bony growth on the pastern bone, suspect ring bone (usually in the front leg).

❖ If the back of the pastern is tender or swollen, suspect inflammation of the suspensory ligament or of the superficial flexor tendon.

FEET

❖ The hooves should face forward and be large, dense, and wide at the heels. There should also be a continuity in the slope (45 to 50 degrees) from the pastern. The coronet band extends around the top of the hoof; this is where the insensitive, protective lamina originates.

❖ If there is some inflammation on the coronet, suspect a quittor condition. Check with your vet.

❖ If the heels are contracted, there are underlying problems. Check with your farrier or blacksmith.

❖ Feet that are not properly aligned with their toes, splaying in or out, can lead to stumbling and brushing, causing undue strain on the structures of the foreleg.

THE BACK

❖ The back should be well-muscled with its length proportional to the body; if it is too long it might be subject to strain or inflammation (cold back).

❖ A weak or hollow back (sway back) might indicate arthritis or weakness in the structures.

❖ Arching upwards (roached back) may indicate a predisposition to arthritis.

❖ Starting at the withers, run your fingers firmly along the spine down toward the tail. Normally, a horse dips its back when pressure is applied as you run your fingers over the muscles of the back. If the animal tenses against your pressure, this is an indication that there may be a problem (muscle inflammation, tightness, cold back), or this may simply be indicative of a horse with a high-strung, sensitive nature.

LOINS

❖ Because they have the least structural support, the loins should be short and well-muscled. If they are poorly muscled, a weak back or cold back results.

❖ If the loins are short but are well-developed compared to the rest of the body, excessive muscle pull may be transmitted to the back, causing it to become tense.

HINDQUARTERS

❖ The hindquarters should be well-developed, muscular and strong, with a broad hip showing a good length from the point of the hip to the hock with proportionally well-muscled gaskins.

❖ An imaginary line sighted from the back of the rump should run through the hock and cannon bone to the ground.

❖ If the back of the rump is very tender, suspect a torn hamstring.

❖ A horse normally tenses his hindquarters upwards when you run your fingers on the croup. If the animal sinks downward and away from pressure, this would be an indication of underlying problems such as serious muscle inflammation or a sacroiliac luxation.

❖ Heat with an associated bump over the sacrum can indicate sacroiliac luxation (hunter bump).

❖ If there is tenderness over the head of the femur, suspect trochanteric bursitis.

STIFLES

❖ The stifles should be well-defined, with no bumps around the joint.

❖ If the stifle feels hot or swollen, suspect either arthritis or patellar problems.

❖ The gaskin should be strong since it originates most of the muscle action needed for hock and foot movements.

❖ If there is swelling or heat over the tibia (gaskin), suspect a tear in the peroneus tertius.

HOCKS

❖ The hocks should be strong with a clean outline and flat on the sides with a rounded point at the back (tuber calcanei bone).

❖ A bony growth at the front of the hock indicates *spavin* (a degenerative joint condition causing lameness).

❖ If there is swelling and heat behind the hock, suspect:
   a) *Curb* (tearing of the ligament, especially with young horses).
   b) *Thoroughpin* (inflammation of the synovial sheath of the deep flexor tendon).
   c) *Capped hock* (inflammation of the bursa between the skin and the tuber calcis).

❖ Hocks might be close together (cow hocks) or wide apart (bowed hocks); both conditions indicate a slight weakness in the structure.

❖ Straight hocks might cause excessive strain on the stifle joint, which in turn could cause undue strain on the Achilles tendon.

Check the lower aspect of the hind leg as you did for the foreleg. The conformation points and characteristics are essentially the same.

EVALUATION OF THE HORSE'S WEIGHT DISTRIBUTION: THE FLOAT LINE

Draw an imaginary line between the center of oscillation of the foreleg (upper third of scapula) and the center of articulation for the hind limb (point of hip). This is called the *"float line"* and it should be close to horizontal (see figure 9.1).

However, it would be more desirable if the point of the foreleg were slightly higher than the point at the hind leg than if the reverse were true. When the point at the hind leg is slightly higher than the point of the foreleg, the weight of the horse would tend to be distributed more toward the front end, causing it to be out of balance and therefore apt to develop stress, leading to more serious problems such as inflammation of the muscle fibers, or worse, in the tendons or ligaments of the front quarters.

ACTION AND SOUNDNESS

The Walk

When evaluating how a horse moves, have the horse walk in a straight line away from you, turn around, and walk back toward you. To assess the walk, stand where you can watch the front and rear of the horse and then position yourself so you can see the side. The horse should move easily and freely, balanced equally in front and behind and evenly in the shoulders and hips. Check the length of stride, the rhythmic cadence of the four-beat gait at the walk, and that the feet are lifted clear off the ground; watch for whether or not he "tracks up." Pay attention to the flexibility of the joints. The movements should flow easily, showing ease and strength. A horse that is a little sore will be slightly "off," moving his legs unevenly.

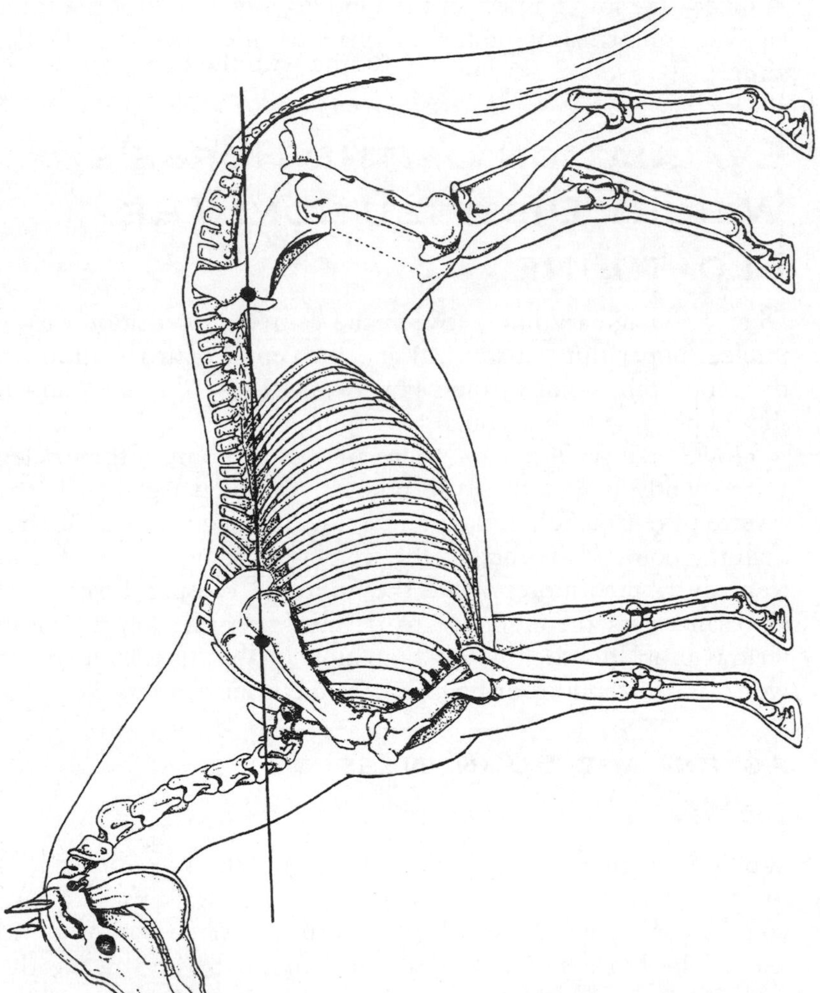

9.1 Float Line Diagram

The walk is the best gait to use when checking for weak or sore muscles because the muscles are relaxed and move freely during this action. If there is restriction of muscular origin, you will see it readily at the walk, whereas during the trot the overall action of the muscles (working as a unit) would mask any specific muscle tension (i.e., the horse "works out" of the soreness).

The Trot

Repeat the previous drill, but this time with the horse trotting in the same sequence as mentioned in assessing movement at the walk. The trot should be supple and even, the gait springing, with joints well-flexed. Listen to the rhythmic two-beat cadence of the trot; it should be even. At this pace, a horse will definitely favor a hurt limb. If lameness at a walk is due to a sore muscle, the lameness might very well appear less pronounced at a trot. This is due to the masking effect of the muscle groups working strongly together at the faster gait. The horse should hold his head fairly steady at the trot.

If lame in a front leg, the horse will raise his head as the lame leg strikes the ground.

If lame in the hindquarters, the horse will drop his head as the lame leg strikes the ground.

Any lameness that is still obvious at a trot could indicate that the problem lies deeper, for example, in a ligament or joint.

Watch for:

* *Dishing* (foot thrown outward), toe flipping.
* *Plaiting/lacing* (placing one foot in front of the other due to a narrow chest).
* *Brushing* (due to feet turned outward, hurt fetlock inside).
* *Forging* (hind feet strike front feet).

The sound horse should hold his head fairly steady at the trot.

Record all your findings in a case study form (see chapter 16). The conformation check-up routine helps you determine abnormalities and understand certain aspects of the signs and symptoms manifested by the horse. The ground check routine contributes greatly to your evaluation and helps you decide the best course of action for your horse's treatment.

A solid knowledge of equine conformation is important as it helps you better understand the different criteriums of selection for movement. So many breeds are available today that a classical understanding of proper conformation will assist you in evaluating muscular conditions and faulty gaits. This understanding will build up your confidence in your application of equine massage.

10

BODY PARTS AND THEIR STRESS POINTS

To improve the quality of your work you need to know more about the stress points found in the horse's head and neck, shoulders and forelegs, back and rib cage, and hindquarters and hind legs.

For each stress point (SP), you will learn:

- ❖ Its location in the muscle groups
- ❖ The motion it affects
- ❖ Its signs and symptoms
- ❖ The way it feels on palpation
- ❖ Important structures involved

In turn, such knowledge coupled with your massage skills will directly affect your horse's performance capabilities, permitting greater flexibility and coordination and thus more power.

THE HEAD AND NECK

A horse uses his head and neck to keep the rest of his body in balance during motion. Therefore, the flexibility of both head and neck is vital to good performance.

The way the horse carries his head will affect his stride. A very high head carriage will cause very high leg action with a short stride. A long-necked horse with average head carriage will extend the leg and have a long stride. A short-necked horse with an average head carriage will bend the knees and have a short stride because of the short neck.

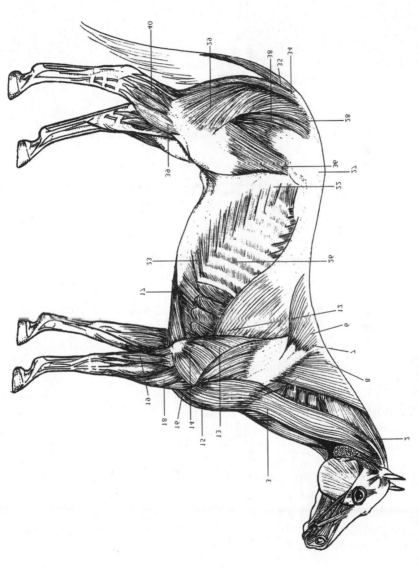

10.1 Superficial Muscle Layer with Stress Point Location

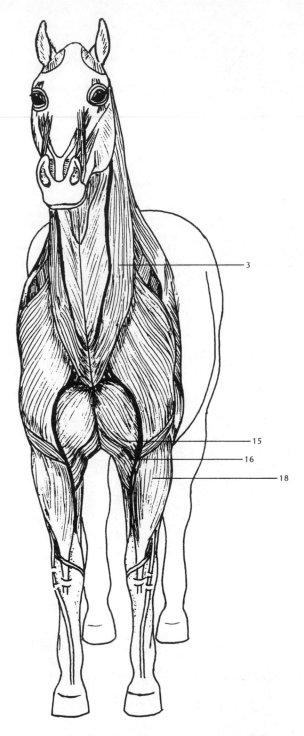

10.2 Front Muscles with Stress Point Location

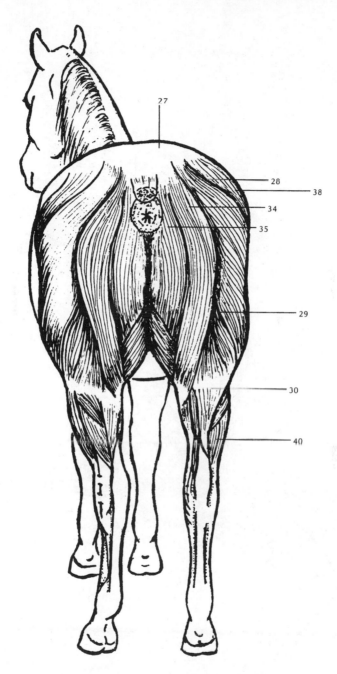

10.3 Back Muscles with Stress Point Location

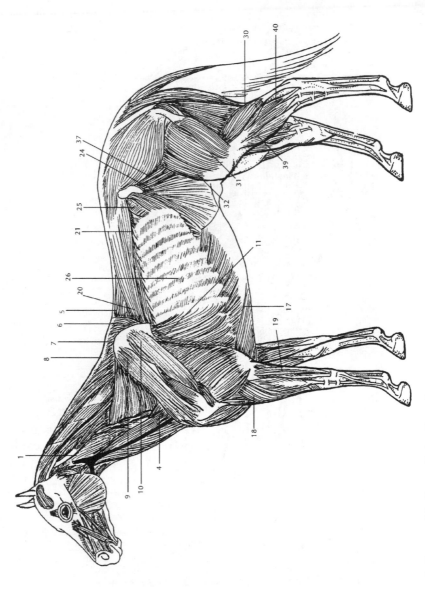

10.4 *Deep Muscle Layer with Stress Point Location*

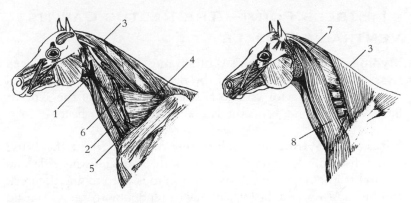

**10.5 Head and Neck Section (Deep and Superficial Muscle Layers)
with Associated Stress Point Location**

(A) Deep Muscle Layer
  [1] SP 1 rectus capitis ventralis muscle
  [2] SP 4 sternothyrohyoid and
       omohyoid muscles
  [3] ligamentum nuchae
  [4] serratus cervicis muscle

[5] scalene muscle
[6] intervertebral muscles

(B) Superficial Muscle Layer
  [7] SP 2 splenius cervicis muscle
  [8] SP 3 brachiocephalic muscle

A heavy head will create more stress on the neck, especially if the neck is long. The lighter the head, proportionally, the better. The angle of the head relative to the neck will affect breathing.

A good neck is one of a horse's most important features. A long neck gives a horse a mechanical advantage in balancing himself by making a wide range of adjustments along the length of his body during any athletic movements. The 7 cervical vertebrae have considerable lateral and vertical flexibility; they act as a blueprint for the shape of the neck. The cervical spine curves twice like a gentle "S" seen from the right side. The length of the neck varies from breed to breed because each breed has different sizes of vertebrae. The "S" curve is extreme in Saddlebreds, average in Thoroughbreds, and almost flat in Quarter Horses.

The ligamentum nuchae (nuchal ligament) is a strong ligament that runs from the poll to the withers, where the splenius muscle attaches to it. When the splenius muscle contracts it raises the neck; it lowers the neck as the muscle relaxes. The multifidus cervices and the rectus capitis lateralis muscles assist lateral rotation of the head. Remember that during motion all the muscle groups of the body work at once, ever ready to assist the horse in any situation.

#1 STRESS POINT—THE RECTUS CAPITIS VENTRALIS MUSCLE

Myology: The rectus capitis ventralis muscle (located in the deep layer) is found on each side of the neck attaching to the cervical vertebrae, running forward to anchor at the base of the skull. It flexes the head and assists the lateral rotation of the head.

Signs and Symptoms: When this muscle is tight the horse shows discomfort, pulling the head to that side, resisting sideways motion to the opposite side and continuously stretching the neck and head. At rest, the horse will have a tendency to keep his head low, continuously stretching it to relieve muscular tension. In motion, he will clearly show head discomfort.

Treatment: When you apply pressure to SP 1, the horse will respond with some skin twitching along the neck and by dropping his head. If the stress point is very tender the horse will flinch and perhaps try to pull away from the pressure. This is a sign of excessive tightness and stress; if you feel heat, suspect inflammation.

Stress Point 1 is located on the origin tendon, third cervical vertebra. The whole muscle will feel tight from its origin all the way to its attachment on the skull. It may feel very tender to the horse.

#2 STRESS POINT—THE SPLENIUS CERVICIS MUSCLE

Myology: The splenius cervicis (located in the superficial layer) is on each side of the neck, attaching on the base of the skull and upper cervical vertebrae and running parallel toward the body to anchor along the first thoracic vertebra. When both sides contract simultaneously, they extend the neck, bringing the head up (extension). When contracting unilaterally, the muscle turns the head and neck to the side (lateral flexion).

Signs and Symptoms: When the muscle is tight, the horse shows discomfort by extending the neck or by pulling the head and neck to the affected side. The horse also resists movements to the opposite side. At rest, the animal will have a tendency to keep the head low, continuously stretching it to relieve the muscular tension. In motion, he will clearly show neck and head discomfort.

Treatment: When you apply pressure to SP 2 the horse will respond with some skin twitching along the neck and by dropping his head. If the stress point is very tender the horse will flinch, perhaps trying to pull away from the pressure. This is a sign of excessive tightness and stress; if you feel heat, suspect inflammation.

Stress Point 2 is felt as a rigid knot with flinching in the neck. It is located on the insertion tendon of the splenius muscle at the base of the skull. The whole muscle will feel tight along its course. This point may feel very tender to the horse.

#3 STRESS POINT—THE BRACHIOCEPHALIC MUSCLE

Myology: The brachiocephalic muscle (located in the superficial layer) runs on each side of the neck, attaching on the base of the skull and first cervical vertebra and running downwards to anchor on the upper end of the humerus (point of shoulder). When both sides contract simultaneously during motion they bring the point of the shoulder up toward the head. When one side of the brachiocephalic muscle contracts, the horse will move his neck to that side.

Signs and Symptoms: When the muscles are tight, the horse shows discomfort by stretching his neck upwards or to the opposite side during rest periods. During motion, the horse is fine on straight lines, but on circles he will be off. Eventually he will be off on all movements.

Treatment: When you apply pressure to SP 3, the horse will respond with skin twitching along the neck and by stretching his head to the opposite side. If the stress point is very tender the horse will flinch, perhaps trying to pull away from the pressure. This is a sign of excessive tightness and stress; if you feel heat, suspect inflammation.

Stress Point 3 will be felt as a rigid knot three quarters of the way down from the poll, with flinching at the point of shoulder. It feels very tender to the horse. The whole muscle will feel tight along its course.

#4 STRESS POINT—THE STERNO-THYROHYOID AND OMOHYOID MUSCLES

Myology: The sternothyrohyoid and omohyoid muscles (located in the deep layer) run on each side of the neck. They attach from the first cervical vertebra and run down and attach to the middle of the anterior edge of the scapula (shoulder blade). These muscles contribute to lateral neck flexion and to rotation of the head.

Signs and Symptoms: When one muscle is tight, the horse shows discomfort, stretching his neck to the opposite side. In action, the horse resists movement to the direction opposite to the muscle with the stress point.

Treatment: When you apply pressure to SP 4, the horse will respond with some skin twitching along the neck and by stretching his head to the opposite side. If the stress point is very tender the horse will flinch, perhaps trying to pull away from the pressure. This is a sign of excessive tightness and stress; if you feel heat, suspect inflammation.

Stress Point 4 will be felt as a rigid knot in front of the anterior (closer to the neck) edge of the shoulder blade. The active stress point will be very tender to the horse. The whole muscle will feel tight along its course.

OTHER TENSION AREAS IN THE NECK

The *ligamentum nuchae:* Runs from the poll all the way to the withers and provides a strong attachment support for all neck muscles. Muscle squeezing applied along its length will do wonders to relax this strong ligament.

The *serratus cervicis:* Found on both sides of the neck, this muscle attaches on the upper edge of the scapula and runs forward to attach on the cervical spine. Its contraction causes the scapula to move forward during retraction of the foreleg.

The *scalene muscles:* Found on both sides of the neck, these muscles attach along the cervical vertebrae and run upward to attach to the base of the skull. The contraction of one scalene muscle will cause the head to rotate to the corresponding side.

The *intervertebral muscles:* These small muscles run on each side of the vertebral column and attach on every second vertebra. Their contraction causes the neck to rotate on itself (torque) as well as assists lateral flexion of the neck. Stretching of the neck muscles (see chapter 8) will help bring these deep muscles into relaxation.

THE SHOULDERS

Powerful, flexible, pain-free shoulders are essential for peak athletic performance. A horse uses his shoulders to stretch the legs forward while extending the front legs and to fold the legs up tight in front of the body when jumping. A horse with prominent withers usually shows freer shoulder rotation.

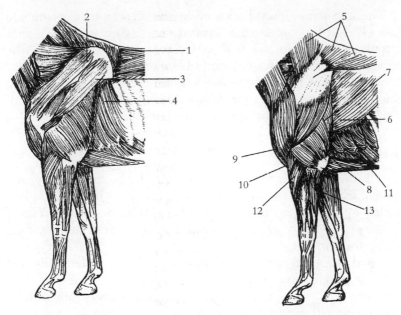

10.6 Shoulder and Foreleg Section (Deep and Superficial Muscle Layers) with Associated Stress Point Location

(A) Deep Muscle Layer
  [1] SP 5 spinalis dorsi muscle
  [2] SP 9 supraspinatus muscle
  [3] SP 10 infraspinatus muscle
  [4] SP 11 thoracic part of the serrate muscle

(B) Superficial Muscle Layer
  [5] SP 6,7,8 trapezius and rhomboid muscles
  [6] SP 12 latissimus dorsi muscle
  [7] SP 13 upper end of triceps muscle

[8] SP 14 lower end of triceps muscle

[9] SP 15 cranial superficial pectoral muscle

[10] SP 16 caudal superficial pectoral muscle

[11] SP 17 caudal deep pectoral muscle

[12] SP 18 radial carpal extensor of foreleg

[13] SP 19 lateral carpal flexor of foreleg

The shoulder joint is formed by the scapula and humerus. Visually noticeable points are: the upper edge of the scapula (by the withers), the scapular spine, the point of shoulder (head of humerus), and the point of elbow (head of the ulna).

THE SCAPULA

The scapula has no direct joint linkage with the horse's trunk. The scapula is attached by a muscular sling that supports the thorax and reduces concussion from the front legs. The slope of the scapula and the angle formed by its junction with the humerus provides shock absorption and has much to do with the smoothness of gait of a riding horse.

The scapula is moved backward by the serratus thoracis muscle (SP 11) and forward by the serratus cervicis muscle. The upper scapula is linked to the withers by the rhomboid muscle, the trapezius muscle (SP 6 to 8), and the deltoid muscle.

The scapular spine bisects the length of the scapula, separating the supraspinatus muscle (SP 9) and the infraspinatus muscle (SP 10). These two last muscles secure the shoulder joint.

THE HUMERUS

The humerus moves forward when pulled by the brachiocephalic muscle (SP 3) and the biceps muscle, and moves backward when pulled by the triceps muscle (SP 13, 14). The pectoral group of muscles (SP 15 to 17) assists both actions as well as providing adduction motion.

Good flexibility and muscle power at the shoulder joint will ensure a high level of performance from the forelegs during jumping and galloping. Long, sloping shoulders are valued because the shoulder joint can go higher and the humerus can become almost vertical—the best combination for a longer stride. The longer the humerus, the longer the stride.

After each training session, follow with complete stretching exercises for the foreleg. Watch for discomfort, resistance, or restriction in the range of motion of that limb. Take notes! Follow with a gentle massage emphasizing drainage. Check thoroughly all related stress points.

#5 STRESS POINT—THE SPINALIS DORSI MUSCLE

Myology: The spinalis dorsi muscle (located in the deep layer) attaches to the spinous processes of the first few thoracic vertebrae (withers) and upper rib attachment; it runs backwards and down the sides of the horse to fix on the lower ribs. Its contraction contributes to the spinal extension and to lateral flexion of the horse's body.

Signs and Symptoms: When this muscle is tight, the horse shows pronounced soreness over the withers. The horse reacts to the tightening of the girth. During movement, the animal resists the downward movement of his head and lateral movement to the side opposite the tightness.

Treatment: When you apply pressure to SP 5, the horse will respond with some skin twitching along the back muscles and the upper shoulder. He might drop his head. If the stress point is very tender the horse will flinch, and perhaps try to pull away from the pressure. This is a sign of excessive tightness and stress; if you feel heat, suspect inflammation.

Stress point 5 is felt as a deep rigid knot. It is located on the insertion tendon of the spinalis dorsi muscle, along the crest of the withers at the level of the ninth thoracic vertebra. It feels very tender to the horse. The whole muscle will feel tight along its course.

#6, 7, AND 8 STRESS POINTS—THE TRAPEZIUS AND RHOMBOID MUSCLES

Myology: The trapezius (located in the superficial layer) and rhomboid muscles (located in the deep layer) attach on the lower cervical and upper thoracic vertebrae (wither area) as well as the nuchal ligament. The rhomboid runs down to attach on the upper part of the scapula. The trapezius muscle runs downward to attach along the scapular spine. Both muscles draw the scapula upwards and either forwards or backwards, depending on the action in play. The cervical part of the trapezius pulls the scapula forward and the thoracic part of the trapezius pulls the scapula backward.

Signs and Symptoms: When the muscles are tight, the horse reacts to the tightening of the girth. When in action, the animal loses flexibility in his shoulder movement, which results in reduced motion, poor coordination, and loss of power from the foreleg. All this will trigger other compensating stress points among other muscle groups, both in the shoulder and in the hindquarters.

Treatment: When you apply pressure to SP 6, 7 and 8, the horse will respond with some skin twitching along the shoulder and eventually along the back or neck; he might drop his head. If the stress point is very tender, the horse will flinch, perhaps trying to pull away from the pressure. This is a sign of excessive tightness and stress; if you feel heat, suspect inflammation.

Stress points 6, 7 and 8 will be felt as tight lines running from withers to scapula, which will feel very tender to the horse. Both muscles will feel tight all along their course.

#9 STRESS POINT—THE SUPRASPINATUS MUSCLE

Myology: The supraspinatus muscle (located in the deep layer) anchors on the anterior (or cranial) part of the scapula and attaches on the anterior aspect of the head of the humerus. The supraspinatus and infraspinatus muscles play a very important role in prevention of lateral dislocation of the shoulder joint. Any lateral work (for example, side pass) will put stress on these two muscles. When contracting, the supraspinatus muscle extends the shoulder joint as well as prevents lateral dislocation.

Signs and Symptoms: When this muscle is tight, the horse will hold the leg bent at the knee (flexed) due to the referred pain (the occurrence of pain in an area of the body compensating for an injury or soreness in a corresponding portion of the body) into the shoulder joint.

The referred pain affects the shoulder joint because the supraspinatus lower tendon attaches in the fascia that surrounds the shoulder joint. So when this muscle aches the soreness spreads right over the joint capsule fascia. During movement, this tightness causes lameness in the shoulder, resulting in abnormal stride of the foreleg in all planes, therefore affecting the horse's gait.

Treatment: When you apply pressure to SP 9, the horse will respond with skin twitching along the shoulder and he might drop the leg on the same side. If the stress point is very tender, the horse will flinch and perhaps stamp his feet on the same side or try to pull away from the pressure. This is a sign of excessive tightness and stress; if you feel heat, suspect inflammation.

Stress point 9 will be felt as a large, tight knot in the upper end of the muscle. It will feel very tender to the horse. The whole muscle will feel tight along its course.

#10 Stress Point—The Infraspinatus Muscle

Myology: The infraspinatus muscle (located in the deep layer) anchors on the posterior (or caudal) part of the scapula and attaches on the posterior aspect of the head of the humerus. The infraspinatus and supraspinatus muscles play a very important role in prevention of lateral dislocation of the shoulder joint. Any lateral work (e.g., half-pass, cutting) will cause stress within these two muscles. When contracting, these muscles flex the shoulder joint as well as prevent lateral dislocation. They also assist in abduction and outward rotation of the leg.

Signs and Symptoms: When the muscles are tight, the horse will hold his leg bent (flexed) at the knee as a result of the referred pain in the shoulder joint. The referred pain affects the shoulder joint because the infraspinatus lower tendon attaches in the fascia that surrounds the shoulder joint. So when this muscle aches the soreness spreads right over the joint capsule fascia.

During movement, the stress causes lameness in the overall shoulder motion, resulting in abnormal stride of the foreleg in all planes and affecting the general gait.

Treatment: When you apply pressure to SP 10, the horse will respond with skin twitching along the shoulder and he might drop the leg on the same side. If the stress point is very tender, the horse will flinch and perhaps stamp his feet on the same side or try to pull away from the pressure. This is a sign of excessive tightness and stress; if you feel heat, suspect inflammation.

Stress point 10 will be felt as a large, tight knot in the upper end of the muscle. It may feel very tender to the horse. The whole muscle will feel tight all along its course.

#11 STRESS POINT—THE THORACIC PART OF THE SERRATE MUSCLE

Myology: The thoracic serrate muscle (located in the deep layer) attaches to the ribs, runs upwards and anchors on the posterior edge of the scapula. When contracting, it moves the scapula backwards, allowing the shoulder joint to come up. At rest, it contributes to adjusting the trunk to its proper level.

Signs and Symptoms: When the muscle is tight, the horse reacts to the tightening of the girth. During movement, the tightness causes lameness in the side where it appears. The stride will be stilted on that side (especially when the girth is tight), interfering with the flexibility of the shoulder.

Treatment: When you apply pressure to SP 11, the horse will respond with skin twitching along the thorax and the upper shoulder, and sometimes along the back muscles. If the stress point is very tender, the horse will flinch and perhaps stamp his feet on the same side or try to pull away from the pressure. This is a sign of excessive tightness and stress; if you feel heat, suspect inflammation.

Stress point 11 will be felt as a large, tight knot by the upper posterior edge of the scapula. It will feel very tender to the horse. The whole muscle might feel tight along its course.

#12 STRESS POINT—THE LATISSIMUS DORSI MUSCLE

Myology: The latissimus muscle (located in the superficial layer) attaches along the thoracic aspect of the spine from the first thoracic vertebra all the way to the lumbar vertebrae. It runs down on each side to attach on the upper medial aspect of the humerus of the foreleg. Its contraction is one of the main sources of power for the retraction of the foreleg. It also contributes to the medial (inward) rotation of the foreleg.

Signs and Symptoms: When the muscle is tight, the horse reacts to the tightening of the girth. During movement, the tightness causes lameness in the side where it appears. The stride will be shortened on that side and the retraction power will be reduced.

Treatment: When you apply pressure to SP 12, the horse will respond with skin twitching along the thorax and the shoulder, and sometimes along the back muscles. If the stress point is very tender, the horse will flinch and perhaps stamp his feet on the same side or try to pull away from the pressure. This is a sign of excessive tightness and stress; if you feel heat, suspect inflammation.

Stress point 12 will be felt as a large, tight knot by the lower aspect of the muscle near the edge of the triceps muscle. It feels very tender to the horse. The whole muscle might feel tight along its course, depending on the severity of the stress.

#13 Stress Point—The Upper End of the Triceps Muscle

Myology: The triceps muscle (located in the superficial layer) attaches on the posterior edge of the scapula, running downwards to anchor on the point of elbow. When the triceps muscle contracts it causes the shoulder joint to flex.

Signs and Symptoms: When the muscle is tight, the horse will hold his leg bent (flexed) and will not put weight on it while at rest. During action, the horse will show lameness with a shortened stride; he will jump flat or hang a leg.

Treatment: When you apply pressure to SP 13, the horse will respond with skin twitching along the shoulder; he might flex his knee. If the stress point is very tender, the horse will flinch and perhaps stamp his feet on the same side or try to pull away from the pressure. This is a sign of excessive tightness and stress; if you feel heat, suspect inflammation.

Stress point 13 will be felt as a small knot against the middle posterior edge of the scapula, which may be very tender to the horse. A tight line of fibers will also be felt across the muscle.

#14 STRESS POINT—THE LOWER END OF THE TRICEPS MUSCLE

Myology: The triceps muscle (located in the superficial layer) attaches on the posterior edge of the scapula, running downward to anchor on the point of elbow. It extends and locks the elbow joint.

Signs and Symptoms: When the muscle is tight and the horse is at rest, he will hold his leg bent (flexed) and will not lock the knee joint completely. During movement, the animal will show lameness with a shortened stride.

Treatment: When you apply pressure to SP 14, the horse will respond with skin twitching along the shoulder and he might flex his knee. If the stress point is very tender, the horse will flinch and perhaps stamp his feet on the same side or try to pull away from the pressure. This is a sign of excessive tightness and stress; if you feel heat, suspect inflammation.

Stress point 14 will be felt as a rigid knot of tissues at the point of elbow. It may feel very tender to the horse. The whole muscle might feel tight along its course, depending on the severity of the stress.

#15 STRESS POINT—THE CRANIAL SUPERFICIAL PECTORAL MUSCLE

Myology: The cranial superficial pectoral muscle (located in the superficial layer) attaches to the sternum and upper ribs. It runs downwards to each side to attach to the medial (internal) aspect of the humerus. Its contraction assists the protraction, controls the adduction, and assists the lateral movement of the foreleg.

Signs and Symptoms: When tight, the muscle affects the stride and resists the abduction (lateral) movement of the foreleg.

Treatment: When you apply pressure to SP 15, the horse will respond with skin twitching along the chest and point of shoulder. If the stress point is very tender, the horse will flinch or try to pull away from the pressure. This is a sign of excessive tightness and stress; if you feel heat, suspect inflammation.

Stress point 15 will be felt as a rigid knot of tissues at the point it attaches to the humerus, and it will feel very tender to the horse. The whole muscle might show tightness along its course, depending on the severity of the stress.

#16 Stress Point—The Caudal Superficial Pectoral Muscle

Myology: The caudal superficial pectoral muscle (located in the superficial layer) attaches on the sternum and ribs, running laterally on both sides to attach on the medial (internal) aspect of the humerus. Its contraction causes adduction of the foreleg.

Signs and Symptoms: When tight, the muscle affects the stride and restricts the abduction movement of the foreleg.

Treatment: When you apply pressure to SP 16, the horse will respond with skin twitching on the inside of the leg and the chest. If the stress point is very tender, the horse will flinch and perhaps stamp his feet on the same side or try to pull away from the pressure. This is a sign of excessive tightness and stress; if you feel heat, suspect inflammation.

Stress point 16 will be felt as a rigid knot of tissues by the attachment point on the humerus. It may feel very tender to the horse. The whole muscle might show tightness along its course.

#17 Stress Point—The Caudal Deep Pectoral Muscle

Myology: The caudal deep pectoral muscle (located in the superficial layer) attaches on the sternum and lower ribs. It runs forward to attach to the medial (internal) aspect of the humerus. During concentric contraction, it draws the foreleg backwards as well as assists in the adduction (medial) movement of the leg. During eccentric contraction this muscle assists in the abduction (lateral) movement of the foreleg.

Signs and Symptoms: When this muscle is tight, the horse reacts to the tightening of the girth. During movement, the animal shows shortened extension of the foreleg and becomes stilted.

Treatment: When you apply pressure to SP 17, the horse will respond with skin twitching along the lower thorax. If the stress point is very tender, the horse will flinch or try to pull away from the pressure. This is a sign of excessive tightness and stress; if you feel heat, suspect inflammation.

Stress point 17 will be felt as a rigid knot of tissues on the origin tendon over the sternum. It will be a very sensitive area with a tight line of muscle fibers running forward along its course.

#18 STRESS POINT—THE RADIAL CARPAL EXTENSOR MUSCLES OF THE FORELEG

Myology: The extensor muscles (located in the superficial layer) attach on the lower end of the humerus, running downwards to attach on the anterior aspect of the pastern bones. Their contraction causes the fetlock joint to extend (or dorsi flex).

Signs and Symptoms: When these muscles are tight they limit the extension of the hoof during protraction of the leg.

Treatment: When you apply pressure to SP 18, the horse will respond with some skin twitching along the foreleg and the point of shoulder. If the stress point is very tender, the horse will flinch and perhaps stamp his feet on the same side or try to pull away from the pressure. This is a sign of excessive tightness and stress; if you feel heat, suspect inflammation.

Stress point 18 will be felt as a rigid knot of tissues by the attachment point on the humerus. It feels very tender to the horse. The whole muscle might show tightness along its course.

#19 STRESS POINT—THE LATERAL CARPAL FLEXOR MUSCLES OF THE FORELEG

Myology: The flexor muscles (located in the superficial layer) attach on the upper aspect of the ulna. They run downwards to attach on the posterior aspect of the pasterns. Their contraction causes the fetlock joint to flex.

Signs and Symptoms: When tight, these muscles limit the flexion of the hoof during retraction of the leg.

Treatment: When you apply pressure to SP 19, the horse will respond with some skin twitching along the foreleg and the point of shoulder. If the stress point is very tender, the horse will flinch and perhaps stamp his feet on the same side or try to pull away from the pressure. This is a sign of excessive tightness and stress; if you feel heat, suspect inflammation.

Stress point 19 will be felt as a rigid knot of tissues by the attachment point on the ulna. It feels very tender to the horse. The whole muscle might show tightness along its course.

THE BACK AND RIB CAGE

The vertebral column and the rib cage are made up of strong bones, ligaments, and muscles. These structures provide anchoring for strong muscle groups.

The muscles that prevent the back from sagging are the spinalis dorsi muscle (SP 5), the longissimus dorsi muscle (SP 20), and the iliocostalis dorsi (SP 21) muscle.

The external and internal oblique muscles (SP 22, 23, and 24), the transverse abdominal muscles (SP 25), and the intercostal muscles (SP 26) all stabilize the rib cage during movement. They also strongly contribute to the flexion of the back. The other muscle groups associated with protraction and retraction of the limbs have a second function in supporting the backbone.

Always check these stress points (SP 20, 21, 38) to prevent a "cold back." After exercising, massage them thoroughly to prevent inflammation. If stress point tenderness persists, check the saddle, the padding, and flaws in the rider's style.

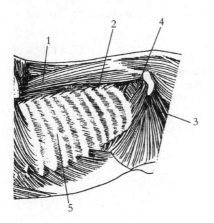 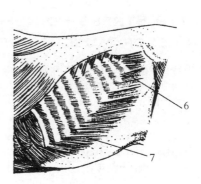

10.7 Back and Rib Cage Section (Deep and Superficial Muscle Layers) with Associated Stress Point Location

(A) Deep Muscle Layer
 [1] SP 20 longissimus dorsi muscle
 [2] SP 21 iliocostalis dorsi muscle
 [3] SP 24 internal abdominal oblique muscle
 [4] SP 25 transverse abdominal muscle (pubic attachment)
 [5] SP 26 intercostal muscles

(B) Superficial Muscle Layer
 [6] SP 22 external abdominal oblique muscle (hip attachment)
 [7] SP 23 external abdominal oblique muscle (rib cage attachment)

#20 STRESS POINT—THE LONGISSIMUS DORSI MUSCLE (FORWARD ATTACHMENT)

Myology: The longissimus dorsi muscle (located in the deep layer) runs along the spine from the withers to the point of the croup. It attaches along all the vertebrae (both thoracic and lumbar) and the ribs. The longissimus dorsi muscle extends along the back and loins and also causes lateral flexion to the side of the unilateral contraction.

Signs and Symptoms: When this muscle is tight, the horse shows soreness over the back when pressure such as saddling or grooming is put on it. During movement, the animal is very uncomfortable and will lose coordinated power.

Treatment: When you apply pressure to SP 20, the horse will respond with skin twitching along the back muscles. If the stress point is very tender, the horse will flinch or try to pull away from the pressure. This is a sign of excessive tightness and stress; if you feel heat, suspect inflammation.

Stress point 20 will be felt as a rigid knot in front of the withers. It feels very tender to the horse. The whole muscle might show tightness along its course, depending on the severity of the stress.

#21 STRESS POINT—THE ILIOCOSTALIS DORSI MUSCLE

Myology: The iliocostalis dorsi muscle (located in the deep layer) runs from the withers, attaches on the ribs, and continues backwards to the point of the hip. Its contraction causes lateral flexion of the trunk and assists in the extension of the back.

Signs and Symptoms: When this muscle is tight and pressure is put on it, the horse shows soreness. The horse will show restriction in lateral bending.

Treatment: When you apply pressure to SP 21, the horse will respond with skin twitching along the back muscles. If the stress point is very tender, the horse will flinch or try to pull away from the pressure. This is a sign of excessive tightness and stress; if you feel heat, suspect inflammation.

Stress point 21 will be felt as a rigid knot against the last rib. It is a very sensitive area. The whole muscle might show tightness along its course, depending on the severity of the stress.

#22 STRESS POINT—THE EXTERNAL ABDOMINAL OBLIQUE MUSCLE (HIP ATTACHMENT)

Myology: The external abdominal oblique muscle (located in the superficial layer) attaches from the anterior aspect of the hip and runs downwards to anchor on the ribs. Together with the internal oblique muscle, it aids in the contraction of the abdomen and assists in lateral bending.

Signs and Symptoms: When this muscle is tight, the horse shows restricted lateral movement.

Treatment: When you apply pressure to SP 22, the horse will respond with skin twitching along the abdomen or by relaxing his hind leg. If the stress point is very tender, the horse will flinch or try to pull away from the pressure and eventually raise his hind leg. This is a sign of excessive tightness and stress; if you feel heat, suspect inflammation.

Stress point 22 will be felt as a small knot along the edge of the hip bone. It is a very sensitive area. The whole muscle might show tightness along its course, depending on the severity of the stress.

#23 STRESS POINT—THE EXTERNAL ABDOMINAL OBLIQUE MUSCLE (RIB CAGE ATTACHMENT)

Myology: The external abdominal oblique muscle (located in the superficial layer) attaches to the anterior aspect of the hip and runs downwards to anchor on the ribs. Together with the internal oblique muscle it aids in the contraction of the abdomen and assists in lateral bending.

Signs and Symptoms: When this muscle is tight, the horse shows general discomfort and restricted lateral movement.

Treatment: When you apply pressure to SP 23, the horse will respond with skin twitching along the abdomen. If the stress point is very tender, the horse will flinch or try to pull away from the pressure. This is a sign of excessive tightness and stress; if you feel heat, suspect inflammation.

Stress point 23 will be felt as a tight, thick muscle knot at the area where the tenth rib attaches to the sternum.

#24 STRESS POINT—THE INTERNAL ABDOMINAL OBLIQUE MUSCLE

Myology: The internal abdominal oblique muscle (located in the deep layer) attaches to the anterior aspect of the hip and runs downwards to anchor on the ribs. With the external abdominal oblique muscle, it aids in the contraction of the abdomen and assists in lateral bending.

Signs and Symptoms: When this muscle is tight, the horse shows restricted lateral movement.

Treatment: When you apply pressure to SP 24, the horse will respond with skin twitching along the abdomen or by relaxing his hind leg. If the stress point is very tender, the horse will flinch; he might stamp his hind foot on the same side or try to pull away from the pressure. This is a sign of excessive tightness and stress; if you feel heat, suspect inflammation.

   Stress point 24 will be felt as a tight, thickened ridge in the middle of the muscle, a couple of inches below the origin attachment. It is a very sensitive area. The whole muscle might show tightness along its course, depending on the severity of the stress.

#25 STRESS POINT—THE TRANSVERSE ABDOMINAL MUSCLE (PUBIC ATTACHMENT)

Myology: The transverse abdominal muscle (located in the deep layer) attaches to the lumbar spine and runs downwards and backwards to anchor on the hip bones. Its contraction aids in the contraction of the abdomen and assists in lateral bending.

Signs and Symptoms: When this muscle is tight, the horse shows general discomfort and a shorter stride in the hind legs.

Treatment: When you apply pressure to SP 25, the horse will respond with skin twitching along the abdomen or by letting go of his hind leg. If the stress point is very tender, the horse will flinch; he might stamp his hind foot on the same side or try to pull away from the pressure. This is a sign of excessive tightness and stress; if you feel heat, suspect inflammation.

   Stress point 25 will be felt as a tight, thickened muscle a few inches in front of the point of the hip. It is a very sensitive area. The whole muscle might show tightness along its course, depending on the severity of the stress.

#26 STRESS POINT—THE INTERCOSTAL MUSCLES

Myology: The intercostal muscles (located in the deep layer) attach from rib to rib along the entire rib cage. Their contraction causes the thorax to compress during exhalation.

Signs and Symptoms: When these muscles are tight, the horse's breathing is shallow due to the lack of expansion of the rib cage.

Treatment: When you apply pressure to SP 26, the horse will respond with skin twitching along the thorax and abdomen. If the stress point is very tender, the horse will flinch or try to pull away from the pressure. This is a sign of excessive tightness and stress; if you feel heat, suspect inflammation.

Stress point 26 will be felt as a tight muscle knot between the tenth and eleventh ribs. This is a very sensitive area. The whole intercostal muscle might show tightness all around the rib cage, depending on the severity of the stress.

THE HINDQUARTERS AND HIND LEGS

The conformation of the hindquarters and hind legs will determine the horse's performance ability in a given sport. There are breed-specific variations in the natural angles formed by the joints of the hind legs.

The more angle at the joints (sloping pelvis, angular stifle and hock), the greater the predisposition for sprinting or jumping. The straighter the joint (nearly horizontal pelvis, straight stifle and hock), the greater the predisposition for a long stride; for example, the stride of a racehorse (the longer the muscle, the more ground covered with each stride).

The bony areas of the hindquarters that can be palpated are: the point of croup (ilium); point of buttock (ischium), point of hip (femur), and stifle joint (femur, tibia, and patella).

The bulky muscles of the hindquarters anchor on the lumbar spine and the pelvis; they run downward and attach to the femur and tibia of the hind leg. The muscles moving the femur (thigh) are the gluteus accessories (SP 38), the iliacus and psoas muscles (SP 37), the biceps femoris (SP 28), the gluteus maximus (SP 27), and the tensor fasciae latae (SP 36). The muscles that move the tibia (gaskin) are the gastrocnemius (SP 30), the belly of biceps femoris (SP 29), the semitendinosus (SP 34), and the semimembranosus (SP 35). Follow each training session with a thorough stretching

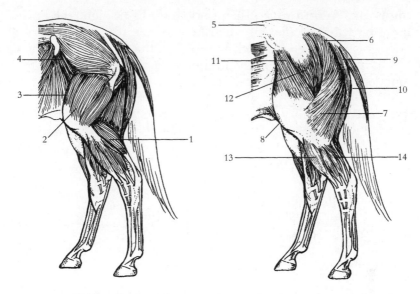

10.8 Hindquarter Section (Deep and Superficial Muscle Layers) with Associated Stress Point Location

(A) Deep Muscle Layer
[1] SP 30 gastrocnemius muscle
[2] SP 31 vastus lateralis muscle
[3] SP 32 rectus femoris muscle
[4] SP 37 iliacus muscle

(B) Superficial Muscle Layer
[5] SP 27 junction of gluteus muscles and longissimus dorsi muscle
[6] SP 28 biceps femoris muscle
[7] SP 29 belly of biceps femoris muscle

[8] SP 33 adductor muscles
[9] SP 34 semitendinosus muscle
[10] SP 35 semimembranosus muscle
[11] SP 36 tensor fasciae latae muscle
[12] SP 38 superficial gluteus muscle
[13] SP 39 long digital extensor muscles
[14] SP 40 long digital flexor muscles

exercise of the hind legs. Thoroughly massage the hindquarters, emphasizing drainage, and check all main stress points.

#27 Stress Point—Junction of the Gluteus Muscles and the Longissimus Dorsi Muscles

Myology: The gluteus muscle (located in the superficial layer) anchors on the lumbar spine, runs downwards, and attaches on the femur. The longissimus dorsi muscle (located in the deep layer) runs along the spine from the withers to the point of croup, attaching onto the thoracic vertebrae and the ribs and inserting on the lumbar vertebrae. These muscles are involved in forward motion (protraction).

Signs and Symptoms: When these muscles are tight, the horse keeps his legs bent (flexed) when he is at rest. If the animal sinks down or sags when his back is touched, this is a sure sign of a "cold back." During movement, the horse shows lameness in the hind legs and loss of power on protraction.

Treatment: When you apply pressure to SP 27, the horse will respond with skin twitching along the back muscles and the hindquarters; he might flex the stifle on the same side. If the stress point is very tender, the horse will flinch or try to pull away from the pressure. This is a sign of excessive tightness and stress; if you feel heat, suspect inflammation.

Stress point 27 will be felt as a rigid knot a couple of inches away from the spine at the level of the point of croup. It is a very sensitive area. Both muscles might show tightness along their course, depending on the severity of the stress.

#28 STRESS POINT—THE BICEPS FEMORIS MUSCLE

Myology: The biceps femoris muscle (located in the superficial layer) anchors on the lumbar spine and runs downwards to attach on the tibia (gaskin). It flexes the stifle and hock joints in protraction, and extends and abducts the limb in retraction. It is the major component of the hamstring group of muscles.

Signs and Symptoms: When this muscle is tight, the horse will hold his leg loose (flexed) or will try to stretch the leg by tucking under the hind end. During movement, the horse shows lameness and shortened protraction.

Treatment: When you apply pressure to SP 28, the horse will respond with skin twitching along the hindquarters and he might flex the stifle on the same side. If the stress point is very tender, the horse will flinch or try to pull away from the pressure. This is a sign of excessive tightness and stress; if you feel heat, suspect inflammation.

Stress point 28 will be felt as a tight knot a couple of inches away from the spine, past the point of croup. This is a very sensitive area. The whole muscle might show tightness along its course, depending on the severity of the stress.

#29 STRESS POINT—THE BELLY OF THE BICEPS FEMORIS MUSCLE

Myology: The biceps femoris muscle (located in the superficial layer) anchors on the lumbar spine and runs downward to attach on the tibia. Here at the bifurcation area, the biceps femoris serves both the stifle and the hock; it flexes the stifle and hock joints in protraction and extends and abducts the hind leg during retraction.

Signs and Symptoms: When this muscle is tight, the horse will hold his leg loose (flexed) and will scuff his hind leg when walking. During movement, the animal will show a shortening in the forward movement (protraction).

Treatment: When you apply pressure to SP 29, the horse will respond with skin twitching on the hindquarters and he might flex the stifle on the same side. If the stress point is very tender, the horse will flinch or try to pull away from the pressure. This is a sign of excessive tightness and stress; if you feel heat, suspect inflammation. This particular stress point needs pressure applied inwards and sideways. The idea is to make the muscle move from side to side. SP 29 should be worked in conjunction with SP 28.

Stress point 29 will be felt as a thickening of muscle fibers at the bifurcation of the muscle. It is a sensitive area. The whole muscle might show tightness along its course, depending on the severity of the stress.

#30 STRESS POINT—THE GASTROCNEMIUS MUSCLE

Myology: The gastrocnemius muscle (located in the deep layer) attaches on the femur, running downwards and backwards to attach on the point of hock. It flexes the stifle joint and extends the hock joint.

Signs and Symptoms: When this muscle is tight, the horse will hold his leg loose (flexed) and will show discomfort when standing. During movement, the horse will show lameness in the hind leg and a restricted forward motion.

Treatment: When you apply pressure to SP 30, the horse will respond with skin twitching along the hind leg and he might flex the stifle on the same side. If the stress point is very tender, the horse will flinch or try to pull away from the pressure. This is a sign of excessive tightness and stress; if you feel heat, suspect inflammation.

Stress point 30 will be felt as a tight, hardened bundle of fibers three inches above the hock joint. It is a sensitive area. The whole muscle might show tightness along its course, depending on the severity of the stress.

#31 STRESS POINT—THE VASTUS LATERALIS MUSCLE

Myology: The vastus lateralis muscle (located in the deep layer) attaches to the ilium and runs forward and downward to attach on the femoral fascia covering the patella. Its action flexes the stifle joint and contributes to abduction of the hind leg.

Signs and Symptoms: When this muscle is tight, the horse will hold his leg loose (flexed) and will show discomfort when standing. During movement, the horse will be lame in the hind leg, with forward motion and abduction of the hind leg restricted.

Treatment: When you apply pressure to SP 31, the horse will respond with skin twitching along the hindquarters and he might flex the stifle on the same side. If the stress point is very tender, the horse will flinch or try to pull away from the pressure. This is a sign of excessive tightness and stress; if you feel heat, suspect inflammation.

Stress point 31 will be felt as a tight, hardened bundle of fibers behind and 2 inches above the stifle joint. It is a sensitive area. The whole muscle might show tightness along its course, depending on the severity of the stress.

#32 STRESS POINT—THE RECTUS FEMORIS MUSCLE

Myology: The rectus femoris muscle (located in the deep layer) attaches to the ilium and runs forward and downward to fix on the femoral fascia covering the patella. Its action flexes the stifle joint.

Signs and Symptoms: When the muscle is tight, the horse will hold his leg loose (flexed) and will show discomfort when standing. During movement, the horse will be lame, with forward motion of the hind leg restricted.

Treatment: When you apply pressure to SP 32, the horse will respond with skin twitching along the hindquarters and he might flex the stifle on the same side. If the stress point is very tender, the horse will flinch or try to pull away from the pressure. This is a sign of excessive tightness and stress; if you feel heat, suspect inflammation.

Stress point 32 will be felt as a tight, hardened bundle of fibers 2 inches above the stifle joint. It is a sensitive area. The whole muscle might show tightness along its course, depending on the severity of the stress.

#33 STRESS POINT—THE ADDUCTOR MUSCLES

Myology: The adductor muscles (located in the superficial and deep layer) attach to the ischium and run downward to insert on the medial condyle of the femur (medial aspect of the stifle). Their contraction causes the hind leg to adduct (move inward).

Signs and Symptoms: When this muscle is tight, the horse will hold his leg loose (flexed) and will show discomfort when standing. During movement the forward and backward motion of the hind leg will be restricted; the animal will resist abduction of this limb.

Treatment: When you apply pressure to SP 33, the horse will respond with skin twitching along the inside of the hindquarters and he might flex the stifle on the same side. If the stress point is very tender, the horse will flinch or try to pull away from the pressure, possibly kicking. This is a sign of excessive tightness and stress; if you feel heat, suspect inflammation.

Stress point 33 will be felt as a tight, hardened bundle of fibers on the inside of the leg, 2 inches above the stifle joint. It is a sensitive area. The whole muscle group might show tightness along its course, depending on the severity of the stress.

#34 STRESS POINT—THE SEMITENDINOSUS MUSCLE

Myology: The semitendinosus muscle (located in the superficial layer) attaches on the lumbar spine and runs downward to anchor on the hock joint (tuber calcis). Its contraction causes extension of the hip and the hock joint, flexes the stifle, and rotates the leg inwards.

Signs and Symptoms: When this muscle is tight, the horse will hold his leg loose (flexed) when at rest or will try to stretch it by tucking the leg under his hind end. During movement, the horse shows lameness in the hindquarter, with shortened protraction and discomfort in straightening the stifle.

Treatment: When you apply pressure to SP 34, the horse will respond with skin twitching along the hindquarters and he might flex the stifle on the same side. If the stress point is very tender, the horse will flinch or try to pull away from the pressure. This is a sign of excessive tightness and stress; if you feel heat, suspect inflammation.

Stress point 34 will be felt as a rigid knot or as a tight line of muscle fibers at the origin tendon attachment on the sacrum. It is a sensitive area. The whole muscle might show tightness along its course, depending on the severity of the stress.

#35 Stress Point—The Semimembranosus Muscle

Myology: The semimembranosus muscle (located in the superficial layer) attaches to the lumbar spine, runs downward, and attaches to the hock joint. It extends the hip joint and the fetlock, flexes the stifle, and adducts the leg.

Signs and Symptoms: When this muscle is tight, the horse will hold his leg loose (flexed) when at rest or will try to stretch it by tucking it under his hind end. During movement, the horse shows lameness in the hind leg with shortening of protraction, resists lateral movement, and tracks inward during protraction.

Treatment: When you apply pressure to SP 35, the horse will respond with skin twitching along the hindquarters and he might flex the stifle on the same side. If the stress point is very tender, the horse will flinch or try to pull away from the pressure, or may even kick. This is a sign of excessive tightness and stress; if you feel heat, suspect inflammation.

Stress point 35 will be felt as a rigid knot at the origin attachment (sacrum) with a tight line of muscle fibers running downward. It is a sensitive area. The whole muscle might show tightness along its course, depending on the severity of the stress.

#36 Stress Point—The Tensor Fasciae Latae Muscle

Myology: The tensor fasciae latae (located in the superficial layer) runs from the point of the hip to the distal (lower) end of the femur. Its contraction causes flexion of the stifle joint.

Signs and Symptoms: When this muscle is tight, the horse will hold his leg loose (flexed) when at rest or will try to stretch it by tucking it under his hind end. During movement, the horse throws the leg outward on protraction and resists lateral movements.

Treatment: When you apply pressure to SP 36, the horse will respond with skin twitching along the hindquarters and he might flex the stifle on the same side. If the stress point is very tender, the horse will flinch or try to pull away from the pressure. This is a sign of excessive tightness and stress; if you feel heat, suspect inflammation.

Stress point 36 will be felt as a rigid knot over the origin attachment, on the point of the hip. It is a sensitive area. The whole muscle might show tightness along its course, depending on the severity of the stress.

#37 STRESS POINT—THE ILIACUS MUSCLE

Myology: The iliacus muscle (located in the deep layer) runs from the point of the hip to the distal end of the femur. Its contraction causes the hip joint to flex, assisting the outward rotation of the thigh.

Signs and Symptoms: When this muscle is tight, the horse will hold his leg loose (flexed) when at rest, drawing it inward or trying to tuck it under the hind end. During action, the horse shows discomfort in the back and in leg movements, especially during circles.

Treatment: When you apply pressure to SP 37, the horse will respond with skin twitching along the back muscles and the hindquarters. If the stress point is very tender, the horse will flinch or try to pull away from the pressure. This is a sign of excessive tightness and stress; if you feel heat, suspect inflammation.

Stress point 37 will be felt as a tight line of muscle fibers all along its course. It is a very sensitive area. The whole muscle might show tightness along its course, depending on the severity of the stress.

#38 STRESS POINT—THE SUPERFICIAL GLUTEUS MUSCLE

Myology: The superficial gluteus muscle (located in the superficial layer) runs from the lumbar spine to anchor on the hip. Its contraction assists the main gluteus muscles in extension of the hip as well as in outward rotation of the thigh.

Signs and Symptoms: When this muscle is tight, the horse shows discomfort in his back, with restricted hip motion and shortened protraction of the hind leg. This stress point always shows up in back problems.

Treatment: When you apply pressure to SP 38, the horse will respond with skin twitching along the hindquarters and he might flex the stifle on the same side. If the stress point is very tender, the horse will flinch or try to pull away from the pressure. This is a sign of excessive tightness and stress; if you feel heat, suspect inflammation.

Stress point 38 will be felt as a rigid knot approximately 2 inches behind the point of the hip. It is a sensitive area. The whole muscle might show tightness along its course, depending on the severity of the stress.

#39 STRESS POINT—THE LONG DIGITAL EXTENSOR MUSCLES

Myology: The long digital extensor muscles (located in the superficial layer) attach to the upper aspect of the tibia. They run downwards to fix on the anterior (front) aspect of the pastern bones. Their contraction causes the hock joint to flex and the fetlock joint to extend (dorsi flex).

Signs and Symptoms: When these muscles are tight, extension of the hoof during the protraction of the leg is limited, resulting in a shorter stride.

Treatment: When you apply pressure to SP 39, the horse will respond with skin twitching along the hind leg and he might flex the stifle on the same side. If the stress point is very tender, the horse will flinch or try to pull away from the pressure. This is a sign of excessive tightness and stress; if you feel heat, suspect inflammation.

Stress point 39 will be felt as a rigid knot of tissues below its attachment point on the tibia. It feels very tender to the horse. The whole muscle might show tightness along its course.

#40 STRESS POINT—THE LONG DIGITAL FLEXOR MUSCLES

Myology: The long digital flexor muscles (located in the superficial layer) attach to the upper aspect of the tibia and fibula. They run downwards to fix on the posterior (back) aspect of the pastern

bones. Their contraction causes the hock to extend and the fetlock joint to flex.

Signs and Symptoms: When these muscles are tight, flexion of
the hoof during retraction of the leg is limited, resulting in loss of
power.

Treatment: When you apply pressure to SP 40, the horse will
respond with skin twitching along the hind leg and he might flex
the stifle on the same side. If the stress point is very tender, the
horse will flinch or try to pull away from the pressure. This is a
sign of excessive tightness and stress; if you feel heat, suspect
inflammation.

Stress point 40 will be felt as a rigid knot of tissues next to the
attachment point on the fibula. It feels very tender to the horse.
The whole muscle might show tightness along its course.

*Having a thorough knowledge of all the stress points found on the
body of the horse will contribute tremendously to the quality of
your massage work.*

STRESS POINT CHECK-UP
ROUTINE

The stress point check-up routine is divided into three sequences.
But, before you start, to best evaluate potential stress point areas in
your horse, take note of his history (type of training, accidents,
traumas) and current training program (chapter 15). Keep in mind
the horse's conformation and way of going (chapter 9). Then, first
evaluate all 40 stress points on each side of the animal to get direct
feedback on your horse's physiological state. This will tell you
which part of the body needs emphasis. Second, using the stress
point technique, work the whole body of the horse, spending
more time on the areas showing active stress points.

Finally, go over the whole horse again, strongly emphasizing
drainage. Remember to use hydrotherapy (cold application) over
tender stress points when needed. Complete your work with a
thorough stretching routine.

It took a certain amount of time for these stress points to
develop, so it will probably take a few treatments before you see
full recovery. Be patient; you will see improvement right from the
start of your massage.

Take notes so that you can assess the progress of your work and
its effect on the horse. After your first evaluation, you can consider
giving small local treatments of 20 to 30 minutes to the most

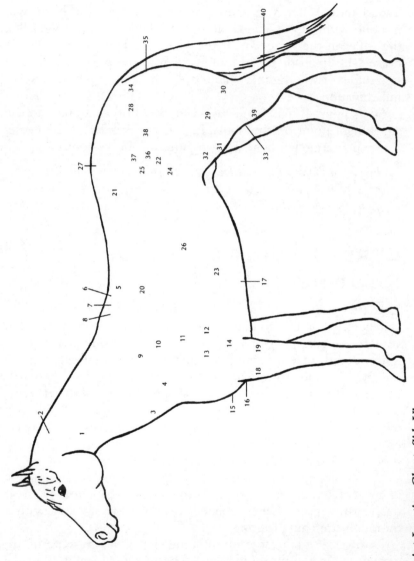

10.9 Stress Point Location Chart, Side View

GENERAL STRESS POINT CHART

	MUSCLE NAME	MUSCLE FUNCTION
1.	Rectus capitis ventralis muscle	Flexion and lateral flexion of the head
2.	Splenius cervicis muscle	Lateral flexion of the head
3.	Brachiocephalic muscle	Sideways head and neck movement, lifts foreleg
4.	Sternothyrohyoid and omohyoid muscles	Flexes neck to the side, rotates head to opposite side
5.	Spinalis dorsi muscle	Extends the back
6.	Rhomboids and trapezius muscles	Draws scapula upwards, forwards and backward
7.	Rhomboids and trapezius muscles	Draws scapula upwards, forwards and backward
8.	Rhomboids and trapezius muscles	Draws scapula upwards, forwards and backward
9.	Supraspinatus muscle	Extension of shoulder joint, prevents dislocation
10.	Infraspinatus muscle	Abduction, rotation of shoulder joint, prevents dislocation
11.	Thoracic part of serrate muscle	Draws scapula backwards, draws trunk upwards (adjustment)
12.	Latissimus dorsi muscle	Draws leg backward
13.	Triceps (upper end) muscle	Flexes shoulder joint
14.	Triceps (lower end) muscle	Extends and locks the elbow joint
15.	Cranial superficial pectoral muscle	Adducts foreleg during movement
16.	Caudal superficial pectoral muscle	Adducts foreleg during movement
17.	Caudal deep pectoral muscle	Draws foreleg backwards
18.	Radial carpal extensor muscle	Extends hoof during movement
19.	Lateral carpal flexor muscle	Flexes hoof during movement

(continues)

	Muscle Name	Muscle Function
20.	Longissimus dorsi muscle	Extends back and loins, lateral (forward attachment) flexion
21.	Iliocostalis dorsi muscle	Lateral flexion of the trunk
22.	External abdominal oblique muscle	Flexes trunk straight and laterally (hip attachment)
23.	External abdominal oblique muscle	Flexes trunk straight and laterally (rib cage attachment)
24.	Internal abdominal oblique muscle	Flexes trunk straight and laterally
25.	Transverse abdominal muscle	Flexes trunk straight and laterally
26.	Intercostal (10th rib) muscle	Flexes trunk straight and laterally
27.	Junction of gluteus muscles	Forward propulsion
28.	Biceps femoris muscle	Extends and abducts hind leg (hip and hock flex stifle)
29.	Biceps femoris muscle (belly part)	Flexes the stifle and the hock joint
30.	Gastrocnemius muscle	Extension of hock, flexion of stifle joint
31.	Lateral vastus muscle (stifle)	Flexion of hip/femur
32.	Rectus femoris muscle (stifle)	Flexion of hip/femur
33.	Adductor muscles (femur insertion)	Adducts hind leg
34.	Semitendinosus muscle	Extends hip and hock joints; flexes stifle and rotates leg inward
35.	Semimembranosus muscle	Extends hip joint
36.	Tensor fasciae latae muscle	Flexes hip joint and extends stifle
37.	Iliacus muscle	Flexes hip joint and rotates thigh outward
38.	Superficial gluteus muscle	Extends hip, rotates thigh outward
39.	Long digital extensor muscle	Extends the hoof
40.	Long digital flexor muscle	Flexes the hoof

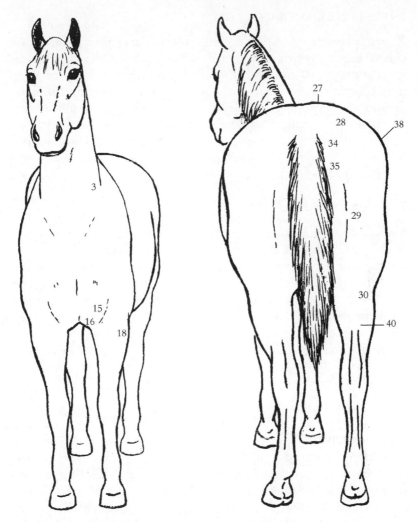

10.10 Stress Point Location Chart, Front/Rear View

active stress points in order to provide relief. Hydrotherapy (chapter 4) and stretching exercises (chapter 8) are useful additions to these short treatments.

A thorough knowledge of these 40 stress points will allow you to make more accurate evaluations and thus ensure better treatments. Remember that the whole muscle structure of the horse works simultaneously and that consequently you will most likely find more than one stress point.

FIRST SEQUENCE

After applying a relaxation massage routine, use light strokings or effleurages to go from point to point, evaluating all 40 points in approximately 10 minutes. Palpate lightly with the tip of your thumb or fingers to determine the degree of tension and inflammation (if any heat or swelling is present) at each point. Remember the four T's—tension, texture, tenderness, and temperature. As you go along, note the areas that need work. At the end of this pass, record your findings to remind yourself of the area that will need more attention.

The Head and Neck

Use gentle muscle squeezing. Start with the ears, massaging thoroughly from the poll down (a few inches) to the throatlatch. Feel the transverse processes of the cervical vertebrae and check if the vertebrae are aligned. Then flow into strokings or effleurage to check the stress points and the main muscles that attach to the head: the rectus capitis ventralis (SP 1), the splenius muscle (SP 2), the brachiocephalic muscle (SP 3), the sternothyrohyoid and omohyoid (SP 4), and the ligamentum nuchae (nuchal ligament).

The Shoulder

With gentle muscle squeezing, check the stress points over the withers (SP 5 to 8). Then with light stroking go down over the scapula to check stress points related to that bone (SP 9 to 11). Flow over the triceps muscle to check its stress points (SP 13, 14) and the one pertaining to the latissimus dorsi (SP 12). Stroke gently to the front of the shoulder to check the pectoral muscle and its stress points (SP 15 to 17). Keep stroking down the leg to check the flexor and extensor of the foreleg (SP 18, 19). Assess the joints with a light palpation. Look for any inflammation, swelling, or abnormal bone formations. Then weave your strokes into light effleurages going up the leg, over the shoulder, and up to the withers.

The Back and Chest

Continue with some gentle strokings to assess the back muscles, the longissimus dorsi and iliocostalis dorsi muscles (SP 20, 21). Weave your strokes to the abdominal muscle, the internal and external oblique muscles, and the intercostal muscles (SP 22 to 26).

The Hindquarters and Hind Legs

Follow with strokings to the muscles of the hindquarters, starting with the gluteus maximus (SP 27). Move to the semitendinosus and the semimembranosus muscles (SP 34, 35), the biceps femoris (SP 28, 29), and the gastrocnemius (SP 30). Gently go over the stifle area to check the quadriceps group of muscles, especially the vastus lateralis (SP 31,). Then gently effleurage on the inside leg to check the adductor group (SP 33). Continue by stroking down to the long digital extensor and long digital flexor muscles (SP 39, 40). From there, effleurage up the leg all the way to the flank, where you will check the iliacus, the tensor fasciae latae and the superficial gluteus muscles (SP 36 to 38). Weave some gentle strokes back to the withers and up the neck.

This completes the first side. Duplicate your assessment routine on the other side of the animal.

Feel free to make changes in this sequence, which is only intended to give you an idea on where to start. Write down your observations before proceeding to the second phase of the stress point routine.

SECOND SEQUENCE

Start the second pass of the routine at the poll. This time use heavier massage movements such as wringings or firmer effleurages to stir up the circulation, especially in the areas that need work. Then proceed to lightly massage every stress point, spending more time on the areas that need it the most. Be careful not to overwork any particular point. Mostly use the stress point technique interspersed with lots of drainage moves (effleurages, compressions, wringings).

If some stress points are not active, spend only enough time on them to trigger a reflex in the Golgi nerve cells; 30 seconds to a minute is plenty when the stress point is not inflamed. When dealing with active stress points, take the time to release them totally, using lighter pressure for a longer period of time; some chronic stress points might take from 2 to 3 minutes. Be careful not to overwork the muscle tissues, and remember to drain thoroughly with effleurages every 20 to 30 seconds.

You will feel the progressive release of the stress point through your fingers. Depending on the origin of the stress point, it may take 1 to 5 massage sessions to release it completely. Emphasize drainage in between points.

During this second pass, depending on the level of stress in the animal worked on, you might spend from 30 minutes to over an hour all together working the various stress points on both sides of the horse.

THIRD SEQUENCE

Go through the whole routine again, this time mostly emphasizing thorough drainage. Use lots of effleurage, wringing, and compression moves. Pay special attention to the areas that have shown particular stress. As you go over the active stress points you should feel them relieved, showing less tightness or inflammation. Finish with lots of stroking to induce relaxation. Keep this third pass under 15 minutes.

Stress points will show tremendous improvement after only one massage session, unless the problem was caused by a direct trauma or an old injury.

Do not try to overachieve on the first treatment. Several sessions will produce a better effect and give the horse time to become accustomed to this form of deep work.

Take notes from the start to track the progress of your treatment. As you develop a schedule of treatments for the horse and become familiar with his common areas of stress, you might reduce the check-up routine to half-hour sessions, working only stress points that particularly need it.

Always drain thoroughly after using the stress point technique. If inflammation is present, use cold hydrotherapy to soothe the nerve endings and assist circulation. It is good for the animal to have a little exercise (for 5 minutes) after such treatment (longeing, walk/trot) unless contraindicated. Stretching exercises performed regularly will allow for a more complete treatment.

THE "TROUBLE SPOTS" ROUTINE

The routine for trouble spots is designed to deal with problems that commonly occur and to prevent their corresponding stress points from developing and the eventual trigger points from forming. This routine is a nice complement to a maintenance routine, especially if your animal exercises regularly.

As you check these areas and detect a strong level of inflammation, apply the ice cup massage technique (chapter 4) for a few minutes to decrease the sensitivity of the nerve endings and reduce the inflammation. If, however, you decide not to perform this routine in combination with the maintenance routine, begin your work with the short version of the relaxation routine to calm and prepare the horse, then start the trouble spot routine at the neck with the first trouble-spot area.

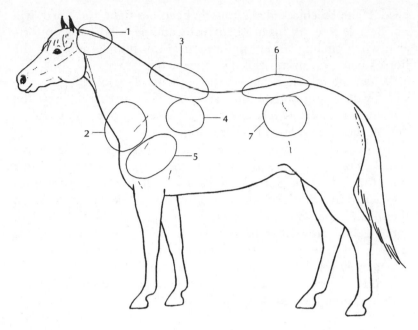

10.11 The "Trouble Spots" Routine Outline

STEP 1: THE UPPER NECK

Work the entire upper neck where the splenius cervicis and the upper rhomboid muscles attach, as well as the ligamentum nuchae attachment at the occiput, between the ears and behind the skull. This is an area of constant stress for a horse that engages in strenuous activities.

Use several light effleurage moves, followed by some gentle muscle wringings to warm up the whole upper neck. Take the time to relax the muscle fibers in that area with lots of thumb kneadings. This work will prevent the formation of SP 1 and SP 2. Then apply some muscle squeezing along the crest of the neck, starting with a 10-pound pressure and progressing to 15 or 20 pounds, depending on the degree of tension that you find. Use your judgment. If the area is tender, the horse will react by moving away from the pressure or by arching the neck against it. If you move too quickly into heavier pressure you might make the existing tension worse. Use several effleurages or strokings to flow to the next trouble spot.

STEP 2: THE POINT OF SHOULDER

The next trouble spot is found in the brachiocephalic muscle of the lower neck. This muscle is involved in the protraction of the foreleg, the head carriage, and side movements of the neck and head. If the brachiocephalic muscle becomes tight, the horse will not be able to carry his head correctly and he will be uncomfortable when circling. Severe tightening of this muscle results in the horse's being off in most of his movements.

When the muscle is tender, the animal will react to light pressure by flinching and pulling away. As you work this area, the horse will most likely relax into the treatment, dropping his shoulder on the same side you are treating.

To massage this area, start with light strokings of the whole muscle. Follow with gentle, smooth effleurages to drain the neck from top to bottom. Stir up circulation with 2 or 3 sets of wringings across the width of the neck. Then apply kneadings to loosen the muscle fibers and prevent the formation of SP 3. Follow with some gentle cross-fiber frictions over the whole length of the muscle. Intersperse with thorough effleurages to drain the area. Then apply gentle compressions to the entire length of the muscle. Follow with effleurages to drain the neck thoroughly, and finish with some light strokings to flow to the next trouble spot.

STEP 3: THE WITHERS

The withers area is a skeletal attachment site for the rhomboid and the trapezius muscles, which are directly involved in the movement of the scapula. The repetitive movement of any gait, and the stress of a potentially difficult maneuver (for example, the impact of landing after a jump) in combination with less-than-perfectly-fitting tack or poor footing, can cause irritation of the withers.

As you reach this area with strokings, move on to warm up the muscles with effleurages and wringings. Then use gentle muscle squeezings (5 to 10 pounds of pressure) to assess the degree of inflammation or irritation. Thoroughly drain the area with lots of effleurages and use kneadings to loosen the muscle fibers. This will prevent the formation of SP 6, 7, and 8. Follow with effleurages to thoroughly drain the withers area. Then apply gentle friction across the length of the fibers, starting gently with moderate pressure and rhythm, working progressively deeper for a period of 2 minutes. Intersperse with effleurages every 20 seconds to drain the area as you work. Keep track of time to avoid overworking the fibers. Follow with generous drainage (effleurages). Finish with light strokings and move over to check the fourth trouble spot.

STEP 4: THE UPPER SHOULDER

The forward attachment of the longissimus dorsi is located behind and a few inches down from the top of the withers. Irritation and inflammation of this area can result from ill-fitting tack or from an extensive workload. When the area is irritated, tension can be felt in one or both sides of this muscle, and will eventually lead to the formation of SP 5 and SP 20.

Take time to warm up the area with lots of gentle effleurages and wringings over the whole muscle. Then use kneadings to relax the muscle fibers and prevent the formation of SP 5. If sore, the horse will probably flinch while arching his back or move away from your pressure; the degree of reaction shown will be indicative of the amount of inflammation present. If you detect a strong level of inflammation, apply the ice massage technique (chapter 4) for a few minutes to decrease the sensitivity of the nerve endings while reducing the inflammation. Follow with light frictions across the muscle to loosen its fibers. Intersperse with effleurages every 20 seconds. When finished, thoroughly drain the whole muscle and then use light strokings to move to the next trouble spot.

STEP 5: THE LOWER SHOULDER

The infraspinatus muscle is one of the most important muscles of the shoulder; it works in conjunction with the supraspinatus, the rhomboid, and the teres minor muscles. These muscles serve to prevent lateral dislocation of the shoulder. Besides being a primary mover of the shoulder joint (protraction and retraction), the infraspinatus is directly involved in lateral movements, such as half-passes.

Abrupt shifts from side to side, such as in cutting, polo, and horseball, render the infraspinatus very susceptible to strain. When the muscle is sore, the horse will exhibit signs of lameness and restricted movement in the foreleg of the injured side. Start massaging this area with light effleurages. The horse might flinch or, if feeling very tender, move away from your pressure. So start working lightly with lots of effleurages; alternate with wringings to warm up the area. Then apply light kneadings to relax the muscle fibers and prevent the formation of SP 9 and SP 10. Follow with effleurages. Then friction the entire muscle back and forth for 2 minutes to loosen its fibers. Intersperse with effleurages every 20 seconds. Follow with compressions along the entire length of the muscle. Finish with lots of effleurages. Use strokings to move to the next trouble spot.

STEP 6: THE CROUP

The longissimus dorsi (back attachment) and the gluteus maximus muscle join in the croup area, a very sensitive or even tender area most of the time. When massaging, approach the loin delicately with light strokings and gentle effleurages (5 to 8 pounds of pressure).

When the loin is inflamed or knotted, the horse will sink or sag in response to your pressure. Apply ice massage first to numb the nerve endings of the area you are treating. Then stimulate circulation thoroughly with wringings and compressions. Intersperse with effleurages every 30 seconds. Use kneadings to relax the muscle fibers and prevent the formation of SP 21. Follow with light frictions along the entire muscle. Thoroughly drain the area with effleurages. Apply palmar compressions along the length of the whole muscle to complete the treatment. Finish with a thorough effleurage and light strokings to move to the next trouble spot.

STEP 7: THE POINT OF HIP

The hip attachment of the tensor fasciae latae (TFL) area just below the point of the hip is a very critical spot. This is where both the TFL muscle and the iliacus muscle attach. These two muscles are strong hip flexors. Furthermore, the TFL muscle plays a role in extending the stifle during retraction of the hind leg.

When this area is stressed, the horse will show discomfort on the same side during lateral movement and will tend to throw his leg outward during protraction. Be careful and very gentle when starting to work this area. If the area appears very tender at first touch, use the ice massage technique prior to the treatment.

Stimulate circulation with gentle effleurages and wringings. Apply compressions with a moderate to heavy pressure (10 or 15 to 20 pounds) along the TFL muscle. Then use kneadings to relax the muscle fibers of these two muscles and prevent the formation of SP 36 and SP 37. Intersperse with effleurages. Then apply cross-fiber frictions over the entire muscle. Alternate with effleurages every 30 seconds. After the massage, apply cold to ease the nerve endings and flush circulation. Finish with a thorough effleurage drainage.

A general stretching of the horse (chapter 8) is particularly good to complete this routine. Active exercise (unsaddled) for the horse after the massage is a good follow-up, but keep any lateral work to a minimum at first, especially if the shoulder and TFL muscles were tight. To finish the routine, apply lots of light strokings over the horse's entire body to give him a sense of relaxation.

TREATMENTS

The word *treatment* refers to a massage application over a localized body part without delivering a full-body routine. Treatments are designed to deal with specific problems such as cold back, neck stiffness, leg soreness, and so on. Apply the relaxation routine (short version) for a few minutes to calm and prepare your horse before starting your treatment.

The duration of a treatment varies with the situation at hand and the goals you want to achieve. In most acute situations (the first 24 hours) and when no contraindications prevail, a treatment should last 15 to 20 minutes, or maybe 30 minutes if the tissues treated are not too inflamed.

In subacute situations (24 to 72 hours), the treatment can last from 30 to 45 minutes. In chronic situations (over 72 hours), an hour-long treatment is not uncommon. Keep in mind the degree of inflammation in the tissues, the number of stress points and trigger points present, and the overall state of the structures you are working on. Proceed cautiously. Remember to use hydrotherapy (chapter 4) to enhance the effect of your massage work, as well as stretching exercises (chapter 8). If no severe inflammation or bad spasms are present among the structures you are working, follow your massage session with a mild, unsaddled exercise period (such as walking or light trotting on a longe) to complete the treatment, but avoid a strenuous workout.

BACK TREATMENT

Most of us have seen horses with cold backs ranging from mildly to severely tender, sometimes accompanied by inflammation of the muscle fibers. (Pages 206–215 describe the different structures and muscle groups and related stress points of the back.) The back muscles affected by this condition are the longissimus dorsi (SP 20), the iliocostalis dorsi (SP 21), and occasionally the spinalis dorsi (SP 5). Cold back is a common problem that is usually associated with ill-fitting saddles, incorrect shoeing, and incorrectly balanced riders. A simple and efficient way to help your horse with this painful condition is to apply a light massage treatment before and after riding. Place more emphasis on the massage given after riding, because warm back muscles can take a more vigorous massage that will soothe any stiffness and prevent the formation of trigger points.

After you apply the relaxation routine (short version) for a few minutes to calm and prepare your horse, begin your massage treatment with the SEW approach (chapter 5) along the entire back, from the withers to the rump, on both sides of the spine. Follow with effleurages 3 to 5 times, progressively increasing your pressure from 3 or 5 pounds to 10 or 12 pounds. Then proceed to wringings across the entire back, 2 or 3 times, to increase circulation. Your pressure should be around 10 pounds. Use effleurages in between each sequence. You might consider using some light hacking moves (10 to 12 pounds of pressure) along the entire back to reach deep in the muscle structure. Complete with some effleurages. Then proceed to check each of the associated stress points (SP 5, 20, 21, 27) and treat them when necessary, using the stress point technique (chapter 5). If the animal appears very tender, also check SP 6, 7, 8, and 25, which are sometimes affected when severe symptoms of tension are present in the back. Apply the trigger point technique (chapter 5) to treat any trigger point that appears inflamed. Use lots of effleurages to thoroughly drain the entire back. Once you have checked and relieved the associated stress and trigger points, gently apply finger frictions along the course of the longissimus dorsi and the iliocostalis dorsi muscles to further loosen and relax the muscle fibers. Intersperse with lots of effleurages and finish your treatment with the WES approach (chapter 5) over the entire back. To enhance the effect of the massage therapy, consider hydrotherapy (chapter 4) before and after your treatment as well as some stretching exercises (chapter 8) when your massage work is done.

NECK TREATMENT

Because the horse's head acts as a counterweight to keep the animal in balance, the neck plays a key role in locomotion. You will notice that his head goes down as the rear leg is brought forward. This counterweight action is more animated at the canter, but it can also be seen at the walk. The neck must be strong and flexible; this counterweight action is fundamental to the horse as he executes smooth transitions and maintains a regular gait. Neck stiffness can restrict the lateral flexion of the neck, which in turn restricts the gait. A simple and efficient way to help your horse with this condition is to use gentle massage moves over the entire neck before and after riding. Emphasize the post-riding massage to prevent muscle stiffness. It is more beneficial to massage when the animal is warm, since the muscles can take more vigorous massage to clear away lactic acid buildup that may have developed during the workout. Familiarize yourself with the structure of the neck in order to improve your massage treatments.

After applying the relaxation massage routine (short version) for a few minutes to calm and prepare your horse, begin your treatment with the SEW approach by stroking the entire neck on both sides. Then apply 10 to 15 light effleurages (3 to 5 pounds of pressure) from the poll to the withers. Follow with some gentle wringings (5 pounds of pressure) across the side of the neck 2 or 3 times to stimulate circulation. Intersperse with lots of effleurages to drain circulation in the neck toward the heart. Then perform muscle squeezings along the crest of the neck, beginning at the poll and working down to the withers. Repeat this sequence 2 or 3 times, working into a medium pressure (8 to 10 pounds) and gradually increasing your pressure to about 15 to 20 pounds by the last repetition of the move. The thickly muscled, strong necks of ponies, Morgans, and draft horses can take more pressure. Once this work is completed, use some effleurages to drain from the poll to the shoulders. Then using thumb or finger kneadings, check the related stress points of the neck (SP 1 to 4 and occasionally 7 to 9 if the symptoms of stiffness are strong). Apply the stress point technique (chapter 5) to treat any point that appears inflamed. Apply the trigger point technique (chapter 5) to treat any trigger point that appears inflamed. Then use lots of effleurages to thoroughly drain the entire neck. Finish with some light strokings to soothe the horse. Repeat the whole procedure on the other side. If after this treatment the horse's neck seems to be tight, apply some neck rocking movements. With one hand on the crest and the other on the bottom of the neck, gently rock the top and bottom of the neck back and forth. Do this along the entire length of the neck. Finish with the WES approach with plenty of effleurages. Consider using hydrotherapy (chapter 4) before and after your treatment to further the effects of the massage.

After massaging both sides, stretch the neck (chapter 8) to the sides; stretching up and stretching down will relax the muscle groups of the neck further. Remember that neck tension is more often than not an indication of a hind or back problem.

THE FOREQUARTERS TREATMENT

The forequarters are considered to be the horse's "power steering." High levels of training put great physical demands on the muscles of the shoulders, chest, and forelegs. Also, a horse experiencing tension or discomfort in his hindquarters will shift more of his weight to the forequarters in order to relieve the pain in the hindquarters. If not attended to quickly, the tension in the forelegs might develop into a more serious problem, such as inflammation of the muscle fibers, or worse, the tendons or ligaments. If your horse shows signs of stiffness or discomfort in the front when asked to turn one way or the other, this is a sure indication of tension buildup.

To help prevent tension buildup, apply a light massage treatment before and after riding, with emphasis on the post-ride massage, to keep the muscles from becoming stiff and sore. Once the horse has exercised, his muscles are warmed up and are able to take a more vigorous massage to relieve stiffness and clear lactic acid buildup.

After you apply the relaxation routine for a few minutes, begin your treatment with the SEW approach covering the entire area of the shoulder, chest, and forelegs. Follow with some effleurages, moving from the withers to the point of shoulder and then around the chest. Your pressure should start at 3 to 5 pounds, gradually building with 2 or 3 passes to 8 or 10 pounds. Keeping your rhythm smooth and consistent, weave your moves into wringings, using 8 to 10 pounds of pressure, across the muscle group of the shoulder and chest 2 to 3 times to stimulate deep circulation. Intersperse with effleurages every second pass. Compressions and muscle squeezings (8 to 10 pounds of pressure) can be performed over the large triceps muscle as well as the pectoral muscles. Repeat 4 to 6 times and finish with effleurages. When working the chest, do not forget the "armpit" area where the leg and chest meet. This site may show signs of tension because the muscles are involved in the adduction (inward motion) and abduction (outward motion) of the foreleg. Loosen the muscles with muscle squeezing and thumb kneading (5 to 8 pounds of pressure), finishing with effleurages.

Once the shoulder and chest areas are well warmed up, move to the legs. Start at the elbow using alternating upward effleurages with 3 to 5 pounds of pressure, slowly working your way down the knee and eventually to the pastern. Use a fairly light pressure (3 pounds) on the structures below the knee since there is no muscle tissue there. Once you have worked your way down the leg, use long gliding effleurages going upward from the fetlock to the shoulder, repeating 2 or 3 times.

If your horse shows signs of tenderness or inflammation, keep your pressure light and your treatment time short. Otherwise, the muscles are now ready for deeper work. Check each of the associated stress points, from SP 5 to SP 19, and treat them when necessary, using the stress point technique (chapter 5). If the animal appears very tender and strong symptoms of tension are present, also check the stress points of the neck, back, and hindquarters, which are sometimes affected by compensation. Apply the trigger point technique (chapter 5) to treat any trigger point that appears inflamed. Use lots of effleurages to thoroughly drain the points treated. Once this work is completed, gently apply finger frictions along the course of the affected muscles to loosen and relax their muscle fibers. Intersperse with lots of effleurages. Finish your treatment with the WES approach over the entire forequarters. Duplicate this whole treatment on the other leg of the horse.

If inflammation symptoms are present, consider using hydrotherapy (chapter 4) before and after your treatment to enhance the effect of the massage. Stretching (chapter 8) the forequarters at the end of your treatment will also contribute greatly to the positive effect of your massage therapy work.

THE HINDQUARTERS TREATMENT

The hindquarters are considered to be the "engine" of the horse. High levels of training put great physical demands on the hindquarters. This chapter outlines the different structures and muscle groups and the related stress points of the hindquarters. To help your horse with the demands made on his hindquarters, apply a light massage treatment before and after riding, with more emphasis on the post-ride massage, to prevent the muscles from becoming stiff and sore. Once the exercise has warmed the horse's muscles, they are able to take a more vigorous massage that will soothe any stiffness and will clear lactic acid buildup.

After you apply the relaxation massage routine for a few minutes, begin your treatment with the SEW approach covering the entire hindquarters. Then drain with some effleurages, starting on the back, moving across the rump to the croup; then go across the hip and move down toward the stifle. Your pressure should start at 3 to 5 pounds gradually building to 8 or 10 pounds within 2 or 3 passes. Follow with some muscle wringings (10 pounds of pressure) across the muscle. Intersperse with effleurages every second movement. Repeat 6 to 8 times. Use fist compressions over the hamstring muscle group to stir deep circulation, finishing with effleurages. Then work the upper leg thoroughly, both on the inside and outside, from the stifle to the hock. Use wringings, picking ups, and thumb kneadings, interspersed every second move with effleurages draining toward the heart.

To drain the hind leg thoroughly, start at the stifle, using alternating upward effleurages (3 to 5 pounds of pressure), slowly working your way down to the hock and eventually to the pasterns. Use a fairly light pressure on the structures below the hock, since there is no muscle tissue there—only tendons, vessels, ligaments, and bones. Once you have worked your way down the leg, use long gliding effleurages, going upward from the fetlock to the stifle. Repeat 3 to 5 times to cover all parts of the leg. To soothe the horse, finish with strokings along the entire hind leg.

If your horse shows signs of tenderness, keep your pressure light and your treatment time short. Otherwise, the muscles are now ready for stronger work. Use muscle compressions (fist or palm of the hand) along the course of the larger muscle groups. Intersperse with effleurages every 20 to 30 seconds. Then apply some finger or thumb kneadings on the muscle attachments along the vertebral column, femur, stifle, and hock. Intersperse with effleurages every 20 seconds.

Check each of the associated stress points, from SP 27 to SP 40, and treat them if necessary, using the stress point technique (chapter 5). If the horse appears very tender and shows strong symptoms of tension, also check the stress points of the back, abdomen, and neck, which are sometimes affected by compensation. Apply the trigger point technique (chapter 5) to treat any trigger point that appears inflamed. Use lots of effleurages to thoroughly drain these points after you have worked them. Next, gently apply finger frictions along the course of the gluteus muscles, the hamstring group of muscle, the tensor fasciae latae, and the iliacus muscle to loosen and relax their muscle fibers. Intersperse with lots of effleurages every 30 seconds and finish your treatment using the WES approach over the entire back.

If inflammation is present, consider using hydrotherapy (chapter 4) before and after your massage treatment to enhance the effect of the massage therapy. Stretching (chapter 8) the hindquarters at the end of your treatment will also contribute greatly to the positive effect of your massage therapy work.

With practice you will become familiar with each treatment and routine, and will discover what works best for your horse.

To know all the 40 stress points common to the active horse will give you a strong advantage when massaging your horse. With practice you will become familiar with each location. The trouble spot routine will keep your horse at the top of its fitness. This knowledge of the equine stress point will improve the quality of your work and will bring lasting results.

11

EQUINE MYOFASCIAL MASSAGE

Myofascial therapy is probably one of the most important evolutions in alternative medicine. Today, more and more massage and physical therapists are using the myofascial technique for preventive, maintenance, and recovery treatments. Since the horse's musculoskeletal anatomy and physiology are so similar to humans, this beneficial technique can easily be adapted to the horse.

Myofascial therapy specializes in dealing with the myofascial system of the body, which includes fascial layers, fascial bands, retinaculum, ligaments, and tendons. Any kind of tissue irritation, discomfort, or injury will reflect on the entire myofascial system causing referred pain and restrictions in movement, eventually affecting the entire quality and quantity of motion, gait, and posture of the subject.

Flexibility of the fascia, muscles, ligaments, and joints plays an important role in enhancing performance, rehabilitation, and wellness of the active horse. Regular massage and proper stretching provide the basis for optimal agility, coordination, speed, and most importantly, flexibility. It is important to remember that the primary obstacle to optimal flexibility is the tightness of the surrounding muscles and fascia of a joint, or group of joints.

From human practice we know that most people find myofascial release sessions very relaxing. However, because these sessions are deep reaching, they can trigger major energy releases and changes, resulting in temporary feelings from tiredness to stimulation. These reactions are usually considered a good sign, showing that the body is going through the healing process. Allow your animal plenty of rest after your session. During the course of several myofascial release sessions your horse will regain a more balanced posture, regular gait, and more vitality, as his body is realigned and freed from pain.

The myofascial massage starts with a visual evaluation followed by a palpation to evaluate the entire fascial system. Then a three-dimensional, hands-on application of sustained pressure and movement into the fascial system is used to eliminate the fascial restrictions. This approach will further help you to feel, touch, and listen to your horse's real needs.

Myofascial massage, combined with regular massage, allows you to contribute to proper equine massage maintenance, while deepening the bonds of trust and compassion with your horse.

THE FASCIAL SYSTEM

The fascial system of the horse is similar to our own. It can be seen as a multi-layer body wrapping, weaving in layers throughout the body with fascial sheaths wrapping the muscles, blood vessels, nerves, and organs, giving our body structural integrity and strength. You could visualize the fascia layer as a big stocking that wraps the body but is flexible. Because of this, stress recorded in any area of the body will affect all other areas of the body as well. Furthermore, the fascial network serves as an extensive water storage system, facilitating the regulation of the homeostasis of the body by contributing to the removal of toxins.

11.1 Superficial Fascial Layer Illustrated as a Stocking

WHAT IS FASCIA?

Fascia is a tough, whitish, collagenous fiber known as *connective tissue*. Fascia spreads throughout the entire body in a 3-dimensional way. As its name implies, the connective tissue (fascia) connects everything and everything is interconnected. Fascia is found everywhere without interruption, functioning as a web. This web gives strength and support to the entire body from head to toe.

Connective tissue is made up of *collagen* which gives fascia its physical strength, *elastin* which gives fascia elasticity where it is required (skin, blood vessels), and a polysaccharide *gel complex,* a substance that fills the space between fibers and allows the fibers to slide over each other with minimal friction. This combination of collagen, elastin, and gel complex forms a three-dimensional, interdependent fascial system of strength, support, elasticity, and cushion, allowing for greater absorption of compressive force and mechanical stresses. If injured, dehydrated, or under repetitive or continuous stress, the hardening of the gel complex is equivalent to pouring glue into the interstitial space resulting in a hard, non-giving fasciae. This decreases the fascia's flexibility and elasticity. Over time, the hardened fascia will cause the animal to first develop restricted movements and eventually an abnormal gait.

THE FASCIAL SYSTEM AND ITS FUNCTIONS

The fascial system is divided into two basic categories: subcutaneous and subserous.

The *subcutaneous fascia* has two distinct layers that form continuous sheets over the entire body, superficial and deep, and it connects the skin, muscles, and skeletal structures. The subcutaneous fascial system consists of layers of loose and dense connective

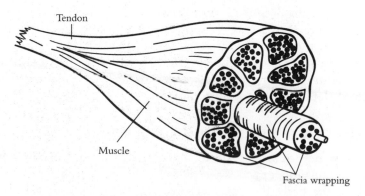

11.2 Fascial Covering of Muscle, Muscle Fibers, and Bundles

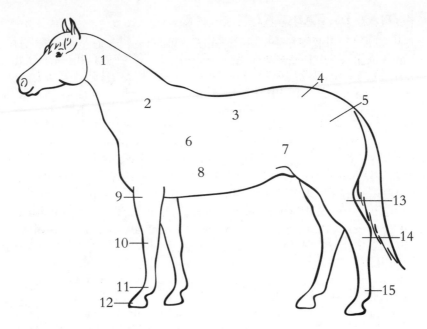

11.3 Fascial Denomination

(1) cervical fascia
(2) omobrachial fascia
(3) thoracolumbar fascia
(4) gluteal fascia
(5) femoral fascia
(6) thorax fascia
(7) fascia latae
(8) abdominal fascia

(9) antebrachial fascia
(10) carpal fascia
(11) metacarpal fascia
(12) digital fascia
(13) crural fascia
(14) tarsal fascia
(15) metatarsal fascia

tissue that make up the "fascial bands." In turn these fascial bands make up the superficial and deep fascia layers, the loose fascia, the retinaculum, the ligaments, and tendons. The fascia system surrounds, protects, separates, supports, and connects everything throughout the entire body.

Subserous fascia lines the body cavities, such as the pelvis and rib cage. The subserous fascia protects the organs by suspending them to the skeletal and muscle structures.

PHYSICAL PROPERTIES OF FASCIA

Fascia as a shock absorber: The collagen, elastin, and gel complex combination provides the fascia with strength and elasticity, allowing the body to resist mechanical stress, both internally and externally.

Fascia as a tension sensor: Another property of the fascia is its ability to conduct micro-currents created by the body. When the fascia is stimulated, it sends information back to the central nervous system affecting proprioceptive information. In this way, fascia acts as a sensor of mechanical tension.

Fascia as water storage: The fascia is able to store water. Hydrated fibrous tissue creates a smooth coating, allowing fascia structures to glide over each other without friction. When a horse gets dehydrated its smooth, hydrated matrix changes consistency, creating adherence to tissues as if they were partially glued. This gluing creates tension, fatigue, and leads to ischemia and build up of metabolic toxins.

Fascia and scar tissue: Proportional to the amount of scar tissue formation, the fascia becomes rigid and loses its flexibility.

Fascial knots: When the fascia is irritated, it contracts and twists and turns throughout the body. The fascia becomes rigid and loses its flexibility. Fascia reorganizes itself along the lines of tension created and imposed by pain on the body, providing support and protection from further trauma. Based on those patterns, layers of fascia start to glue to one another, resulting in fascial knots. Over time this phenomenon alters the gait, flexibility, and muscle power of the animal.

Fascia and the autonomic nervous system: The fascia has a close relationship to the autonomic nervous system to the extent that autonomic ganglia are embedded into the fascial matrix. Human studies have suggested that autonomic dysfunction may arise from fascial dysfunction. Fascial disruption affects circulation and nourishment of these autonomic ganglia, resulting in aberrant dysfunction of the smooth muscle such as poor digestion or cardiac irregularity.

Fascia as an information exchange network: Fascia is considered a semi-conducting communication network, conveying bioelectric signals between every part of the body along the fascial lines. Therefore, the ever changing aspect of the fascial system profoundly influences every other aspect of the body (muscles, nerves, blood vessels, bones, and organs) and their interrelationship.

Fascial Restrictions—Cross-links

The formation of elastocollagenous cross-links within the connective tissue (fascia) is often seen following a trauma, a mechanical irritation, or inflammation. These cross-links form restrictions at the nodal points where the various layers of fascia are designed to glide over each other. This reduces the gliding motion, causing a reduction in the quantity and the quality of motion. This affects the horse's gait, which in turn affects his performance.

Fascia and Muscle Imbalance

Sometimes over-training or under-training schedules result in an imbalance in the muscle groups of the horse. This in turn leads to strains or tears, especially during quick acceleration or deceleration movements, or strong pushes. The pain triggered by such strains or tears will affect the entire fascia system, as the animal will compensate in order to avoid the pain and maintain optimal performance.

Fascia and Emotional Memory

Horses, like humans, have an innate protective mechanism that keeps record of any type of trauma (physical, mental, and nutritional) in order to avoid this trauma again. This coding of traumatic experiences is termed *"emotional memory."* When working with myofascial release, you will most likely find some restriction barriers that will trigger an emotional memory in the animal. Always observe the feedback signs your horse expresses and progress cautiously. A change in breathing rhythms or an intense expression in the eyes are very revealing of this condition.

PREPARATION

Preparation is crucial as it will insure the good development of your session. It will also save you time and help you avoid mistakes. Remember the old axiom "Being prepared is half the battle." Being prepared will allow you to work at your best ability for the benefit of your animal.

ATTITUDE

Whenever you apply myofascial massage techniques, it is important to be relaxed. Become focused and very attentive, constantly assessing the sensations your fingers give you as well as observing your horse's feedback signs.

Do not let your mind wander. We have a tendency to let our left brain dominate, leading to rationalization and criticism thereby reducing our perceptions. By practicing relaxation, we allow the right brain to dominate, giving us more nonverbal intuition. Consider taking gentle and regular deep breaths; it will help you stay focused, yet relaxed. When you allow both hemispheres of your brain to function in harmony, the balance will enhance your perception and effectiveness.

OBSERVATION

Develop a keen sense of observation and a sharp eye to detect any musculoskeletal asymmetries in the horse's posture at rest, when moving, or when playing. First look at your horse globally, comparing the various body parts in relation to each other: note the size, proportion, and alignment. Get a general impression of the horse's state of health and fitness, and the quality of the muscular structure, section by section. Next, observe any physical restrictions in his various gaits: walk, trot, and canter. This simple act of observation can already reveal a lot to you.

TOUCH—THE FOUR T'S

Using the four T's—tension, texture, tenderness, and temperature (see chapter 3) can tell you a lot. Before you proceed with treatment, please review the section on the four T's.

PRESSURE, CONTACT, AND RHYTHM

Pressure: The pressure used in myofascial release is very gentle. The evolution of myofascial release techniques in many human disciplines has taught us that in order to get the release of fascial restriction we only need to exert a light pressure and/or stretch for a period of time over the area of myofascial restriction. The fluidity of the movements coupled with light pressure allows for a better relaxation of the tissues.

During myofascial release you will mostly use pressure starting at 1 pound and building up to 3 to 5 pounds, sometimes 10 to 12, depending on the size of the horse and the location you are working on.

Contact: To maximize your hand contact with the fascial layers of your horse, keep your hands flexible at all times, molding them to his body parts. As you always start your contact with light pressure, your hands will give your horse a pleasurable sensation of comfort. Then gently build your pressure to the point where you meet the barrier and wait for release. The comforting touch will relax your horse and help him accept the soreness that is sometimes associated with this process. Then as you progressively release your pressure, the same comforting touch will give your horse a feeling of continuity, ensuring connection and comfort.

Rhythm: In this context, rhythm refers to the frequency at which you apply your techniques and the movements in between techniques. A gentle, almost slow rhythm of 1 stroke per second is best in between different technique applications.

FEEDBACK FROM THE HORSE

Being able to accurately read the feedback signs your horse gives you during the application of myofascial massage will greatly contribute to the smooth evolution of your work (see chapter 2). During your application, keep looking at the horse's eyes. They are his most expressive feature. Any discomfort will cause him to open his eyes, then tense his lips and move his head up.

When needed, use a calming voice to ease your horse's anxiety. If necessary, delay your work until your horse is in a better frame of mind. You do not want to create a worse situation by forcing the issue.

Remember, when waiting on the tissue barrier to release during the application, you only need to follow the tissue motion as it releases. Do not be eager to induce it. If you exert too much pressure you risk causing unnecessary soreness, if not pain, depending on the nature and the location of the restrictions. Right after the release has occurred, the horse might raise his head and open his eyes widely as a sign of a "feel good" sensation. Because you know your horse best, you will be quickly and intuitively able to read and interpret his feedback signs, allowing you to adjust your work accordingly.

EMOTIONAL RELEASE

In the human practice of myofascial release it is theorized that the energy created by a life stress, trauma, or anxiety converts into a fascial restriction and an unresolved psychological issue. The body records this unfortunate episode as a physical sensation (pain!), an emotional sensation (I don't like it!), and an intellectual awareness (stay away!), both at the conscious and subconscious level. Even after the experience has passed and the body heals, the fascia remains restricted(with its emotional and intellectual connection), both consciously and subconsciously. This myofascial restriction is there to "protect" against further trauma. Professional therapists call this process "tissue memory."

When facilitating a myofascial release, you most likely will trigger some tissue memories; so be very gentle, as your horse needs to release not only the physical fascial restrictions but also the correlated emotional and intellectual memories. It is important to honor this process and create the most positive environment for your horse so he feels at ease. While the horse might never forget a particular incident, over the course of several sessions he will be able to let go of the associated fear and reactive anxiety.

Positioning the Horse

Working in the horse's stall is best. Do not use a halter or any crossties. The horse should be free to move so he can best position himself for maximum benefit and release.

Timing

During a myofascial release the time component of the release is very important. Due to the nature of the tissue and the associated tissue memory, usually several minutes are required for total release. The various sensations felt during the elongation part of the technique will let you know when the barriers have all been released. When your horse seems to focus on the sensation with his eyes half closed, it usually means that your horse has finally reached the point where the myofascial release occurs(where the tissue memories let go). This is what professionals refer to as a "still point." Give your horse a few moments before moving to the next still point.

Palpation Evaluation

Your manual palpation routine will allow you to test your horse's entire musculoskeletal structure and to ensure that no contraindications are present. **Pay attention** to any abnormal swelling, heat, inflammation, tissue hardening, muscle knots, or any abnormal reactions from your horse, which could indicate that massage is contraindicated (see chapter 2). Throughout your entire palpation, use a light pressure ranging from 0.5 to 1 pound on average, up to 2 pounds of pressure maximum on large muscled areas or with large horses.

Skin Mobility

Check the skin mobility by placing your hand flat on the skin of any given body part, and moving it slowly in all directions. The skin should move equally in all directions, the exception being when going over the insertion of a muscle's tendon into the bony structures.

If the skin, or muscle, you are palpating does not move well in a particular direction, it indicates that the underlying fascia is restricted. Assess thoroughly the direction of the restriction. This will give you precise direction of where to apply the appropriate myofascial release movement; usually into the direction of the restriction.

Under normal conditions, the horse's body tissues should be fairly soft and pliable. If instead they are hot, tender, and eventually hard, you have found where the problem is! If the tissues feel leathery, lumpy, or even like wire, it indicates that the fascia has tightened considerably and that its gel complex has solidified.

MYOFASCIAL RELEASE TECHNIQUES

By the term "technique" I refer to specific movements performed in a pattern and done in an orderly fashion in order to obtain the desired effect.

DOUBLE-HANDS FRICTION TECHNIQUE

The double-hands friction technique is a good opening myofascial technique in prelude to other myofascial massage techniques. Performed in a light fashion, it is a great technique to evaluate

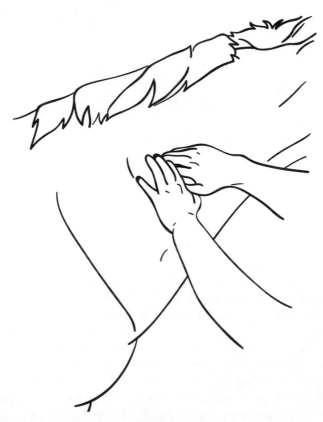

11.4 Double-Hands Friction Technique Done Over the Neck

large muscle groups. When done with a heavier pressure, this friction technique is very efficient in loosening the cross-links and warming up the gel complex.

The double-hands friction technique is performed in the same way as in regular massage, with both hands side by side, applying a downward pressure with the fingertips right into the muscle. Then, moving slowly and in a motion perpendicular to the muscle fibers, apply friction movements with your fingertips to the entire length of the muscle group. Proceed smoothly, not erratically, and position yourself properly (relaxed shoulders, elbows slightly flexed, with your wrists positioned in the continuity of the forearms). Your fingers should be at a 90-degree angle from your hands. It is the extension-flexion movement of the fingers that produces the strumming motion. Always start with a light pressure, so a sensation of "well-being" is passed onto your horse. If you progress deeper, the sensation might change and become sharper. Monitor your horse's feedback through the entire process.

CROSS-HANDS TECHNIQUE

The cross-hands technique gets its name from the position in which your hands are held during the application of this technique. The cross-hands technique is used to release both superficial and deep myofascial restrictions over large areas, anywhere over the horse's body. After you have assessed the area and identified the location and sense of the restrictions with your palpations, warm up the area with regular massage using the SEW approach (see chapter 5). Then in a relaxed manner, cross your hands and position them on the part you need to work on. Slowly apply a gentle pressure—1 to 2 pounds —as you open your hands to stretch the elastic component of the restriction. Keep stretching until you come to a barrier where your hands will stop naturally. Do not force beyond this natural barrier. Just hold a steady pressure to maintain the stretch. The stretch should last at least 1 to 2 minutes, the equivalent of 7 to 15 regular full breaths. Sometimes it might take up to 3 minutes before the release occurs, depending on the amount of cross-links present in the myofascial tissues and the state of the gel complex. The steadiness of the sustained pressure is the key to the success of the myofascial release.

Just before the release occurs, you may feel heat building up or a throbbing sensation under your hands called the therapeutic pulse. The horse will feel it too with a slight increase in discomfort. As the restrictions are being released, you will feel motion under your hands. Go with that motion, sustaining your pressure as long as the motion persists. It is usually a sign of softening and pain relief for the horse.

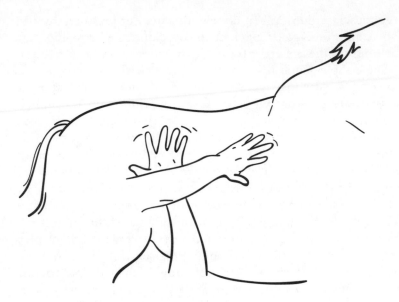

11.5 Cross-Hands Technique Over Back

For small areas, a variation of this technique is performed using the fingertips instead of the full hands. Using the fingertips or thumbs is ideal for smaller areas, especially less accessible areas such as the horse's hind legs and forelegs. When working tiny areas, like a section of fascia around a particular joint (retinaculum of knee joint for example), you will find the cross-hands technique delivered with the thumbs most efficient.

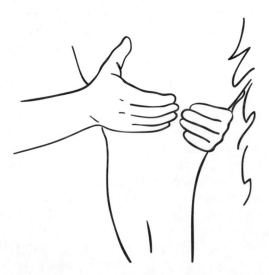

11.6 Cross-Hands Technique Using Fingertips

After the application of the cross–hands technique, you should apply regular massage techniques using the WES approach (see chapter 5) to maximize the benefits of increased circulation to the horse's musculoskeletal structures.

THE STROKING TECHNIQUE

The stroking technique is performed with 1 or 2 fingers, bent at the knuckles. The stroke is primarily used to loosen superficial and deep myofascial restrictions (cross-links) wherever they are found. From human practice we know that the application of the stroking technique can cause some tenderness in the patient and should therefore be applied with extreme caution. The same applies for your horse. Because of the tenderness associated with the stroking technique when going over the restrictions, keep assessing your horse's body language, and reassure him constantly with a gentle, calm voice.

11.7 Stroking Technique Over Neck

When you locate a restriction in one direction, apply some counter pressure with the heel of one hand just in front of the restriction, and with the knuckles of your other hand, perform the stroke in the direction of the restriction. The speed with which you apply the stroke should be fairly slow. Do not stroke too fast as it would be painful to the horse. Furthermore, the slower pace gives you the time to appreciate the quality of your touch over the tissue you are stretching, providing valuable feedback on the elongation and release of the myofascial layer.

THE HAND PRESSURE TECHNIQUE

The hand pressure technique is very efficient in helping to realign the bony structures and release the myofascial restrictions found deep and close to the bony structures such as vertebrae, ribs, hipbones, or other body parts on the limbs. Warm up the area with regular massage using the SEW approach (see chapter 5) before applying the pressure technique.

The pressure technique consists of exerting a gentle, yet firm, pressure over the key area with the palm of your hand and gently stretching it in the direction the restriction is felt. Hold this pressure for 2 to 3 minutes or until you feel the restriction "give in"— heat sensation and tissues moving ["melting'] under your pressure. Ensure your hand doesn't glide over the horse's coat during this

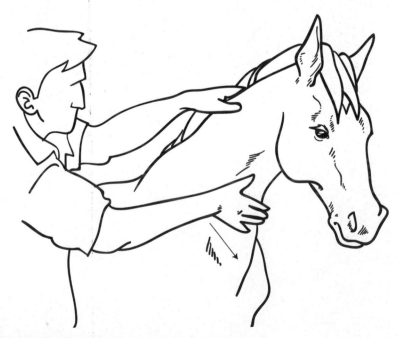

11.8 Hand Pressure Technique Over Lower Neck

process. As the myofascial restriction unwinds, keep following the path of restriction, barrier after barrier. When the movement stops, the release is complete.

Following the application of this technique, you might want to apply some more regular massage movements using the WES approach (see chapter 5) to relax the entire muscle structure and increase circulation in that particular area.

The knowledge of these myofascial massage release techniques is a great addition to your massage skills. Your awareness of the myofascial system and how to work with it will become very important in helping you realign the fascial system and the muscular systems. For more in-depth information on myofascial massage, consult the author's work, Equine Myofascial Massage, Foundation Course.

12

"Equine TMJ problem" is a word combination that usually gets a strong response from people, usually a worried one. Due to the importance of good contact at the bit, for the hands of the rider to delicately direct the horse, a healthy temporomandibular joint (TMJ) is important for the proper performance of the equine athlete. Also, being part of the mastication (chewing) apparatus of the horse, a good TMJ is vital for his good health. Poor performance of the TMJ will result in poor mastication and absorption of foods and their nutrients, which often lead to digestive complications.

Massage treatment for the Equine Temporomandibular Joint Dysfunction Syndrome (ETDS) works in harmony with the horse as a noninvasive approach that assesses the muscle tone and stiffness, finds imbalances, and helps correct these imbalances. Early detection helps you maximize your animal's well-being, as well as save on recovery time, not to mention save money.

The temporomandibular condition is characterized by pain and/or dysfunction of the temporomandibular joint with associated pain or discomfort around the ear, teeth, or other referred areas of the head, and with masticatory muscle tenderness, possible clicking noises in the TMJ when moving the mandible, and/or limited range of motion of the jaw. ETDS affects the horse's joint of the jaw and of the cranium, in a unilateral (one-sided), or bilateral (both sides) way.

The human TMJ condition is a very well-known, well-documented, and well-treated condition. Due to the comparable physiology with the horse, all human research on this condition has helped the management of Equine TMJ Dysfunction Syndrome to come a long way. As much as this TMJ condition is seen more rarely with horses than with humans, it usually is more severe for the horse. This is due to the fact that the lower, horizontal portion of the horse's mandible, known as the "ramus," is twice as long as in the human. When chewing, this extra leverage will affect the equine TMJ with greater force, causing more severe damage to the structures.

ANATOMY OF THE EQUINE TMJ

SKELETAL STRUCTURE

The bony structures of the equine TMJ are the temporal bone of the skull and the mandible. The mandible articulates on either side of the skull, at the temporomandibular joints.

When the horse chews, the mandible moves in a rotating fashion (medio-lateral), with minimal cranio-caudal displacement. This movement forms a figure 8 during mastication.

TEMPOROMANDIBULAR ARTICULATION

The temporomandibular joint is a unique joint that simultaneously combines a synovial and a condylar joint; it links the condylar process of the mandible to the articular surface of the temporal bone.

12.1 Bones of the TMJ

(1) skull   *(2) mandible*

❖ A *synovial joint* is a special form of articulation, which permits the union of the bony elements by surrounding them with an articular capsule enclosing a cavity lined by a synovial membrane that produces the transparent, viscid fluid called synovia. The *synovial fluid* provides lubrication to the joint.

❖ A *condylar joint* is a joint in which an oval head of one bone moves in an elliptical cavity of another, permitting all movements except an axial rotation. This combination allows the TMJ free motion to open by hinge action, then to glide sideways in order to perform many different movements, principally for good mastication.

Inside the TMJ there is a thick, fibro, cartilaginous, interarticular disk located between the mandible and the temporal bones, dividing the synovial joint capsule into 2 cavities. The disc function is to improve the performing functions of the TMJ against mechanical constraints. The hinge movement occurs in the lower cavity, and the lateral gliding and slight protrusive movements (anterior and posterior movements of the mandible) occur in the upper, more capacious cavity, where the oval head of the mandible articulates in the elliptical cavity of the temporal bone of the skull. On each of its sides, the temporomandibular joint gets extra

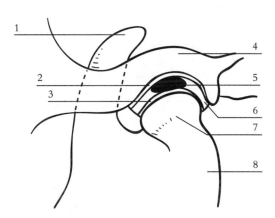

12.2 Lateral View of the TMJ

(1) cronoid apophysis
(2) disco-temporal articulation
(3) disco-mandibular articulation
(4) zygomatic arch
(5) articular disc
(6) articular capsule
(7) head of mandible
(8) neck of mandible

support from a collateral and a caudal ligament. Palpation of the TMJ will reveal the placement of this joint.

NERVE SUPPLY

The facial (adjust) nerve and the mandibular nerve provide the nerve supply to the TMJ. These two nerves divide into many branches as seen in figure 12.3:

- ❖ The caudal auricular nerve
- ❖ The rostral auricular nerve
- ❖ The mesenteric nerve (not seen in figure 12.3)
- ❖ The mandibular alveolar nerve
- ❖ The mylohyoid nerve (not seen in figure 12.3)
- ❖ The masticatory nerve
- ❖ The pterygoid nerve (not seen in figure 12.3)
- ❖ The infraorbital nerve
- ❖ The cervical branch of the facial nerve

12.3 Nerve Supply of the TMJ

(1) rostral auricular nerve   (5) caudal auricular nerve
(2) infraorbital nerve   (6) facial nerve
(3) masticatory nerve   (7) cervical branch of facial nerve
(4) mandibular alveolar nerve

Vascular Supply

The common carotid artery and the external jugular vein provide the blood circulation to and from the upper neck and head area. These vessels divide themselves into many branches. The most adjacent vessels to the TMJ are:

❖ The occipital artery and vein located posterior to the TMJ

❖ The transverse facial artery and vein, located laterally to the TMJ

❖ The masseteric artery and vein, located latero-distally to the TMJ

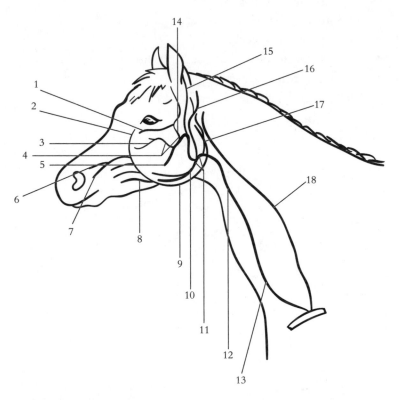

12.4 Arteries of the TMJ

(1) supra orbital artery
(2) angular artery [eye]
(3) intraorbital artery
(4) maxillary artery
(5) mandibular alveolar artery
(6) dorsal nasal artery
(7) lateral nasal artery
(8) facial artery
(9) masseteric artery

(10) linguofacial artery
(11) external carotid artery
(12) thyroid artery
(13) common carotid artery
(14) superficial temporal artery
(15) caudal auricular artery
(16) occipital artery
(17) internal carotid artery
(18) vertebral artery

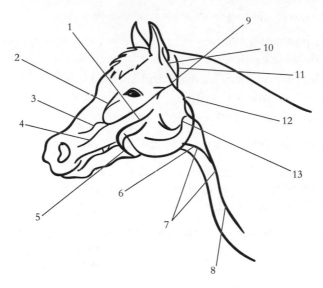

12.5 Veins of the TMJ

(1) deep facial vein
(2) angular vein of the eye
(3) dorsal nasal vein
(4) lateral nasal vein
(5) facial vein
(6) buccal vein
(7) external linguofaciabular vein

(8) external jugular vein
(9) transverse facial vein
(10) rostral auricular vein
(11) dorsal auricular vein
(12) maximillary vein
(13) masseteric vein

FASCIA OF THE HEAD

A continuation of the cervical fascia, both the deep and superficial layers, the fascia of the head may be divided into 2 groups:

❖ The *superficial fascia,* which forms an almost continuous layer except over the natural orifices—the eyes, nostrils, mouth, and ears—and provides attachment for the various cutaneous muscles

❖ The *deep fascia,* which can be further subdivided into the temporal fascia, the buccal fascia, and the pharyngeal fascia

MUSCLES OF MASTICATION

A good knowledge of the anatomy of the muscles and bones involved in the proper functioning of the TMJ is crucial for your understanding of their interrelation. It will contribute greatly to your expertise in assessing this condition and in treating it with massage.

The muscles responsible for closing the jaw are:

❖ The masseter muscle
❖ The temporalis muscle
❖ The pterygoideus medialis and lateralis
❖ The buccinator muscle
❖ The mylohyoideus muscle

The muscles responsible for opening the jaw are:

❖ The digastricus muscle
❖ The occipitomandibularis (deep) muscle
❖ The sternothyroideus muscle

The lateral swinging of the jaw from side to side during mastication is achieved by the alternate, unilateral contraction of the pterygoideus muscle—both the medialis and lateralis bundles on each side. Take note that the mandibular nerve lies between the two muscle bundles, so when applying massage over that area, start with a gentle pressure and only increase your pressure while observing the feedback signs given by your horse.

When there is a TMJ problem, upon palpation there is usually a marked variation within the temporal and masseter muscles. These muscles will be more developed on the side where most of

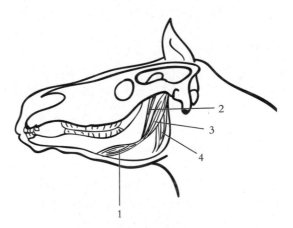

12.6 Muscles of the Jaw, Deep

(1) rostral portion of digastricus muscle
(2) stylohyoid
(3) digastricus (caudal portion)
(4) occipitomandibular portion of digastricus

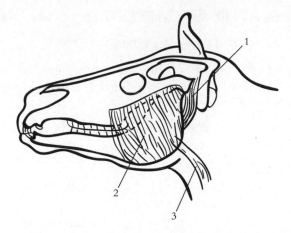

12.7 Muscles of the Jaw, Superficial

(1) occipitomandibularis muscle
(2) masseter muscle
(3) sternothyroideus muscle

the mastication occurs and underdeveloped on the side of little use. The extent of this variation is proportional to the degree of severity of the TMJ dysfunction.

Causes of TMJ Dysfunction Syndrome

The TMJ dysfunction syndrome is caused by inappropriate alignment of the joint and/or laxity of the supporting ligaments and muscles. Many of the following factors can trigger the TMJ dysfunction syndrome to develop:

❖ Dental problem and/or faulty teeth
❖ Upper cervical vertebrae misalignment
❖ Arthritis of the TMJ
❖ Trauma to the jaw, head, or upper neck
❖ Violent traction of the reins and bit
❖ Equine gastric ulcer syndrome

Signs and Symptoms of TMJ Dysfunction Syndrome

Here is a list of some of the most common signs and symptoms associated with TMJ dysfunction syndrome that you may observe in your horse's behavior:

- ❖ The horse starts shaking his head regularly, especially during exercise
- ❖ The horse avoids contact with the bit
- ❖ The horse plays with his tongue (tongue lolling)
- ❖ Some swelling over the joints
- ❖ Spasms, hyper tonicity, or trigger points in the mastication muscles
- ❖ When jaw is closed there might be some bruxism (grinding of the teeth); not to be confused with Equine Gastric Ulcer Syndrome
- ❖ Difficulty opening the mouth when bridling

Upon visual and palpation evaluation, you may encounter the following symptoms, even if minimal, in the early development stage:

- ❖ Muscle, fascia, and ligament tightness
- ❖ Jaw moving unevenly to one side
- ❖ Mastication action is tender to perform
- ❖ Mastication action only happens on one side
- ❖ There might be some restriction to open the jaw properly and fully
- ❖ There begins to be an offset alignment between the upper and lower rows of teeth
- ❖ Noticeable wear of the molars
- ❖ There might be some trigger points in the mastication muscles

TMJ Problems

Two types of lesions can develop in the TMJ due to the articular disc slipping forward or backward from its normal position as seen in figure 12.8.

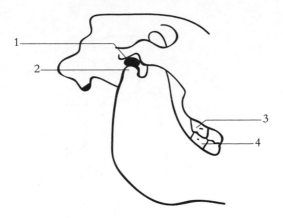

12.8 Healthy TMJ

(1) disc
(2) temporo-mandibular articulation
(3) third molar [maxillary]
(4) third molar [mandible]

CAUDAL LESION

A *caudal lesion* of the TMJ is a situation where the articular disc has slipped forward, and the head of the mandible has slipped backward, touching the temporal bone at the zygomatic arch, by the retro-articular process landmark as seen in figure 12.9. This will result in a reduced mouth opening for the horse and a greater difficulty in feeding himself.

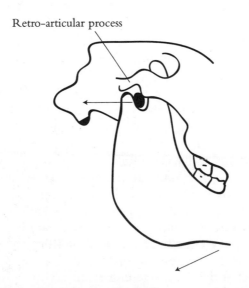

12.9 Caudal Lesion of the TMJ

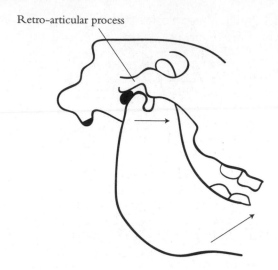

Retro-articular process

12.10 Rostral Lesion of the TMJ

ROSTRAL LESION

A *rostral lesion* of the TMJ is a situation where the articular disc has slipped backward, behind the head of the mandible, and between the retro-articular process of the zygomatic arch of the temporal bone as seen in figure 12.10, causing the mandible to protract.

If only one side is affected, the mandible will move towards the side opposite the luxation. The horse will be able to open his mouth, but will have problems closing it. This might cause him some difficulty in feeding.

PALPATION

As you proceed with palpation, constantly assess the horse's feedback signs (especially his eyes) to evaluate the presence of pain from inflamed muscles, ligaments, or the joint itself. Palpate the masseter, the temporalis, the pterygoideus medialis and lateralis, the occipitomandibularis, the digastricus, and the buccinator muscles for tone, tenderness, inflammation, and the eventual presence of trigger points and stress points. Referring to figures 12.4 and 12.5, note where the veins, arteries, and nerves are located. It is important to know what lies under your fingers.

Palpate the TMJ joint by placing your index finger on the horse's face in front of and slightly below the auditory canal of the ear (do not place your fingers in the auditory canal). With your other hand, force the horse to open and close his jaw. You should be able to tell if the jaw is opening evenly. During your palpation you may feel and/or hear a small "click." This is a sign of joint restriction and muscle tension.

CHECKING THE PROTRACTION AND THE RETRACTION OF THE MANDIBLE

Place yourself in front of the horse's mouth with one hand on the bridge of the horse's nose and the other on his mandible. Gently push the maxilla to the rear (caudally) while pulling the mandible to the front (rostrally). You should feel some play. If the horse's jaw protrudes, that is a good sign. Lack of protrusion could indicate a TMJ condition. Then reverse your pressure over the mandible to evaluate the movement to the rear (caudally). Lack of retraction could also indicate a TMJ condition.

Restriction in the protraction or retraction of the mandible could be revealing of a disc problem in the TMJ. It could also reveal muscular spasms, restriction of the hyoid bone, or some restrictions at the occiput and first cervical level, as well as a problem with dentition.

CHECKING THE LATERO-LATERAL MOVEMENT OF THE MANDIBLE

Stand in front of the horse's mouth, with one hand on the bridge of the horse's nose and the other on the mandible. While holding the maxillary steady, move the mandible to one side and then to the other. Do this gently, but firmly. Note if there is any restriction going to the right and then to the left.

Lack of free movement can be revealing of lesions at the teeth level, the disc level of the TMJ, or the occiput and first cervical vertebrae level; or of some muscle spasms.

CHECKING THE INCISIVE LINES

Examine the incisor teeth and the incisor lines. Gently open the lips of the horse's mouth. If the TMJs are healthy, the middle of the maxillary incisors should be aligned with the middle of the mandible incisors. The gum line between the incisor teeth should be aligned. If not, the direction of the deviation reveals the tighter TMJ side.

MASSAGE GUIDELINES FOR ETDS

The massage routine presented here is designed for the maintenance of the temporomandibular joint and the prevention of ETDS. The sequencing of the routine is important. Follow it

12.11 Checking Incisor Teeth

when starting your practice. Later, you can adjust the sequences to your liking, as you develop a feel for the horse, his needs, and what works best for him. Always monitor the horse's body language for feedback signs, especially his eyes.

Note: This routine is not suited for an acute phase of the ETDS condition. If the inflammatory symptoms are strong, massage is contraindicated. Please, first contact your veterinarian for the best course of action.

MASSAGE GOALS

Here are the goals for your massage session:

❖ To warm-up the upper neck and jaw area

❖ To promote circulation of fluids

❖ To reduce stiffness and pain/discomfort

❖ To reduce excessive fibrotic tissue formation

❖ To stretch for full mobility

❖ To reduce the compensatory muscular tension from indirectly affected structures

DURATION

The duration of this massage session varies according to the situation at hand and the goals you want to achieve. On average, it should last about 20 minutes. If inflammatory symptoms are present, keep your massage short to avoid soreness and use more cold hydrotherapy. Always check the horse's feedback signs, especially his eyes. Also, apply the neck stretching exercises (see chapter 8) either during or at the end of your massage session to maximize the flexibility of the tissues and joints you are working on.

THE RELAXATION MASSAGE ROUTINE

For the benefit of your work, I strongly recommend you apply the short version of the relaxation routine (see chapter 6) before starting your massage session over the TMJ.

NECK STRETCHES

Neck stretches will greatly contribute to the success of your massage applications for the horse with ETDS. Stretching the neck of a horse that shows signs of ETDS gives you feedback on the state of health of his muscles, fascia, and ligament structures, particularly in regard to their elasticity and tone. Any restriction during stretches reveals the actual location of tension (see chapter 8, page 176).

MASSAGE ROUTINE FOR ETDS

Following the application of the relaxation massage routine, start the massage routine for ETDS on the horse's left side. Spend a moment quietly breathing and talking softly with the animal. Then, gently place the palm of your left hand on the ridge of the horse's nose, and with your right hand start some gentle circular effleurage over the neck for a couple of minutes. Follow with the application of the SEW approach (see chapter 5) to warm up the entire neck area from the withers to the poll on both sides.

Then, begin loosening the muscles of mastication with your thumbs and/or fingers by kneading. If you find any trigger points and/or stress points, relieve them using the corresponding massage technique (see chapter 5). Apply the origin-insertion massage technique to the following muscles: the masseter, the temporalis, the pterygoideus medialis and lateralis, the buccinator, the mylohyoideus, the digastricus, the occipitomandibularis (deep), and the sternothyroideus. Use effleurage moves every 10 to 20 seconds to thoroughly drain the part you are working on. Work one side, then the other.

12.12 Kneading of the Cheeks

Now, apply some finger friction movements along the lower jawbone, the maxillary arch, and the base of the ears (be gentle!), the occipital portion of the cranium, and the upper vertebrae. For this part of the massage routine, you should consider working both sides, starting with the left. Always start with a very gentle pressure, progressively increasing to 5 pounds of pressure. You do not need more pressure.

Important recommendation: If an aspect appears tight, just work that area a little longer, not stronger. Intersperse with effleurage every 10 seconds. Please, study the anatomical structure thoroughly, so you know what to expect underneath your fingers (see figures 12.1 to 12.7). Be careful not to apply too much pressure over the nerve loop just below and in front of the ears, as well as over nerve endings.

When done, use the WES approach—Wringing, Effleurage, and Stroking—to thoroughly drain the areas you just worked on (see chapter 5). For this exercise, work one side at a time.

Next, take the ear at its base; pull it gently forward toward yourself, and with the other hand open the mouth exactly as you would to make the horse accept the bit. This action will relax tension in the swallowing mechanism; it will also work well in relaxing the upper neck. Use a lot of effleurages to drain the cheeks toward the ears and neck. Then place one hand on each ear, and starting very lightly, pull them outwardly for 3 to 5 seconds and gently release. Repeat 2 or 3 times.

12.13 Finger Friction of Cheeks A, B, and C

12.14 Ear Pulling

Follow with stretches (see chapter 8, page 176). First, gently
bring the head of the horse upwards. Use an incentive—a carrot
or biscuit—if needed. Try to hold that stretch for a few seconds.
It will stretch all the throat and lower aspect of the neck, as well
as the cervical fascia. Next, stretch the neck to the left and then to
the right. Place your incentive by the point of hip first, then by
the shoulder or even the withers if possible.

Check the opening of the mouth. Stand in front of the horse's
mouth, and gently place your thumbs on the bars of the maxilla.
Then push progressively toward the horse's back and up to gently
force the horse to open his mouth. Observe carefully the opening
of the mandible. See if it happens evenly on both sides, or if one
side is tighter than the other.

Check the restricted side of the mouth. Still standing in front
of the horse's mouth, gently place one thumb over the bar of the
maxilla on the tight side, and place your other thumb over the bar
of the mandible on the other side. Then, in a progressive manner,
push your thumbs in opposite directions, up over the maxilla,
down on the mandible. See how much movement there is, or how
much resistance there is. Then reverse the position of your thumbs
and check the other side. Compare your findings.

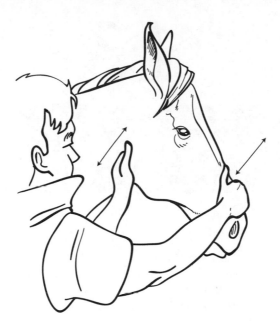

12.15 Jaw Rocking: *Right side of the horse.*

Jaw Rocking

The "jaw rocking" exercise is very efficient to loosen the TMJ deeply. First, stand on the left side of the horse. To perform this movement, place your left hand over the bridge of the horse's nose, and with your right hand gently grab the "angle" of the jaw bone. In a slow motion, gently rock the lower jaw, pushing back and forth. This will stretch the TMJ capsule and its collateral ligaments, and loosen them. When done, use some light stroking movement over that area, and duplicate the exercise on the other side.

Over several sessions, your horse will become more accepting of your massage. You will see some positive signs of improvement, such as the disappearance of the inflammatory symptoms, the jaw movements will be freer, and the horse will be back to his normal self.

Please, complement your massage session with a full body massage to further relax his nervous system and benefit his entire musculoskeletal system.

> The knowledge of equine temporomandibular dysfunction syndrome will help you to detect it and assist your horse's recovery. But most importantly, your awareness of ETDS will help you prevent it. This knowledge is a great addition to your massage skills. For more in-depth information on ETDS and massage therapy for ETDS, consult the author's work Equine Massage Therapy for the Equine Temporomandibular Dysfunction Syndrome.

13

This chapter will discuss the various lines of muscular and fascial compensation existing in the horse, or any quadruped as a matter of fact. When looking at a horse's skeleton, it is important to understand that the skeletal structure is made up of 3 important components:

* ❖ The spine, including the skull
* ❖ The forelimbs
* ❖ The hind limbs

The most important component is the vertebral column and the skull. They respectively secure the spine—a.k.a. the cauda equina—and the central nervous system. The tail of the horse, meaning the coccygeal vertebrae, is considered a part of the sacrum, and it plays an important role in balancing the horse's gait.

The skull and the sacrum are two ends of the same structure. There is an important relationship between the two extremities as they both play a role in the proprioceptor's feedback to the brain. These two extremities are vital for the overall balance of the horse. The deep fascia of one extremity influences the other. If the neck is experiencing discomfort, it will reflect directly over the sacrum. If the sacrum is experiencing discomfort, it will reflect directly on the neck.

Attaching to the spine are the thorax, the hips, and the fore- and hind limbs. The forelimbs are attached to the spine by the scapulas via the shoulder sling of muscles (trapezius, rhomboideus, serratus ventralis cranialis and caudalis, subscapularis). The scapulas move in relation to the thorax.

The hind limbs are attached to the iliums of the hip at the coxofemoral joint, where the head of the femur articulate in the

278

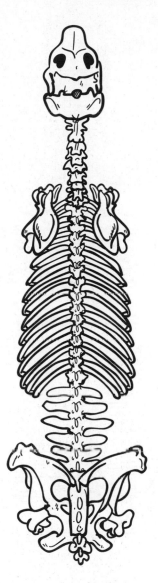

13.1 The Spine and Skull

acetabulum fossa of the hip. The hind limbs move in relation to the hips.

The coxofemoral articulation shows a similarity with the shoulder articulation and the temporomandibular articulation. All three articulations work in concert via muscular and fascial lines.

Figure 13.3 shows the network of 6 diagonal, 3 transversal, and 4 side lines of compensation seen in the horse.

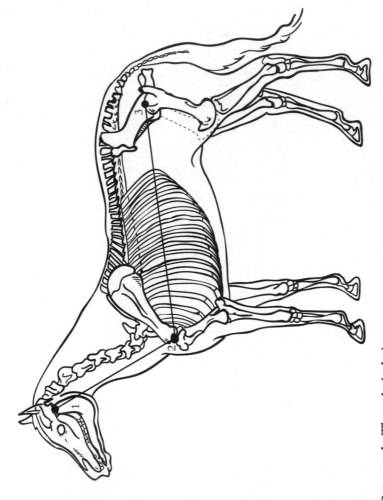

13.2 Relationship Between the Three Articulations

(1) the temporomandibular   (3) the coxo-femoral
(2) the scapulo-humeral

EXTERNAL LINES OF COMPENSATION

Understanding the lines of compensation can show you how a local problem can affect the rest of the horse and interfere with the horse's health and performance. *External lines of compensation* are the lines that affect the outer aspect of the horse, both in its superficial and deep muscle layers. There are 3 types of external lines: diagonal, transversal, and side lines.

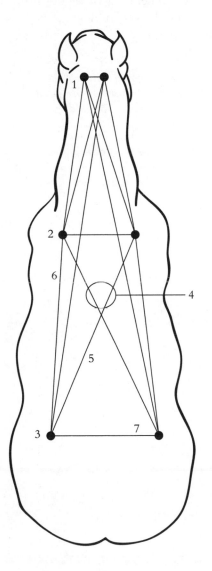

13.3 Lines of Compensation Network

(1) *temporomandibular*
(2) *scapulo-humeral*
(3) *coxo-femoral articulations*
(4) *center of gravity*
(5) *diagonal line of compensation*
(6) *transversal line of compensation*
(7) *side line of compensation*

DIAGONAL LINES OF COMPENSATION

Stress felt in areas on one side of a horse's body will be reflected on areas on the opposite side of the horse's body. Diagonal lines of compensation exist between the skull and shoulders, the shoulders and hips, and the skull and hips.

Between the Skull and Shoulders

The intersection point A of lines 1 and 2 on figure 13.4 is located approximately over the second and third cervical vertebrae, influencing the extensor and the flexor muscles of the neck, as well as the cranial, cervical, and omobrachial fasciae.

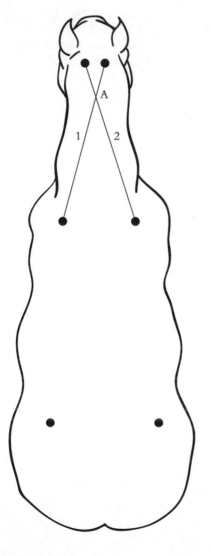

13.4 Diagonal Lines of Compensation Between Skull and Shoulders

(1) between the left shoulder and the right occipital protuberance
(2) between the right shoulder and the left occipital protuberance

Between the Shoulders and Hips

The intersection point B of lines 3 and 4 on figure 13.5 is located approximately over the eleventh and twelfth thoracic vertebrae, influencing the extensor and the flexor muscles of the back, as well as the omobrachial, thoracolumbar, gluteal, and the thorax and abdominal fasciae.

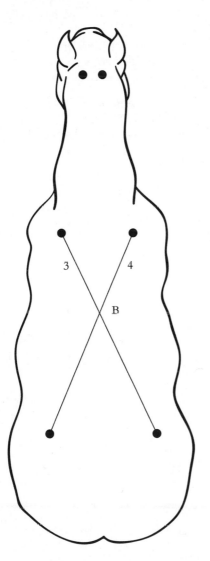

13.5 Diagonal Lines of Compensation Between Shoulders and Hips

(3) between the left shoulder and the right hip
(4) between the right shoulder and the left hip

Between the Skull and Hips

The intersection point C of lines 5 and 6 on figure 13.6 is located approximately over the fourth and sixth cervical vertebrae, influencing the epiaxial and the hypoaxial muscles of the spine, as well as the cranial, cervical, omobrachial, thoracolumbar, gluteal, thorax, and abdominal fasciae. Do not forget to consider the fascia of the limbs as well.

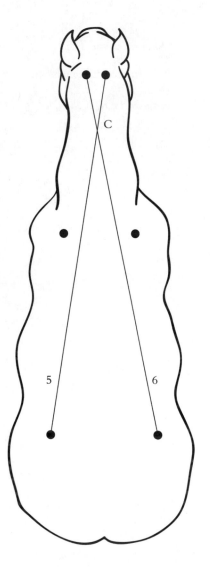

13.6 Diagonal Lines of Compensation Between Skull and Hips

(5) between the left hip and the right occipital protuberance
(6) between the right hip and the left occipital protuberance

Summary of the Diagonal Lines of Compensation

The crossing points A, B, and C will vary slightly length–wise (as in front to back), or even laterally, depending on the horse's gait and speed. Indeed, the horse's conformation, his shoeing, and the terrain he is moving on will also influence the distribution of muscular and fascial tension.

The two mastoid processes of the skull receive four lines of compensation from the other point of anchor. Notice how the hip directly relates to the neck. A bad case of sacrum luxation, or of a L5–L6 sub-luxation, can really influence the neck, affecting the horse's ability to carry his neck smoothly.

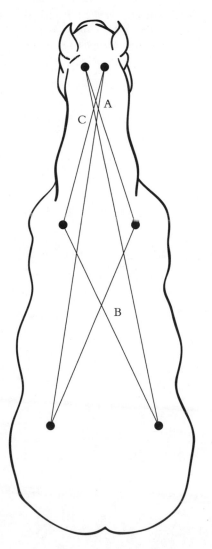

13.7 Diagonal Lines of
Compensation Summary

The hips receive four lines from the other point of anchor. Notice how the neck directly relates to the hips. A bad case of equine TMJ syndrome, or of a C0–C1 sub-luxation, can really influence the hind legs, reducing the energy generated by the horse's engine.

TRANSVERSAL LINES OF COMPENSATION

Transversal means between the two sides of the horse. The transverse plane runs perpendicular to the median plane that divides the body lengthwise in two equal halves. There are three main lines of compensation, those of the skull, the shoulders, and the hips.

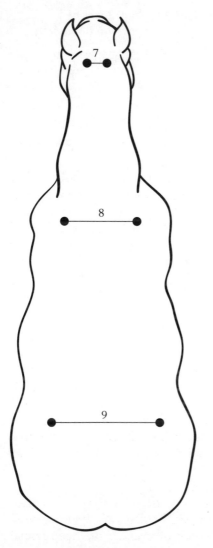

13.8 Transversal Lines of Compensation

It is important to acknowledge these transversal lines of compensation as they play an important role in equine locomotion at all gaits, but especially during the canter and gallop. During resting periods, a horse usually stands on one hind leg while resting the other.

These transversal lines become critical when the horse is recovering from an injury because he will shift his weight to avoid pain. A long period of recovery can lead to some very serious compensatory phenomenas in both the fascia and the muscles.

Lines of the Skull

Line 7 in figure 13.8 marks the transversal line of compensation between the occipital protuberances of the skull, influencing the upper attachment of the extensor and the flexor muscles of the neck, as well as the cervical fascia, and possibly the omobrachial and thoracolumbar fasciae. A bad case of equine TMJ syndrome, or of a C0–C1 sub-luxation, would quickly spread strong muscular and fascia compensation into the entire upper neck, making the horse very tender and reactive at the bit, even with fine hands.

Lines of the Shoulders

Line 8 in figure 13.8 marks the transversal line of compensation between the shoulders, influencing the shoulder girdle muscles, possibly the extensor muscles of the neck and back, as well as the omobrachial and antebrachial fasciae, and possibly the cervical and the thoracolumbar fasciae. Consider also the carpal, metacarpal, and digital fasciae of the lower foreleg. A bad case of uncomfortable shoes, eventually creating the beginning of an abscess, would quickly spread muscular and fascial tension over the entire shoulder area.

Lines of the Hips

Line 9 in figure 13.8 marks the transversal line of compensation between the hips, influencing the hip flexor and hip extensor muscles, possibly the extensor muscles of the back, as well as the gluteal and femoral fasciae, and possibly the thoracolumbar and abdominal fasciae and the fasciae latae. Consider also the crural, tarsal, metatarsal, and digital fasciae of the lower hind leg. Again, a bad case of uncomfortable shoes will eventually create the beginning of an abscess and quickly spread muscular and fascial tension over the entire hip area.

When a horse accidentally slides to the side with one leg underneath his belly, this will seriously affect his deep fascia and ligaments governing that side of the limb. Also, falls from uneven landings when jumping can cause a lot of stress in the deep fascia layers right down to the skeleton.

A myofascial massage technique, labelled the cross-hands technique (see chapter 11), was developed to address these transversal lines of compensation, especially over the hips and the thorax.

SIDE LINES OF COMPENSATION

Side lines are the lines of compensation on the lateral flank of the horse, parallel to the median plane. Side lines of compensation exist on both sides of the neck and trunk.

It is important to acknowledge these side lines of compensation as they play an important role in equine locomotion at all gaits, but especially during the canter and gallop. During resting periods, a horse usually stands on one side while resting the other.

13.9 Side Lines of Compensation

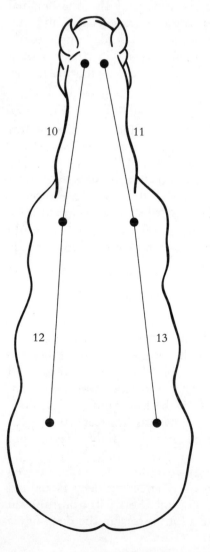

The transversal lines on the same side join forces with the side lines to offer better support. This is critical when the horse is recovering from an injury, favoring one side for a long period of time.

Lines of the Neck

Lines 10 and 11 in figure 13.9 respectively illustrate the side lines of compensation over the left and the right side of the neck, influencing the flexor and extensor muscles of the neck, as well as the cervical and omobrachial fasciae, and possibly the antebrachial fascia.

A bad case of cervical luxation (joint displacement) at any level along the seven vertebrae that comprise the cervical section would quickly cause muscular and fascial compensatory tension on either neck side.

Lines of the Trunk

Lines 12 and 13 in figure 13.9 respectively illustrate the side lines of compensation over the left and the right side of the trunk, influencing the extensor and the flexor muscles of the back, as well as the omobrachial, thoracolumbar, gluteal, and the thorax and abdominal fasciae. Consider also the carpal, metacarpal, and digital fasciae of the lower foreleg, and the crural, tarsal and metatarsal, and digital fasciae of the lower hind leg.

Here, too, a bad case of thoracolumbar or lumbo–sacral luxation (displacement) at any level along the 18 thoracic vertebrae that comprise the thoracic section or the 6 vertebrae that comprise the lumbar section, or the sacrum, getting out of alignment with the hips, would quickly cause muscular and fascial compensatory tension on either side of the body.

Left Side Lines of Compensation Together

Lines 10 and 12 in figure 13.9 reveal the horse's option to brace himself over his left side to further accommodate strong compensation from a problem arising on his right side, or sometimes on his left side.

Right Side Lines of Compensation Together

Lines 11 and 13 in figure 13.9 reveal the horse's option to brace himself over his right side to further accommodate strong compensation from a problem arising on his left side, or sometimes on his right side.

SUMMARY OF THE SIDE LINES AND TRANSVERSAL LINES OF COMPENSATION

These side lines of compensation relayed by the transversal lines are providing a kind of box for the horse: a box that helps him with his own awareness of proprioception in space. When the horse is at rest, using his stay mechanism so he can rest, these lines of compensation prevail.

A horse at "stall rest," recovering from a serious problem such as surgery or a fracture, will quickly develop compensatory tension along those lines. Both the transversal and the side lines of compensation will help him brace himself as a reflex to better

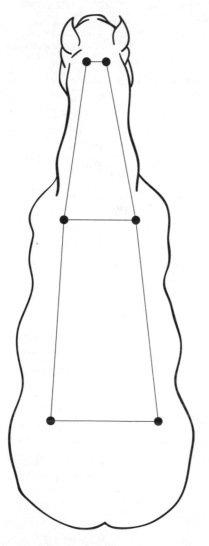

13.10 Transversal and Side Lines
of Compensation Summary

carry himself and avoid discomfort as much as possible. Indeed, depending on the nature of the problem at hand, even the diagonal lines of compensation may be involved.

SUMMARY OF ALL EXTERNAL LINES OF COMPENSATION

This study of all the lines of compensation seen in a horse shows you how a local problem can affect the rest of the body and interfere with the horse's general balance. As stated earlier in this chapter, the coxo-femoral articulation of the hip, the scapulo–humeral articulation of the shoulder articulation, and the temporo-mandibular articulation of the skull work in concert via all the muscular and fascial lines of compensation.

There are some movements that the horse does to the right, some to the left. He also moves his limbs forwards and backwards, adducts and abducts them, sometimes with a minimum of inversion or eversion of the hoof depending on the demands of the rider.

Please make an important note of:

❖ The location of the center of gravity sitting in front of point B, the crossing of the diagonals of compensation between the shoulders and hips

❖ The very busy crossings, points A and C in figure 13.11, over Cervical vertebra #2, 3, and 4 of the neck area

❖ You can quickly see that the withers are a key anchoring area of the equine anatomy. There are an equal amount of lines of compensation on either side of the withers; however, the withers anchor 12 lines of compensation plus the respective transversal lines.

❖ The two mastoid processes of the skull receive six lines of compensation from the other points of anchor plus the respective transversal lines.

❖ The hips receive six lines from the other points of anchor plus the respective transversal lines.

So when there is some restriction developing in any articulations and the associated muscles and fascia, you need to check on all the articulations. This thorough checking will allow you to better determine the source of primary or secondary compensation. This process will also contribute to a much better overall massage and lasting benefits.

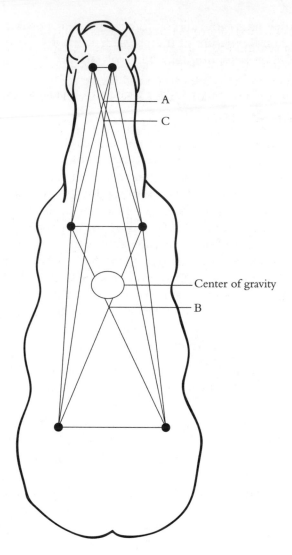

**13.11 External Lines of Compensation
Summary with the Center of Gravity**

INTERNAL LINES OF
COMPENSATION

As shown in figure 13.12, a horse's center of gravity is located along the median plane at the level of the middle of the eighth rib. It is well known that during locomotion the horse chases its own center of gravity. This leaves one wondering about the internal forces at play inside the core of the body cavities and along the spine. Unfortunately, no scientific equine research on this particular topic is available, but common sense prevails.

Figure 13.12 is a projection of the possible internal lines of compensation linking the center of gravity to the skull, shoulder, and hip articulations. Keep in mind that as these 6 lines of compensation converge at the same time to the center of gravity, they constantly influence each other in the overall determination of the horse's balance.

Figure 13.13 is another projection of the internal lines of compensation, this time including both the transversal and the side lines of compensation.

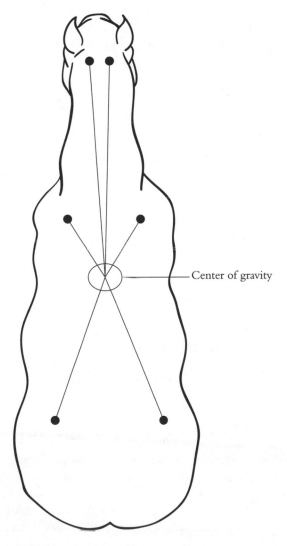

Center of gravity

13.12 Internal Lines of Compensation

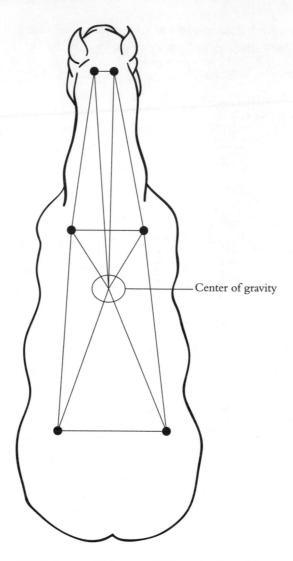

Center of gravity

*13.13 Internal Lines with Transversal and Side
Lines of Compensation*

INTERNAL COMPENSATION FROM THE SKULL

The neck is an important section of the body as it governs the initiation and direction of the horse's locomotion. Many of the equine disciplines such as dressage, jumping, polo, and reining really put a fair amount of stress over the neck structure. Any interference with the center of gravity will affect the neck's deep ligaments, such as:

❖ The ligamentum nuchae
❖ The supraspinous and the infraspinous ligaments

❖ The anterior and posterior longitudinal ligaments

❖ The interspinous ligaments of the spine

It would also be seen in the neck flexor muscles, such as:

❖ The longus capitis

❖ The longus colli

❖ The sternocephalicus

❖ The brachiocephalicus

And the neck extensor muscles, such as:

❖ The splenius

❖ The trapezius

❖ The rhomboideus

❖ The longissimus cervicis

❖ The iliocostalis

INTERNAL COMPENSATION FROM THE SHOULDERS

The shoulders are another very important section of the body as they give the horse stability by supporting the neck, providing suspension, providing steering, and translating the power coming from the hind legs into locomotion. Again, any interference with the center of gravity will affect the shoulder muscle structure, especially its medial aspect, such as:

❖ The subscapularis

❖ The serratus ventralis cervicis and the serratus ventralis thoracis

❖ The rhomboideus

As well as other shoulder muscles like the:

❖ The latissimus dorsi

❖ The trapezius

❖ The deltoideus

❖ The serratus dorsalis cranialis and the serratus dorsalis caudalis

❖ The longissimus cervicis and the rest of the foreleg muscles

INTERNAL COMPENSATION FROM THE HIPS

The hips are also an important section of the body as they provide the power for the horse's locomotion. All of the equine disciplines put a fair amount of stress over the hip structure. Any interference with the center of gravity will affect the hip's deep ligaments, such as:

- ❖ The dorsal sacro–iliac ligament
- ❖ The lumbar supraspinous ligaments
- ❖ The sacrosciatic ligament

It would also affect the medial aspect of the hip flexor muscles, such as:

- ❖ The psoas
- ❖ The iliacus
- ❖ The tensor fascia latae

And the medial aspect of the hip extensor muscles, such as:

- ❖ The gluteal muscle group
- ❖ The hamstring muscle group
- ❖ The rest of the hind leg muscles

Keep in mind that with jumping, the forces of suspension in the thoracic and abdominal cavities will directly add stress on the following muscles:

- ❖ The abdominal group of muscles
- ❖ The serratus dorsalis cranialis and caudalis

The thoracolumbar fascia will influence the hip flexor and extensor muscle groups as well as the deeper muscles of the spine (interspinalis, intertransversii, and rotators).

SUMMARY OF EXTERNAL AND INTERNAL LINES OF COMPENSATION

Figure 13.14 shows how both the external and the internal lines of compensation influence and affect the horse and its center of gravity at all times. Note how the withers and middle of the neck carry a lot of line intersections, emphasizing the stress level in these areas.

A solid knowledge of the equine lines of compensation is important as it helps you better understand the patterns of muscular and fascia compensation. This understanding will build up your confidence during your evaluation of the horse's muscles groups and your application of equine massage.

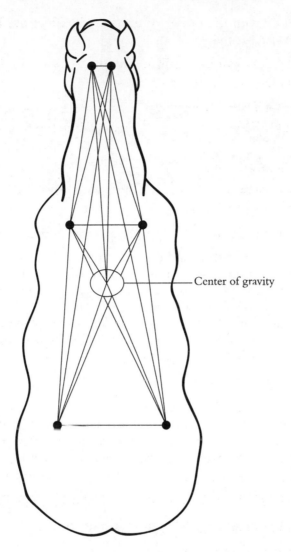

Center of gravity

*13.14 Internal and External Lines of
Compensation with Center of Gravity*

14

SADDLE FITTING

A fair number of muscle and skeletal problems seen in the active horse can be traced back to an ill fitted saddle. A saddle that causes discomfort to a horse not only inhibits the movement of that horse, but also leads to the formation of compensatory tension in both the fascia and the muscular systems as a horse always strives to keep optimal performance in relation to his center of gravity. The scientific definition of a *center of gravity* is: the point at the center of an object's weight distribution where the force of gravity acts. In other words, the center of gravity is that point where an object balances perfectly. The center of gravity in a horse is located at the intersection of the dotted lines as shown in figure 14.1.

Ideally, with the proper saddle, the rider's center of gravity should be above and in line with the horse's center of gravity. During faster paces, when the outline of the horse is lengthened, the center of balance moves forward. However, in dressage, during high collection where the croup is lowered, the center point shifts slightly backwards.

Regardless of the activity, training, and style, a saddle should conform to three basic requirements:

* ❖ The saddle should be comfortable for the horse
* ❖ The saddle should be comfortable for the rider
* ❖ The saddle design should help the rider maintain his/her center of gravity and be symmetrically balanced and aligned with the horse's center of gravity

A saddle that fits your horse well will allow him to perform without discomfort, allowing him to reach his full potential. Comfort for the horse is the result of a correctly fitted and balanced saddle. An unbiased saddle will distribute the weight evenly over the weight-bearing surface of the saddle and onto the back without afflicting the various muscle groups and fascia of the back.

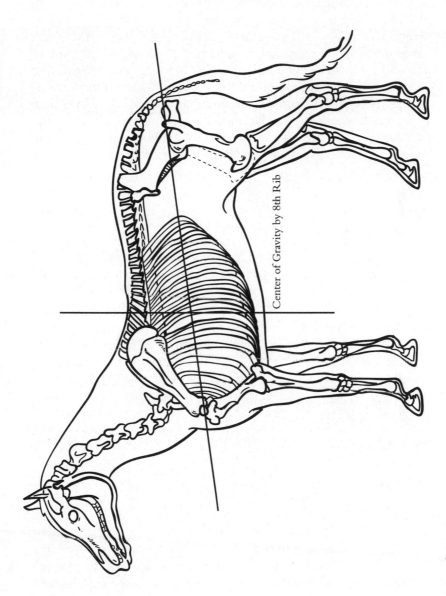

Center of Gravity by 8th Rib

14.1 A Horse's Center of Gravity

SADDLE TREE

The keys to a good saddle are its tree and panels. If the saddle's tree is the correct size, the rest of the completed saddle should follow suit. A saddle should not touch the horse's spine at any point. A badly fitting tree can cause pinching and pressure points in different musculoskeletal structures of the horse's back. The most common problem seen with a badly fitting tree is the pinching of the withers, which causes inflammation to spread directly over the trapezius, the rhomboideus, and the serratus dorsalis cranialis muscles, as well as the thoracic, shoulder, and neck fascia layers. In some cases where the saddle ends up touching the withers, the ligamentum nuchae over the thoracic spinous processes can become inflamed. Usually this type of incident will leave the horse with white hair over the area of contact.

SADDLE PANELS

The condition of the saddle's panels is equally important. To maintain balance they should be evenly and correctly stuffed, to compliment the build of your horse. The bearing surfaces should be equal in size. This will result in a stable and enhanced ride, as it will promote a central seat. For any rider, this will allow your horse to perform at his best.

To properly evaluate if a saddle is well balanced, you need to look at four basic standards:

❖ Even distribution of flock throughout the panels
❖ Close fit without spinal pressure at any point
❖ Overall balance
❖ As broad a bearing surface as possible to spread weight over the back

If, for any given saddle, any of these four points is not met, you can expect musculoskeletal problems to develop in your horse. The latissimus dorsi and the iliocostalis muscles are directly afflicted by the panel's contact as well as the thoracolumbar fascia. A saddle that does not fit your horse properly will cause him discomfort, leading eventually to pain. It will decrease the horse's ability to perform to its full potential. This imbalance will throw the rider's weight off equilibrium. To compensate for this, the rider will sit awkwardly, resulting in poor posture with resulting back stiffness. The horse also will compensate proportionally, resulting in extra muscle and fascial tension along his entire body, directly proportional to the imbalance.

Any incorrect saddle will disfigure any seat or leg aids and the horse might develop a constrained stride, a refusal to canter, a resistance to jumping, an unevenness of ride, or simply a refusal to ride.

If the pommel of the saddle is too high, it will tip the rider back causing excessive pressure in the area of the horse's back. This scenario will cause the horse to compensate with his hindquarters, mostly his gluteal, hamstring, and abdominal muscles, and possibly the tensor fascia latae muscle. This compensation results in a reluctance to work in a rounded outline or hollowness. Over a period of time, the back muscles will develop a dent where the panels touch and the thoracolumbar fascia will also become tense, causing some chronic rigidity over the back. The rider can easily fall behind the movement losing the ability to contain momentum and balance, especially in jumping.

If the pommel of the saddle is too low, it will tip the rider forward causing excessive pressure in the area of the horse's withers and shoulders, possibly limiting the range of motion of both shoulder blade bones. This scenario will cause the horse to tense up and compensate with his shoulder muscles, mostly his rhomboideus and trapezius, the triceps, possibly the serratus group, as well as the pectoral group of muscles and the foreleg muscles, resulting in a reluctance to work in an optimal forward stride. Over a period of time, the shoulder and neck fascia will also become tense, causing some rigidity over the neck action. With a saddle with too low of a pommel, the rider can easily fall out of sink with the movement rhythm, losing the ability to contain momentum and balance, especially in jumping. If there is contact between the saddle and the withers, an inflammation of the withers might result. In such cases, please consult your veterinarian.

The most common ill-fitted saddle problems come from unbalanced panels, which cause the rider's weight to fall to one side. Furthermore, uneven panels with lumps will cause concentrated areas of pressure—a sure way of causing sores and back disorders. This will stress the muscle and fascia of the horse's back causing a well-known problem termed "cold back." It refers to a *myositis,* meaning an inflammation of the muscle fibers of the back and loin muscles.

The horse with a *cold back* displays various signs and symptoms including discomfort when being saddled and/or when the rider is mounting, and during any bending exercises. The horse travels stiff behind, with short strides, and gets tired early. The more inflammation present in the muscles, the more severe the symptoms. The main muscles afflicted by this condition are the longissimus dorsi, the iliocostalis, the thoracolumbar fascia, the serratus dorsalis cranialis (also known as the spinalis dorsi muscle), the serratus dorsalis caudalis, and the abdominal muscles and fascia. They all are affected and show tension and soreness upon palpation. The severity of the symptoms can range from mild to severe soreness. When assessing back problems, consult a veterinarian; his expertise will determine the extent of the problem. If needed, infrared thermography and X rays can help determine the nature and severity of the problem. With this feedback, the veterinarian can deliver a precise diagnosis and decide on the best course of treatment.

Keep in mind that a horse with a sore back as a result of wearing a wrong saddle might prefer working on the rein, causing more muscular compensatory tension to develop in the neck muscles such as the deep splenius, the trapezius, and the rectus capitalis, as well as in the entire neck fascia.

Regardless of the type of ill-fitted saddle you may face, they all will give rise to stiffness and pressure injuries on the horse.

To assist such a horse, massage and hydrotherapy are of great help as they loosen the muscles and increase blood circulation, which in turn provide better oxygenation and nutrition of the tissues. This results in an overall increase of the healing for the sore muscles directly affected by the ill-fitting saddle. Massage will also relieve the compensatory muscular tension seen in the rest of the horse's body.

You can start helping your horse by applying some cold hydrotherapy over the back muscles (see chapter 4). Use cold sponging, ice packs, or the ice cup massage technique for about 10 minutes. This will have an analgesic benefit by numbing the nerve endings located in the sore muscle fibers. It will also cause some vasoconstriction. When you end the cold application, the body will respond with a strong vasodilation to bring blood back to the cool area and bring the cool part back to normal body temperature.

MASSAGE FOR COLD BACK

Start your massage for cold back with some light stroking movements over the entire back to let the horse know your intention to work this area. Follow with some light effleurage movements, going from the withers to the rump. Continue with 2 passes of gentle wringing movements across the entire back, from the withers to the lumbar area and back to the withers. Intersperse with effleurages every 10 to 20 seconds. If the horse appears very sore keep your pressure light and your session brief. It is better to repeat several small sessions and cumulate the benefits than overwork and cause more soreness.

If the horse is not too sore, after your last effleurages you can add some gentle thumb kneading, working the withers area first, moving along the trapezius and rhomboideus muscles, then the longissimus dorsi and the iliocostalis muscles all the way to the lumbar area over the origin tendon of the gluteals. Do not forget to effleurage every 10 to 20 seconds or so. All along, observe the horse's eyes to see his reaction to your pressure. If the horse appears to be enjoying your massage, then continue by using a gentle double hand friction all along the muscles to further loosen the tight fibers. Complete your work with lots of drainage to get circulation moving. Finish your massage application with lots of stroking movements to relax the muscles. Move on to the other side of the horse and repeat the entire sequence. Your entire massage session should last from 20 to 30 minutes, including hydrotherapy time when applicable.

Do not hesitate to re-apply some cold hydrotherapy over the back muscles right after your massage to further numb the nerve endings and to secure a good, lasting vasodilation. Always keep in mind that inflamed tissues are extremely painful. Use a very light pressure at all times and make sure your do not overwork them. In the early stage of cold back, during the acute phase, keep your overall treatment time very short. As the inflammation decreases and becomes more chronic, you can proportionally increase the duration of your massage sessions as well as the pressure used.

According to the severity of the inflammation, 3 to 5 sessions might be necessary to see this condition disappear. Give the horse's back a break for a few days if possible (no saddling) but keep him fit with longeing exercises. Consult your veterinarian to see if some anti-inflammatory medication might be prescribed to assist the horse during his recovery.

Daily care of your horse can speed up the recovery by 40 percent, a considerable benefit that not only helps your animal feel better, but also gets him back to work faster. Your devoted attention in that particular time of pain will strengthen your bond.

If your palpation over the horse's back has shown some abnormality in the alignment of the spinous and transverse processes of the vertebrae, or of the ribs, consult an equine chiropractor. Realigning the spine will greatly contribute to the overall recovery from a cold back.

WARNING

When the back muscle inflammation can be traced to an ill-fitted saddle over the withers, be aware that it can cause the tissues to become bruised. This is serious as there is a *contusion,* meaning a trauma to the blood vessels of the skin and/or muscles attaching onto the withers, with extravasation (leaking) of blood into the tissues. It is characterized by some swelling, heat, and pain, in varying degrees of severity proportional to the damage. When in doubt, please check with your veterinarian. Remember, massage is contraindicated during the acute phase (first 24 hours). However, cold hydrotherapy (ice cup massage technique, ice packs, or cold clay poultices; see chapter 4) is a very efficient way to reduce swelling and inflammation and permit blood clotting.

More rarely, an ill-fitted saddle over the withers can cause an inflammation of the bursa located on top of the backbone in the region of the withers. If untreated, this condition may develop into a more serious condition known as fistulous withers (swelling or abscesses at the withers). If a pustular infection is present, massage is contraindicated until cleared. See your veterinarian for a vaccination against brucellosis. Otherwise, first apply cold packs or use the ice cup massage technique to relieve the inflammation symptoms (see chapter 4). When in the subacute or chronic phase, follow with the massage swelling technique (see chapter 5) and lots of drainage to clear the excess fluid.

Understanding the importance of a good saddle helps you to take better action in the prevention of, or clearing of, a sore back condition. Prevention is everything. A saddle should be re-flocked every 5 to 6 months on average. The quality of the wool used makes a big difference. Talk to your saddle fitter.

15

Not all horses have the same physical ability to do everything that is asked of them. Some types of conformation are structurally better suited to perform in certain disciplines, and some breeds are better suited as well. For example, the breeds listed below excel in specific sports or disciplines:

- *Appaloosas and Paints:* endurance, eventing, western performance
- *Arabians:* show under saddle, endurance
- *Ponies:* hunter, jumper, driving, mounted games
- *Quarter Horses:* western performance, hunter, jumper, racing
- *Saddlebreds:* show under saddle, driving
- *Thoroughbreds:* dressage, hunter, jumper, eventing, racing
- *Warmbloods:* dressage, hunter, jumper, eventing

Each discipline or sport demands the best of the horse's physical capabilities, and of course, some classes demand more than others. The competitive nature of horse sports makes it necessary for the animal to use his entire body at once. Thus stress points (SP) can develop at any time and anywhere in the body. Specific activities definitely trigger the development of particular stress sites, particularly when the horse's conformation is not ideal for the work undertaken. For example, a longer-backed horse may be prone to develop more stress points than a shorter-backed horse. Similarly, a horse with a long cannon bone will tend to be more prone to tendon and ligament problems than a horse with a shorter cannon bone and proportionally shorter tendons and ligaments.

GUIDELINES FOR TREATMENT

Follow these treatment guidelines when working a horse, regardless of sport or discipline.

Hydrotherapy: Apply cold before and after treatment if acute inflammation is present. Use heat or vascular flush if there is chronic tension (see chapter 4).

Massage: Use the stress point check-up routine to evaluate any potential stress points, and the stress point technique (see chapters 10 and 5, respectively) to treat and thoroughly drain them. The nature of the training will help you identify the stress points. Apply any specific massage technique or routine you judge necessary (see chapters 5 and 6). In the case of exhaustion, use the recuperation routine to remove lactic acid buildup.

Always start with a light pressure and pay attention to your horse's feedback signs. Progressively warm up the area you need to work on. Frequently drain the area with lots of effleurages (every 20 or 30 seconds) and always finish with soothing strokings.

Stretching: Stretching exercises (see chapter 8) should be used as appropriate to assist the relaxation of the muscle groups.

The typical activities and disciplines described below will give you an idea of the nature of the stress encountered by a horse taking part in them. Since all muscles work simultaneously to produce smooth and coordinated action, you will rarely find just one stress point. Most likely, you will find several points in various parts of the body due to compensation.

SCHOOL HORSES

School horses can be any breed; they are usually calm and reliable with strong endurance qualities. Often they are older horses with lots of character and plenty of miles on their legs! These horses are used to teach any number of people how to ride. School horses spend hours each day moving in circles at all gaits (mostly walk/trot) with fairly inexperienced riders on their backs. New riders tend to ride with a heavy hand, which may cause the horse to become tense in the neck. Until beginner riders learn to balance on a moving horse, they tend to bounce around in the saddle, causing tenderness and perhaps inflammation in the horse's back muscles.

Problem Areas: Due to the nature of their activity, school horses will most often show neck and back problems in response to stress caused by inexperienced riders. The muscles along the spine (ilio-costalis dorsi and longissimus dorsi) show tension, stress points and, occasionally, inflammation. Use the stress point massage techniques and check stress points (SP) 20 and 21. Use lots of drainage. Sometimes SP 27 will also be sore because of stress in the neck area caused by constant pulling on the reins by the beginner riders. Check the jaw area and SP 1 to 8.

Shoulder and hindquarter stress points need to be checked when the horse is involved in jumping or is frequently used for lessons. Often you will find that older school horses show arthritic pain; gentle massage around the arthritic joint will help them feel better. Check adjacent muscle groups for compensation stress.

PLEASURE HORSES

Because pleasure horses are ridden by several members of a family, they will experience problems similar to those faced by school horses. Sometimes an irregular schedule can cause extra stress: for example, little riding in winter, a lot of riding in spring, little training during the week, a lot of exercise on the weekend. Since family members are often involved in a variety of activities, a pleasure horse may be expected to participate in jumping or western performance.

Even though pleasure horses are versatile, they will develop areas of tenderness as a result of the demands made on them during "fair weather" months, or as a consequence of irregular training schedules and the number of people riding them. A variety of breeds are used for pleasure riding, but those with versatility and a good nature tend to be favored.

Problem Areas: The problems of pleasure horses are very much like those of school horses. Depending on the horse's discipline, breed, conformation, and level of training, other stresses might occur.

Sometimes an irregular training schedule, such as several lazy days followed by a sudden burst of exercise, will cause a horse to tie up. When this happens, exhaustion is the result. The recuperation routine (see chapter 6) is the best course of treatment in this situation. Otherwise, follow the regular treatment guidelines.

HUNTERS

Hunters can be of any breed so long as they are sound and energetic. They need to be agile, smooth, and have a lot of strength and stamina. Of paramount importance is that hunters have good manners around hounds and other horses. The most prized and renowned hunters are those bred in Ireland from Irish draft and Thoroughbred stock. In show competition, riders tend to favor warmbloods, Thoroughbreds, and warmblood crosses.

Problem Areas: Running across uneven, sometimes rough terrain puts stress on the legs of the horse; check SP 12 to 19. Jumping puts stress on the chest, forelimbs, and the entire back during landing; check SP 5 to 8, 15 to 17, 20, and 21. During the takeoff for a jump, the hindquarters are under a tremendous amount of stress; check SP 28, 29, 34, and 35. The level of stress may vary depending on how the hunter is used. For example, in hunting, in which endurance is a factor, fatigue may cause compensation and other stress points to develop. In the show ring, the class a hunter is shown in and the difficulty of the course will be significant factors.

JUMPERS

Show or stadium jumping tests a horse's ability to jump a challenging course, usually within the shortest time possible and with the fewest faults. To participate in this very competitive discipline, a horse needs agility, balance, control, and power. To clear the heights and the spread of the obstacles, a horse calls on extraordinary strength from his muscles and ligaments. Jumpers can be of any breed, but Thoroughbreds and warmbloods dominate. Quarter Horses and crossbreeds are also shown successfully.

Problem Areas: During the take-off stage of the jump a lot of strain (proportionate to the height and spread of the fence) is put on the flexors, extensor muscles, tendons, and ligaments of the hindquarters; check SP 27 to 29 and SP 34 to 40.

Landing puts a good deal of strain on the flexor muscles, tendons, and ligaments of the foreleg (SP 13, 14), the entire shoulder (SP 9 to 11), and the chest muscles (SP 15 to 17) as well as the entire back (SP 5, 20, 21). The impact of the landing causes neck tension (SP 3, 4). Pay attention to the tendons of the foreleg and pasterns, especially if they are long.

Depending on the rider's style, the croup and the side muscles of the back (the spinalis dorsi, longissimus dorsi, and costarum muscles) may be very tense.

Footing is very important. Slippery ground may cause a tendon strain because the horse tenses up to avoid a fall. Ground that is very soft or deep makes it difficult for the horse to pick up his feet. As a result, a ligament sprain may occur in the foot structure because the joint is required to stretch beyond its regular range of motion. Correct shoeing can do much to compensate for less-than-ideal ground conditions.

DRESSAGE HORSES

Dressage horses are trained to perform with elegance and finesse of execution. To accomplish this they must demonstrate control, accuracy, and flexibility, and be extremely sensitive to the rider's aids. Good conformation is essential because of the demands dressage makes on a horse's body. The nature of the work involved in this discipline requires great muscle control and coordination on the part of the horse. Dressage horses at high levels are disciplined specialists whose muscle development and carriage are quite different from that of comparably advanced hunters, jumpers, or eventers.

Today, a high proportion of the horses seen in the dressage arena are German, Dutch, Swedish, and Danish warmbloods, and Andalusians from Spain. However, many Thoroughbreds, Quarter Horses, and a surprising number of Appaloosas do very well at dressage.

Problem Areas: The entire body of the dressage horse has great demands placed up on it, especially the hindquarters. Thus stress may occur in the back, hips, stifles, and hocks. Check the back (SP 21, 22, 25) and the hindquarters (SP 28, 29, 34, 35), as well as the hocks and lower legs.

Lateral work (side passes and bending) contributes to stress buildup in the chest (SP 24), shoulders (SP 9, 10), back (SP 21 to 25), hips (SP 25, 36 to 38), and legs, including the inner legs (SP 15 to 17, 33). Shoulders should move freely; any restriction in the leg extension is unacceptable in dressage. Work the legs thoroughly (stretch when warmed up).

Collection can make the horse tense in the jaw area and develop stress points in the neck (SP 1, 2). Work the jaw, throatlatch, upper neck, and base of the neck.

EVENTING HORSES

Eventing comprises three tests over a period of three days: dressage, stadium jumping, and cross-country. Eventing is an extremely demanding equestrian activity, particularly since each phase's requirements are very different.

To succeed at eventing, or combined training, the horse is required to display courage, intelligence, decisiveness, power, endurance, skill, and obedience. Only a horse capable of using the thrust and shock-absorbing capacity of his hindquarters and fore-quarters correctly will be able to sufficiently reduce the strain on the tendons and muscles to cope with the demands of the three phases of competition. This discipline requires an extraordinarily high level of fitness and competence from both horse and rider. But even those horses that are fit to compete may show signs of tying up or colic, which could be influenced by weather conditions or the stress of the competition itself. Thoroughbreds and warmbloods (Hanoverians, Trakehners, etc.) usually compete in eventing.

Problem Areas: All muscle groups incur a good deal of stress; inflammations and contractures are common, especially in SP 2, 5, 11, 21, 27, 28, and 34. Proper conditioning is very important in building up the tendons, ligaments, and muscles to prevent sprains, strains, inflammations, and stress points.

ENDURANCE HORSES

Competitive trail riding and long-distance riding tests the endurance and stamina of both horse and rider. Endurance competitions take place in an established time frame over distances ranging from 25 miles to 100 miles and over trails with varied terrain, including steep hills and natural obstacles. During the ride, the physical condition of the horse is monitored at regular intervals. At the end of the ride, the horse must show very close to the same physical statistics (pulse and respiration rate, hydration) as he did at the start of the ride.

All breeds of horses compete in endurance, but serious competitors prefer the Arabian horse and Arabian crosses. It is said that the shorter back, very dense bone, and natural ability of Arabians to go for long periods of time with little food or water are what make them a favorite choice for endurance riding.

Problem Areas: Exhaustion, dehydration, electrolyte imbalance, tying up, inflammation, and muscle contractures are the principal problems. The recuperation routine (see chapter 6) is often used on endurance horses right after the race. Tension will develop in the entire body, but especially in the muscles of the back (SP 5, 20, 21, 27).

Polo Ponies

Polo is an exciting and spectacular game in which two opposing teams of four players on horseback use mallets to score goals with a ball.

In order to execute the quick starts, abrupt stops, and sharp 180-degree turns that are of prime importance in the game, the polo "pony" must be extremely well-balanced, agile, fast, competitive, and obedient. Polo ponies must be able to turn on a dime and do flying changes of lead, sliding stops, and neck rein.

The horses commonly used in this sport are not usually more than 15 hands high. Small Thoroughbreds and Quarter Horse crosses are used, but the specially-bred Argentinean Thoroughbreds (Argentinean ponies) are preferred by the high-goal and serious international players.

Problem Areas: All ligaments and muscle groups of the leg are under constant stress. Strains and "fat" (bowed) tendons are common.

The game's quick starts and sharp turns will cause tension buildup, leading to the development of stress points in the horse's hindquarters (SP 27 to 35) and the small of the back (SP 21 to 25). The constant changing of direction and pulling on the reins will cause the upper and lower parts of the neck to develop stress points (SP 1, 2, 3, 8).

The abrupt stops cause tension in the chest muscles (SP 15, 16), rib cage (SP 23 to 26), and abdominal muscles (SP 22 to 25). Also, as a result of the fast pace of the game, lactic acid builds up considerably during this demanding activity; therefore the recuperation routine (see chapter 6) is very helpful, especially after a game.

Western Performance Horses

Western performance competitions include action-packed sports such as reining, cutting, barrel racing, calf-roping, team penning, and steer-wrestling. Each discipline has its own unique and highly technical skills that have to be mastered by both horse and rider.

The horses taking part in these sports must possess great agility and coordination, excellent reflexes, stamina, and a capacity for sudden bursts of speed. The horses most commonly found in these disciplines are Quarter Horses, Pintos, Paints, and Appaloosas.

Problem Areas: Due to the quick starts, stops, and changes of direction associated with these sports, there are several areas of potential tension buildup in western performance horses. Stress points may develop in the hindquarters (SP 27, 34, 35), back (SP 5, 20, 21), base of the neck (SP 3, 4, 8), and shoulders (SP 9, 10, 11, 15), with the possibility of strong tension in the tendons and ligaments of the lower legs.

Reining horses may have stress points in the back and hindquarters, as well as the entire length of the hind legs. The hocks are especially affected since these horses are required to perform spectacular sliding stops that put more stress on these areas than on the rest of the body. The chest and neck muscle groups may also show tension.

When working cows, cutting horses keep their forequarters, head, and neck low while making extremely quick side-to-side movements. The hindquarters, used as pivot points, are well under the horse and carry most of his weight. Consequently, this action will cause cutting horses to show stress points in the neck, shoulders, chest, back, and hindquarters as a result of tension buildup. The tendons and ligaments of the legs, especially the hocks, may also show signs of stress.

GAITED HORSES

Gaited horses, whether under saddle or in harness, have an animated way of moving. Gaited horses typically are smooth-riding, sure-footed, and can be three- or five-gaited. (The three basic gaits are the walk, trot, and canter; further training and ability are required to produce the slow gait and the rack.) Popular breeds include the Tennessee Walking Horse, the American Saddlebred, the Missouri Fox Trotter, the Paso Fino, and the Peruvian Paso.

Problem Areas: The horses that perform these gaits may develop stress points in the muscles of the neck (SP 1 to 4), shoulder and foreleg (SP 6 to 14), chest (SP 15 to 17), abdomen (SP 24), and stifle area (SP 31, 32). Especially affected are those horses that do not perform certain gaits naturally. Unlike the driven horse, the ridden horse may experience tension in the muscles of the back caused by the weight of the rider.

FLAT RACING HORSES

Flat racing has been a popular sport for hundreds of years. Only those horses with exceptional speed and stamina are raced on the flat. Two breeds dominate racing in the United States: the Thoroughbred and the Quarter Horse. They race over different distances and different kinds of tracks, however.

Problem Areas for Thoroughbreds: Thoroughbreds are very long-legged with proportionally long bodies; therefore, their long muscles and tendons could show signs of tension. The neck (SP 1, 2), chest (SP 11 to 17), back (SP 5, 20, 21, 27), and hindquarters (SP 28, 29, 34, 35) may develop tension. Because of the intensity of the race, lactic acid buildup and occasional inflammation may be found in overworked muscles.

Problem Areas for Quarter Horses: Due to the quick starts of the races, the hindquarters of the Quarter Horse tend to show most of the tension and may develop stress points (SP 27, 28, 34, 35). The chest, back, and legs may also experience a lot of tension buildup, resulting in stress points (SP 5 to 11, 17, 20, 21). Because of the intensity of the race (usually sprints on a straightaway), toxin buildup and occasional inflammation may be found in overworked muscles.

STEEPLECHASE HORSES

Thoroughbreds also compete in steeplechase races, at distances of 2 to 4 miles. The horse jumps over massive hedges, fences, and ditches during the course of the race. Steeplechasers share similar qualities of speed and stamina with horses that compete in eventing.

Problem Areas: Steeplechasers may have stress points mostly in the muscles of the back (SP 5 to 8, 20, 21, 27) and hindquarters (SP 28 to 30, 34, 35), but also in the chest (SP 15 to 17) and shoulders (SP 9 to 14) due to a buildup of tension from running and jumping. The tendons and ligaments may also show signs of tension because of the force encountered during the landing phase of the jump. Chances are all the muscle groups will need work. The intensity of racing can cause inflammation of the tissues and trigger a buildup of toxins.

HARNESS RACING HORSES (TROTTERS AND PACERS)

Harness racers are bred for their speed in pulling *sulkies,* which are light, 2-wheeled, single-seat vehicles. Standardbreds are specifically bred for harness racing, which requires speed above all, but also staying power and stamina.

In harness racing, the horse is either a trotter or a pacer. In the *trot,* the opposite front and rear feet push off and land at the same time. In the *pace,* the front and hind feet on the same side push off and land together.

Problem Areas: Trotters and pacers develop problems in the hindquarters (SP 28 to 30, 34, 35), the small of the back (SP 20, 21, 25, 27), the neck, and the jaw (SP 1, 2). The harness may cause tense muscles at the base of the neck and in the chest (SP 3, 4, 15). Both trotters and pacers experience inflammation throughout their bodies because of the repetitive nature of the gaits they perform. Most likely because of the nature of the movement, horses that pace are found to have slightly more tension behind the shoulder and in the rib cage area (SP 11, 12, 23, 26). Pacers do not stretch these muscles as fully as trotters do.

LIGHT HARNESS HORSES

There are almost as many competitive classes in which to drive a light horse as there are for riding them. Each discipline requires a specific type of horse, harness, and vehicle, as well as a specific number of horses in the team (for example, single, double, tandem, four-horse hitch). Even with the variety of horses and vehicles, there are basically only two kinds of harness: the *fine harness,* with a breast collar; and the *heavier harness,* complete with a neck collar and hames.

Many different breeds of horses are used in driving, among them: the Arabian horse, the American Saddlebred, the Hackney horse and the Hackney pony, the Morgan horse, the Hungarian Trotter, the Thoroughbred, the Pony of the Americas, the Connemara Pony, the Shetland Pony, and the Welsh Pony.

Problem Areas: Light harness horses tend to develop stress points as a result of tension buildup in the upper and lower neck (SP 1 to 4), shoulder, and chest area (SP 6 to 12, 15). This tension is due to their high head carriage and pressure from the collar. The horses involved in the more demanding sports of combined driving and western chuck-wagon races not only show tension in the neck, shoulder, and chest, but also in the tendons and ligaments of the lower legs (SP 18, 19, 39, 40). *Wheelers*—horses closest to the wheels of the vehicle—will also show tension in the hindquarters (SP 27, 28, 34, 35) since they are the power of the team.

DRAFT HORSES

Until a few generations ago, draft horses were the engines that provided the power for farming and transportation in most areas of the world. Today, these gentle giant breeds—the Belgian, the Clydesdale, the Percheron, the Shires, and the Suffolk, to name a few—are enjoyed in the show ring and in intense pulling competitions, where a heavy team may pull upwards of 3,000 pounds!

Some farmers and loggers still use them, and so do people who love hayrides.

Draft horses have broad, powerful chests, wide girths, short backs, short and muscular necks, long powerful shoulders, and muscular croups. Their legs are solid, with well-developed quarters, broad feet and short cannons and pasterns.

Problem Areas: Generally, these large horses may show slight tension in the lower neck, chest, and hindquarters. But the horses particularly used in heavy pulling may show stress points in the shoulders (SP 11, 12), chest (SP 15 to 17), hindquarters (SP 27, 28, 35, 36), and legs (SP 18, 19, 29, 30) as a result of tension buildup.

For treatment, follow the guidelines at the beginning of the chapter. Use proper posture, especially with these horses, to ensure that your body weight is used to reach the deeper muscle layers.

A solid understanding of the various breeds of horses will inhance your ability to assess muscular tension in relation to the discipline practiced by that animal.

16

Keeping records of your massage work and findings after each session is as important as keeping records of farrier and veterinarian visits. It will help you better chart the progression of your work.

This chapter gives you a complete set of instructions on how to keep proper records, especially if you plan on practicing as a professional. However, if you will only work on your horse(s), once you have taken a complete initial case study, then you only need to keep updating your findings and work program.

For a complete case study (figures 16.1 to 16.4), your records should contain:

❖ History and background information (to the best of your knowledge) on your horse, such as previous training or accidents and injuries that might have taken place

❖ Personality traits, for example, nasty in stall, biting, kicking, cribbing, weaving, etc.

❖ Medication(s), if any

❖ Type of training he is involved in at the present time, plus his tendencies during training, i.e., trouble picking up leads, bending, lateral work, etc.

❖ Note the overall condition of your horse at the time of each massage. List the various stress points, trigger points, inflammations, swellings, if any, and the finding of your four T's.

❖ If your horse gets hurt (either in training or at play), record what happened, how it happened, when it happened, and where on the horse the injury is located. Also note what treatment was given at the time.

❖ When changing tack (bit, saddle, bridle, harness), record when the change took place, and how the horse responded to the change over the following 7 to 10 days.

316

This information will help you appreciate the progress of your horse following your massage treatments. By keeping thorough notes you will have a clear idea about any changes in the symptoms shown by your horse.

Good records will also give you feedback on the impact of your training program and changes in your horse's life (e.g., traveling, competitions, new barn, etc.). Knowing your horse well will assist you in determining the best maintenance massage program.

With regular massage, you will become aware of signs and symptoms that will tell you when your horse needs veterinary attention much sooner than with just your usual practice of grooming.

You will never look at or touch your horse the same way again. Enjoy your new awareness!

BASIC INFORMATION ABOUT THE HORSE

In this section of the case history you record:

- ❖ The horse's name, breed, pedigree, color, size, weight, age (with date of birth, if known), any acquired scars or congenital markings, conditioning (low, moderate, high), whether the horse is overweight or underweight and, if applicable, the type of work the animal does and has done. Take note of the general health condition (and any signs of disease) of the coat, skin, eyes, pulse, temperature, and respiration; and finally, note the actions, personality, and overall appearance of the horse.
- ❖ The owner's name, address, and telephone number; name and phone number of the establishment where the animal is boarded; the veterinarian in charge; the trainer; and the farrier. Record the name, address, and phone number of any applicable medical insurance company; keep track of all additional relevant information on a separate sheet.

THE MAJOR COMPLAINT

For this section of the case history you want to find out and record as much information as you can regarding the problem you have been solicited to address. The following question outline will help you in this matter:

What: What happened to cause this problem or lameness? What kind of pain or lameness (sharp, dull, or excruciating; constant or intermittent)? Has it changed at all in quality or intensity since the onset? Was the onset gradual or sudden (what was happening before and during the initial signs)? What aggravates the pain? What relieves it? Is it any better or worse in the morning or the evening? How do the symptoms affect the horse in daily life (work, rest, play, etc.)? Is there anything that is difficult or impossible for the horse to do since the onset of the problem?

It is very important to record notes in the owner's own words. Avoid too many direct or specific questions at first, but after the initial conversation, ask away. Recording the signs and symptoms will help you determine if the situation is treatable by massage technique or not.

When: How long ago did it happen? Find out whether the problem is in an acute stage (first 24 hours), a subacute stage (24 to 72 hours), or a chronic stage (after 3 days).

Where: What body parts are affected directly and indirectly by referral pain? (Example: Inflammation of the withers with referred pain along the back muscles and compensatory tightness in the neck and shoulder muscles.) Are there other symptoms associated with the problem, such as weakness, loss of appetite, sweating, abnormal swellings, or fever?

How: How did it happen? In what way? Was an injury or unusual activity involved? Was there a trauma (such as a kick) or did it result from an old injury? Are there any lesions? Has there been too much exercise or a too-heavy workload on the muscle structures? Is there bacterial infection? In some cases, it may be impossible to get any information on how the problem occurred; you'll hear, "He came from the field like this."

THE HISTORY OF THE PRESENT ILLNESS OR PROBLEM

For this section, find out whether the problem has a known history. Have these symptoms occurred previously? Take notes of all details regarding the what, when, where, and how. Discover when the injury or symptoms first occurred and what type of therapy and veterinary work was done at that time.

Find out whether or not there have been changes in the horse's routine: feed change, moving stables or barns, different farrier, shoeing changes, or changes in training.

THE HISTORY OF PAST ILLNESSES OR PROBLEMS

For this section you want to find out:

* ❖ The horse's general health
* ❖ What other injuries have happened to the animal during the course of his life. Record what, when, where, how.
* ❖ Whether the actual problem might be secondary to a previous problem

Do not forget to consider that some problems might be of genetic origin. For example, a bone deformity (scoliosis, lordosis) can cause chronic muscle tension.

CLINICAL EXAMINATION

Palpate and evaluate the overall structures of the body, going over all muscle groups and joints in order to determine the quality and present state of the physiology of the animal. In chapters 9 and 10, you learned how to do a primary assessment in great detail. This is where you use that knowledge to size up the animal as you go along and to modify the assessment process to suit the occasion.

Remember the four T's (tension, texture, tenderness, and temperature; chapter 3).

Also check the horse's conditioning (low, moderate, high), whether he is overweight or underweight, and the condition of his coat, skin, and eyes. Take the pulse and temperature. Check the depth and frequency of respiration. Make a good overall appreciation of the animal.

All this will help you verify your notes and detect problems that may not be obvious at first.

Have the horse exercise in front of you to assess his actions and gait, first at a walk and then at a trot. This activity will help you determine the depth of discomfort and whether the problem is muscular or structural. After the muscles of the horse are warm, include stretching moves to check the range of motion of each limb, the neck, and the back.

Use your stress point check-up routine to assess possible stress point buildup in response to the problem, or to evaluate the level of training when dealing with an athletic horse (chapter 5).

At this point of your case history you should know if there are any contraindications that may apply (chapter 2) and whether you can treat this particular problem or not.

TREATMENT

Now you can decide on the course of your first treatment. Take notes on what you do:

❖ The type of hydrotherapy used when applicable (see chapter 4)

❖ The type of massage routines or techniques used (see chapters 5 and 6)

❖ The type of stretching exercises, if applicable (see chapter 8)

Record the horse's feedback signs during the treatment, the change or relief of the signs and symptoms (if any), and any other relevant information.

PROGRAM

For this section, you estimate how many sessions it will take for a full recovery. At the same time, determine the time frame of the applications; for example, the treatment of chronic tension should require a 45-minute massage session plus 15 minutes of hydrotherapy (one half before and one half after massage) once a day, every day for 5 days.

Specify the type of massage technique to apply or routine to follow. Give such details as the pressure to use, the type and frequency of hydrotherapy to apply, and the type of stretching exercises. The more information you offer, the better the chances of success.

MAINTENANCE

For this section, you determine the maintenance program in conjunction with the recovery process. For example, it might require light exercising such as walking or longeing, circles, figure eights, sand pit work, and so on.

UPDATES

Systematically update your case history by recording the details of each treatment you give to the horse. Note the evolution of the condition, what you did during each treatment, the reaction of the animal, and your prognosis for further treatments and recommended exercises.

A good case history is the foundation of both assessment and treatment. Accurate notes will give you the facts you need to work with. A case history will serve as a guide for further therapy and also as a record which may be of use in the future.

Once you are comfortable with learning how to recognize and describe abnormalities, the time to perform the complete examination and the taking of notes will be greatly reduced.

Maintaining good clinical records of treatment will make it possible for you to accurately discuss problems with veterinarians or other equine therapists. Always consider the recommendations of the veterinarian when determining the course of treatment.

A good case history will show your professionalism and will greatly contribute to your success.

CASE STUDY

Name: _____

Breed: _____

Colour: _____

Size: _____

Weight: _____

Born: _____ Age: _____

Markings: _____

_____

_____

Discipline: _____

Date: _____

EQUINE MASSAGE *Awareness*

Box 1395 Station B, Ottawa, Ontario CANADA K1P 5R4
Tel (613) 789-5422

Owner: _____

Address: _____

_____

Tel: _____

Stable: _____

_____

Tel: _____

Vet: _____

Tel: _____

Farrier: _____

Tel: _____

Conditioning: ☐ Low   ☐ Moderate   ☐ High   ☐ Overweight   ☐ Underweight

Major complaint: What, Where, When, How: _____

_____

History of present illness: _____

History of past illnesse(s): _____

Examination/palpation: _____

_____

_____

Treatment: _____

_____

_____

Maintenance Program: _____

_____

DATE	DATA/EXAM	TX & RESULT	RECOMMEND

16.1 Case Study

CASE STUDY

Name: _Napoleon_
Breed: _1/4 Horse_
Colour: _Buckskin_
Size: _15.2 hh_
Weight: _1,000 lbs_
Born: _1984_ Age: _12yr._
Markings: _Star_
wt. socks - both hind legs

EQUINE MASSAGE Awareness
Box 1395 Station B, Ottawa,
Ontario CANADA K1P 5R4
Tel (613) 789-5422

Owner: _Terry Brown_
Address: _Box 595 Sta. A._
Ottawa, Ont. K1P 0H7
Tel: _(613) 233-6496_
Stable: _(Private) #2180 - 8th Line_
Lanark, Ont.
Tel: _(613) 287-3245_
Vet: _Dr. Jackson_
Tel: _(613) 745-2830_
Farrier: _Karl Roberts_
Tel: _(613) 968-4214_

Discipline: _pleasure, horseball, jumping_
Date: _July 7th/96_

Conditioning: ☐ Low   ☐ Moderate   ☒ High   ☐ Overweight   ☐ Underweight

Major complaint: What, Where, When, How: _Restricted in hind when working circles_
- occasional lameness - sore (R) stifle area.

History of present illness: _occasional lameness - no apparent reason - (horse purchased 1 yr ago)_

History of past illness(es): _Do not know -_

Examination/palpation: _Point of sacrum higher on (R) side. Associated tightness in gluteus mm._
quadriceps + biceps femoris mm - Latissimus dorsi shows tightness & stress pt. at L1 level.
(R) stifle - slight swelling - no inflammation - general tension in both hind legs - withers tender.

Treatment: _Warm-up routine - trigger + stress pt. tech. on muscles of hind legs (R)_
Pumping technique over sacrum - lots of effleurage - drainage + swelling techniques (R)
Stifle - drainage over neck, + back, especially withers. (kneadings + effleurage) - general strech

Maintenance Program: _general maintenance massage + cold hydrotherapy over (R) stifle_
daily. - general stretching routine every other day.
very tight (R) hind
Stretch!

DATE	DATA/EXAM	TX & RESULT	RECOMMEND
July 14/96 1 hr. Tx. (recipt.)	Same condition - 2nd Tx. - More relaxed overall - sp. hind leg (R) - withers much better - still tender - sacrum - normal - stifle tender - little puffy. - no inflammation	- warm-up routine - swelling tech. + drainage over (R) stifle. - general maintenance routine - stress pt. 27, 28, 29 31, 32, 38, 25 + 22. - area tense - friction + drain - withers show s.p. in 5,6,7,8. Tx. - friction + drain. - neck work - rocking, effl., kneading - relaxation. - general stretch - better c (R) hind.	- gentle maintenance routine daily. - cool compress over (R) stifle daily. - reg. stretching routine - exercise - trot {no small - walk } circles
July 22/96 45' (Rec)	- same condition 3rd Tx. - much better overall - less tension - no. inflam. - stifle appears fine! - sacrum still good.	- general warm-up. - general maintenance sp. 27.38 - deep massage along back and (R) rump + hind leg - sp's cleared + drained - good stretches all around!	- general maint. mass. - exercise - walk, trot canter - (no circles yet) circles ok! - stretches
Aug. 24/96 1 hr. Tx. (rec.)	- maintenance visit. - good overall - no inflam. - slight tension - back + withers - sacrum ok! - stifle ok!	- general warm-up. - general maintenance routine. - good tone - light sp's (R) hind - 29-38 - deep work over rump + hind legs - drained - deep work over back + withers. sp. 5,6,78. - cleared + drained. - good stretches!	- maintenance - full exercise program! - stretches

16.2 Example of Filled-out Case Study

INDEX